The Body in Religion

ALSO AVAILABLE FROM BLOOMSBURY

The Religious Life of Dress, Lynne Hume

Shameful Bodies, Michelle Mary Lelwica

The Study of Religion, George D. Chryssides and Ron Geaves

The Body in Religion

Cross-Cultural Perspectives

YUDIT KORNBERG GREENBERG

BLOOMSBURY ACADEMIC
LONDON · NEW YORK · OXFORD · NEW DELHI · SYDNEY

BLOOMSBURY ACADEMIC
Bloomsbury Publishing Plc
50 Bedford Square, London, WC1B 3DP, UK
1385 Broadway, New York, NY 10018, USA

BLOOMSBURY, BLOOMSBURY ACADEMIC and the Diana logo are trademarks of
Bloomsbury Publishing Plc

First published 2018
Reprinted 2018

Cover image © Pallab Seth / Getty Images

A catalogue record for this book is available from the British Library.

ISBN: HB: 978-1-4725-9504-1
PB: 978-1-4725-9503-4
ePDF: 978-1-4725-9505-8
ePub: 978-1-4725-9506-5

Names: Greenberg, Yudit Kornberg, author.
Title: The body in religion : cross-cultural perspectives / Yudit Kornberg Greenberg.
Description: New York : Bloomsbury Academic, 2018. | Includes
bibliographical references and index.
Identifiers: LCCN 2017036053 | ISBN 9781472595041 (hardback) |
ISBN 9781472595034 (paperback)
Subjects: LCSH: Human body–Religious aspects. | BISAC: RELIGION / General. |
RELIGION / Comparative Religion. | SOCIAL SCIENCE / Anthropology / Cultural.
Classification: LCC BL604.B64 G74 2018 | DDC 202/.2–dc23 LC record
available at https://lccn.loc.gov/2017036053

Typeset by Deanta Global Publishing Services, Chennai, India
Printed and bound in the United States of America

To find out more about our authors and books visit www.bloomsbury.com
and sign up for our newsletters.

Table of Contents

List of Illustrations

Acknowledgments

I begin with my appreciation for and acknowledgment of scholars and colleagues who have been trailblazers in the areas of the body, embodiment, and religion. Sarah Coakley's scholarship represents one of the earliest contributions to this nascent field. Her edited volume, *Religion and the Body*, which brings together experts in the history of religion, philosophy, and the social sciences, stimulated my thinking of a cross-cultural approach to the subject. Barbara Holdrege's scholarship on the body in Hinduism, as well as her pioneering work in the comparative study of Hinduism and Judaism influenced my recent work in these areas. Deep gratitude for Karen Pechilis, a wonderful scholar of female gurus and the Bhakti tradition and a dear friend. Appreciations go to George Pati, chair of Body and Religion Group at the American Academy of Religion, for his support of the project. I have enjoyed the collegiality and support of Graham Schweig and Francis Clooney, whose scholarship on divine love and our delightful conversations at the AAR, continue to inspire me.

This project could not have been completed without the encouragement of many friends, colleagues, students, and family. Many thanks to my editor at Bloomsbury, Lalle Pursglove, with whom the idea and vision for this book came together, and for her steady support, advice, and patience with me during the past three years.

Early and continuing support has come from Nanci Adler, who gave her time and energy as the manuscript developed, joined and participated in my class Religion and the Body, helped organize topics, researched, advised, edited, reassured, and of course, laughed with me. I have enjoyed working with you and thank you for your loyalty and perseverance.

Many students who have taken my classes over the past several years have provided me with fresh ideas and helpful suggestions. Issy (Isabella) Beham and Hannah Cody were particularly passionate about the subject. Thank you for your research of various topics in the book, for writing excellent term papers, for asking insightful questions that inspired deep class discussions, and for our regular conversations in my office. My appreciation for the enthusiasm and ideas shared by two excellent students in the Masters of Liberal Arts Program at Rollins, Camellia Gurley and Kristin Abel.

Aislinn Betancourt, Carolina Castaneda, and Mary Robinson: From studying with me in a variety of contexts at Rollins College, undergraduate and graduate courses, our field study experiences in Israel and India, to our fun and stimulating get-togethers in Winter Park, and in the last two months, our group meetings reviewing and editing the manuscript, thank you for your attentiveness, helpful insights, and suggestions for the organization of the manuscript.

My amazingly relational cat Zissel, who insists on sitting on my lap as I flip through printed pages and edit, reminding me to take breaks and give him all the love he deserves: Thank you.

Finally, to my husband and best friend David, who read and edited every chapter of the book with me, asked tough questions, and provided thoughtful insights: My deepest gratitude for your devotion to, and support of my mind, body, and spirit during this journey. Your love, affection, and most importantly, humour are simply the best.

Preface

Our views of the human body continue to change, especially as a result of technological advancements and globalism. Our connected universe with its social media and virtual reality is impacting traditional concepts of self and other. The 2013 Hollywood film "Her" made me acutely aware of the fluid nature of our perceptions and treatment of our bodies. In the film, it is OS 1, a programmed "woman" named Samantha, who despite her being virtual, is able to evoke, inspire, penetrate, and fulfill the inner and outer life of Theodore, a thirty something geek who is in the process of getting a divorce. One of the questions that the film raised for me is what is the future of our embodied existence if, computers are going to be our partners, not only in consuming and producing knowledge, but also in love and relationships? As Swati Chopra (an Indian author writing on topics related to spirituality in contemporary society) articulates on her blog: "Soon, the individual self might come to include body, mind, spirit, and device."

When I thought about this question further, I realized that in a sense, we have had this "problem" of relating to virtual reality for a long time, for millennia. After all, our religions, on the basis of the premise of a supernatural reality, entail beliefs in nonphysical deities who communicate with us virtually. Religious "technology," whether through sacred stories or through rituals aimed at "contact" with the deities, further solidify the phenomenon of interaction with a virtual reality. Chopra predicts the juxtaposition of technology and metaphysics in this way: "The Universal Self might become another name for the omniscient Cloud, within which we all compute." In no way do I wish to deny or question the existential and metaphysical truths or theologies of religious traditions. Rather, what I am suggesting is that we can draw a parallel between religions' idea of a disembodied God with whom we can have an intimate and loving relationship, and some communicative experiences with current technology.

There are other ideas to consider in thinking about religion as contributing to the notion of disembodiment. Since we exist only temporarily in the body, some religions de-emphasize and even denigrate the body, and elevate the soul for its immateriality and eternity. Religions often view the body as a problematic site which needs to be disciplined and ultimately transcended.

Salvation from suffering can only be gained in the afterlife—in a disembodied state. Should we conclude then that from the perspective of religion, it is better to be virtual than to be or have a body?

Theoretically, the answer is yes, if religions were only concerned with a deity, the soul, or the afterlife. However, since religions are also concerned with health, sexuality, family, community, and social justice, our bodies are not only important but also necessary for religions to fulfill their functions as institutions whose goals are to regulate our daily embodied and temporal existence even as they strive to obtain transcendent and eternal life.

Having taught a "Religion and the Body" course at my college for the past decade, I am familiar with the challenges of both teaching and learning such a wide range of topics that spans cultures and religions. I wrote this book for the general and academic community, including university students, both undergraduate and graduate, and professors of religious studies, philosophy, gender studies, and anthropology.

Furthermore, I believe that the notions of the body we inherited from our traditions, as well as the specific issues that emerge from considering the influences of science, technology, and our evolved cultural consciousness on our embodied selves, are topics that have broad interest beyond the academic environment.

As embodied creatures who are subject to decay, old age, and finally death, the body is, or at least should be, on everyone's mind. Food, sex and reproduction, health and healing, and life cycle celebrations are of existential concerns to us all. A controversial "body issue" is the recent decision of the U.S. Supreme Court to legalize same-sex marriage, a decision which over twenty other nations have also made beginning in the year 2000. This monumental decision influences and transforms human notions of the family that human beings have held for several thousand years. Even the most religious among us is invited to think about the body in light of such changes, if only to reaffirm their beliefs for or against such radical changes.

It is my hope that this book will provide its readers with an extensive and accessible introduction to the study of the body in religion. Undertaking such a study will hopefully also contribute to cross-cultural and interreligious dialogue in general. Expanding our knowledge of religions other than our own, and how they conceive of, discipline, and honor the body, will ideally help to overcome cultural barriers and prejudices.

Introduction

I write this book with the belief that studying both subjects "religion" and "body" in and of themselves as well as in relation to each other is essential for understanding who we are as humans, our history, and our future. It appears that the body, in what anthropologist Victor Turner called our "somatic society," is more on our minds today than ever before. Body image, diet, exercise, and longevity are advertised, promoted, and bombarded us in all the various screens that we possess. New exercise techniques and machines promise sculpted bodies and healthy hearts. Yoga is quickly becoming one of the most popular ways to stretch, alleviate stress, and enhance our bodies. Body modifications such as tattoos, piercings, and plastic surgery are omnipresent cross-culturally and transcend class, race, gender, and religion.

Equally important to our body image is our sexual identity. Here, the body and religion interact and collude with one another in much more extreme ways. Gender and sexual identity, especially same-sex sexuality and relations have been "outed" and gradually integrated in our society. Many religions have restrictive expectations concerning the expression of gender and sexuality. Deviations from those expectations may result in negative consequences for the nonconforming person. However, the approval of same-sex marriage by the U.S. Supreme Court as well as in other countries around the world is a transformative moment both for religions and society as a whole. It is indicative of the loosening of religions' authoritarian grip on social trends such as marriage and sexuality. What is interesting is that such steps follow, rather than precede, decisions and practices already implemented into liberal Jewish and Christian denominations.

Religions, both as institutions and in their particular practices such as "life cycle" rituals or "dress codes," are integral to many people's everyday life and to their cultural values. For example, a 2015 Pew poll about religious identity in the United States found that nearly 80 percent of Americans identify with a particular religion, although identifying does not necessarily equal strict adherence to traditional religious views. Cross-culturally, there are disparities for men and women in religious laws and practices of dress, sexual behavior and ritual participation. Secular culture, especially the sexual and feminist revolution of the 1960s, as well as the internet, have contributed to overall openness to critique of traditional views and have already brought about religious reforms in several denominations. These in turn have made an impact on societies by liberalizing deeply rooted notions of self, identity, and authority. Same-sex marriage is the latest but not the last change in the social and religious fabric. At the same time, conservatives are tightening up on their views and practices. These culture wars in the public sphere illuminate both strong conservative religious identities and meaningful religious reforms, demonstrating that religion is still a vital force in the world today.

Furthermore, as technology and biotechnology continue to develop, we face decisions and choices that will alter our bodies and our identity in more radical ways. These technologies provide tools and means to create, alter, transplant, and engineer life, in the process of which they are threatening core religious beliefs. While scientists defend the benefits of stem cell research for example, staunch religionists abhor and denounce such practices, and accuse them of "playing God."

A different angle from which to approach the study of the body in religion comes from the dialogue between religion and science. Science, especially neuroscience and chemistry, is providing us data about our so-called "religious experiences." We can now watch our brain waves on the screen when we meditate and pray. In turn, we can induce "religious" experiences through an array of techniques and external substances. Research is being conducted on the health benefits of religious faith and practices, and their role in the process of healing. These examples show that religion and science of the body are intimately linked without negating or contradicting each other.

An ongoing debate among scholars, especially for feminists, is the question of who makes decisions about our bodies. This question leads to discussions about authority as well as universal ethics versus cultural relativism. For example, should a Westerner judge and sometimes intervene in non-Western practices and rituals such as female genital mutilation (FGM)? While the question of authority may be intra-cultural, rapid trends of globalization and our multicultural society bring us in close proximity with "foreign" practices that we may deem as unethical or even physically and emotionally abusive.

Through the study of religion and the body, we can come to a better understanding of the various "authorities" of the body. Being informed of our traditions by studying the ways in which religions and cultures have controlled our body helps us articulate and challenge hierarchical power structures that have dominated both Eastern and Western cultures. Gender studies and research on women in religion is making strides in recovering and reinterpreting the history of women's roles, as well as creating new religious space and experiences for women to express their spirituality and identity as equal participants in the religious life within their traditions.

Mind-Body dualism

Philosophical dualism generally entails two realities: the physical and measurable, and the nonphysical and immeasurable. This idea raises a number of questions: What is the mind? What is the relationship of mind and body? Mind and brain? Mind and soul? Soul and God? Is one's mind a product of specific religions, philosophies, and cultures? These questions are not new. We are in the good company of Blaise Pascal who declares: "Man is to himself the most prodigious object of nature; because he cannot conceive what body is, and still less what mind is, and less than any other thing how a body can be united with a mind. That is the climax of his difficulties, and yet that is his own being" (*Pensées*, 72).

In the last 2000 years of Western thought and religion, we accepted the relation between the mind and the body as one of conflict, an internal battleground. We inherited this view primarily from the Greeks, chiefly from Plato for whom the body and the soul are distinct substances; the body dies but the mind or soul cannot die. Aristotle provided a closer relationship between the mind and the body than Plato did. He explained the union of body and soul by saying that the soul is the "form" of the body. This means that our soul is essentially our nature as a human being. However, Aristotle associated soul/form with the male and body/matter with the female, contributing to gender binaries and hierarchies. Saint Paul, a Jewish convert to the new religion of Christianity, presents a paradigmatic example of this conflict of mind-body in his teachings, although referring to it in terms of the conflict between "spirit" and "flesh." As he states in Gal. 5:17, "The flesh lusts against the spirit and the spirit against the flesh." In his world view, we have to fight against our emotions and bodily needs in order for God's will to prevail. The early Christian theologian Augustine held a more moderate view of the soul-body relationship. He stated that "man is not a body alone, nor a soul alone, but a being composed of both . . . the soul is not the whole man but the better part of man; the body is not the whole but the inferior part of man . . . and when both are joined they received the name of man" (City of God, Book XIII, Chapter 24).

René Descartes, the father of modern philosophy, is known for his view that the soul is identical with our mind and completely independent of the body. "Cogito ergo sum" (I think therefore I am), is the basis of our identity. Other modern thinkers, stressing individualism, reimagined the soul as free will and intellect. It is ironic that in modern philosophy, especially after Nietzsche, the soul survived even the so-called "death of God."

In modern philosophy, the concept of "will" is analogous to the earlier notions of the soul. We must honor our will for it represents our freedom and our intellect in the fight against our emotions and our bodily needs. In both traditional and modern views, the body needs to be managed for it is at the very least passive, or at most, an obstacle. The Enlightenment version of the self is still prevalent among us. Our intelligence and freewill are in a continuous battle against our flawed body and emotions.

Recently, some philosophers have dropped the category "mind"; instead, they speak about consciousness as brain events. As much as they wish to portray a materialistic view of reality, they maintain traces of dualistic thinking. One of the challenges in a purely materialistic view of reality is that it leaves no room for the belief in an afterlife—a central religious belief.

Another popular idea among philosophers and scientists today is that what we used to refer to as the mind or the soul, that is, some metaphysical entity, is in fact nothing but our brain. This position is called "physicalism," implying that there is nothing but our biochemical, physical being. Another name for this position is "monism"—that there is only one reality and that both mind and body can be reduced to it, that is, that everything can be reduced to atoms. Many of us find this idea of who we are, or of who we are not, problematic, because it threatens to take away our individualism. Despite the advances made in science that might characterize us as logical machines and programs, that is, with our body as the hardware and our soul/mind as the software, we want to hold on to our story of who we are as unique individuals with a gestalt of thoughts, memories, and emotions.

Religion and our bodies

One of the functions of religion is to sanctify aspects of reality and existence and create boundaries between that which is sanctified and that which is not. This distinction was articulated by the modern French sociologist Emil Durkheim in terms of the "sacred" and the "profane," for whom religion is a system of beliefs and practices that define the sacred in terms of group interests and cohesion. Another aim of religion is to help establish moral communities and social order, whereby religions define virtuous as well as forbidden behavior. Religions also address the existential questions of suffering and death, and therefore inform our rituals regarding health, disease, and death. As religions construct the boundaries of the sacred, they also have defined notions of the body as these pertain to the sacred.

Religions have shaped and controlled our bodies in multiple ways. Some of the most apparent ways in which religious practices mark and modify the body can be discerned through the requirements of circumcision, tattoos, shaved heads, beards, and uncut hair. Furthermore, our traditions discipline our bodies through modesty rules that control the body, especially women's bodies. Rules that aim to guard female modesty prescribe dress codes, hair control, and in some contexts, even prohibit public singing for women. Such views and rules often link feminine sexuality and masculine temptation, and place the responsibility of maintaining sexual ethical conduct upon women's behavior.

Food practices are another area of religious disciplining of the body that exercises immense influence in dictating rules and regulations regarding proper and improper, permitted and prohibited foods and their preparations. Sexuality, like food, has been the subject of numerous rules and regulations that discipline the body. In some traditions, there are rules with regard to permitted relations and partners, as well as prescribing permitted times and bodily states appropriate for sexual activity. Other traditions promote the ideals of virginity and celibacy.

Birth and death have also been defined and regulated by religions. Encouraging reproduction has been sanctioned by some religious authorities, while artificial birth control has been condemned and proscribed by others. The births of boys have been causes for celebrations in most traditions. Death has its rules in terms of preparing the body either for burial or for cremation, depending upon one's religion. Gender identity and gender relations have been largely defined and shaped by both religion and culture. Religious taboos of sexual preference and identity include homosexuality and lesbianism, individuals who are gender-ambiguous or those who are transitioning or transgender.

Studying the body in religion invites us to undertake a close reading of primary religious texts. For example, examining creation myths and narratives of God's encounters with humans illuminates particular cultural and religious views of the divine body in relation to the human body, as well as notions of gender and sexuality. In terms of representing the body in texts and art, we find that it is essential to keep in mind the diversity of branches, denominations, streams and attitudes that exist, not only across religions and cultures, but also within their respective communities. Within a single religion, the body is referred to as sacred vessel or a temple, while at other times, the body is denigrated and represented as sinful and pitted against the purity of the soul. This has led to the ways in which religions have represented the body through teachings of shame and guilt, dichotomizing the body against the soul.

Studying the body in religion from a multidisciplinary perspective

The academic study of religion provides students not only an exposition of the major beliefs and practices of religions from their origins through the present, but also a critical and analytic examination of the phenomenology of religion and its key philosophical questions. What is humanity's relationship to the universe? What is the nature of the self? What are the highest possibilities of earthly life? What are the hindrances in achieving these possibilities? How can these hindrances be overcome? What is the final and ultimate purpose and meaning of human life?

In the last three decades, the study of religion has undergone significant changes, becoming more cross-cultural and interdisciplinary, with scholarship of the body representing new trends shaped by anthropology, folklore, cultural, and feminist studies. In addition to the fundamental questions that occupy center stage in the study of religious systems, recent trends consider not only traditional approaches such as the philosophical, historical, and theological that are based on textual analysis and interpretations, but also ethnographic research that reveals distinct and nuanced practices shaped by folk traditions, and that depend upon geographical and cultural contexts of religion. These methodologies of studying religion are challenging monolithic representations of traditions. For example, the scholarship by Caroline Walker Bynum of women in medieval Christianity has provided insights into the ways women managed to assert their spiritual acumen against the authorities of the Catholic Church. Examples of the intersections of anthropology and religion are numerous, illustrated in diverse works, such as Roy Rappaport on the rituals of the Maring community of New Guinea, Karen Brown on priestesses in the voodoo community, and Linda Barnes and Susan Sered's work in health and faith healing.

Our study of the body in religion aims to address perennial questions by focusing on the centrality of the body for our religious and social identity. Our bodies are important because we identify our very selves with our bodies, both physically and symbolically. Our first premise is that religions have marked the body both physically and metaphorically, and therefore, we must excavate the body as the site for conveying and creating religious and social meanings. Our second premise is that often, religious and philosophical representations of the body consist of dualism of mind/body, subject/object, reason/emotion, spirit/matter, transcendence/immanence, and male/female. Such views have lesser or greater degrees of rigidity and hierarchy, which impact the ways that the body is treated in particular traditions.

Our study of the body as a category of analysis in religion is multidisciplinary, combining historical and textual approaches with sociological, anthropological, and feminist theories. Our multi-pronged methodology provides a variety of lenses through which to understand and appreciate the body. One of the earliest works, which combines philosophy and anthropology is Maurice Merleau-Ponty's *Phenomenology of Perception* (1962), in which he critiques the mind-body dualism of Descartes, and develops a new framework for conceptualizing the body and embodiment. With his influential approach, we study the "lived" body in the context of the lived experience of everyday life. With the sociological perspective of thinkers such as Michel Foucault, we discern that the body is not only naturally "given," but also socially constructed. With the insights from the anthropologist Mary Douglas's theory, we highlight how the body is a symbolic system, which conveys the relations between the individual self and society. Other perspectives informing our examination include Michel Foucault's theory of social and political control of the body through religious institutions of power. Furthermore, applying the feminist critique of phallocentric views in Western discourse illuminates how traditional identification of mind/reason with the male, and body/emotions with the female, has contributed to women's lower social and religious status.

A salient premise for our study of the body in religion is that religious beliefs are embodied in religious practice. A few examples of embodiment of religious beliefs in practices are communion, circumcision, and veiling. Communion in Catholic Christianity represents the belief that one needs to consume the flesh and blood of Christ in order to be redeemed. Circumcision embodies the notion of the covenant between Abraham and God. Veiling embodies the belief in female modesty. Numerous other rituals and practices such as cremation, prostration, and the Sabbath are examples of embodied religious beliefs. Cremation embodies the belief that the soul no longer needs the body and in fact is set free to enter another body through reincarnation. Prostration embodies the belief in the humbleness of the worshipper and the greatness of God. The Sabbath as the day of rest symbolizes the notion of God's creation of the world, the importance of attending to the human body and soul by providing it rest and joy, and thereby acknowledging and elevating the human being as co-creators with God. As we study a variety of rituals across religions, we bring to light their interrelationships with theology and philosophical views of the self.

Categories such as body modification and body disciplining in religion not only help to systematize the study of the body, but also offer angles for understanding the paradigm of religion's (and society's) construction or reconstruction of the natural body. With the popularity of tattoos, piercings, and plastic surgery in our society today, it is clear that such "cultural fashions" in fact shape our body. When we study the ways that religions shape our body, we underscore the role religious authorities play in every dimension of life, including the control of hair, dress, gender, sex, food, drink, marital conduct, health, illness, and finally, death.

The category of sustaining the body enables us to address and critique issues of health and healing in religion. It is also important to note the influential role that advances in medical technology and biological engineering have played, determining whose body is normative. Bodies that do not conform to a cultural standard of wholeness are devalued, discriminated against, and marginalized.

While religions have contributed to definitions of health and disease, clergy and religious communities are also in the unique position of augmenting health practices by injecting a spiritual component to the healing process.

Our examination of the body in religion considers both the "lived" body and the ways in which the body has been and continues to be socially constructed and represented in a variety of religious texts and experiences. Other notions of the body include the "divine body," which is represented in text and art, embodied and disembodied. When we consider issues of gender, sexuality, purity, and ritual, we refer to both the lived body and the "social body," since the body has also been a symbol for social cohesion and group identity.

While there are thousands of religions as well as denominations within religions, our study will focus on Hinduism, Buddhism, Jainism, Judaism, Islam, Christianity, Confucianism, Daoism, Sikhism, and a variety of native traditions. Selection of traditions to be examined is based, to a large extent on the author's goal of balancing "major" and better known religions with those that are perhaps lesser known and understood. While there may be traditions not covered in detail in our book, the objective of a thorough analysis of the body in religion is met through the representative set of religions covered.

Our topics range from ancient creation myths to current life extension technologies and the moral and theological questions these and other concepts raise. In between, we will look at a variety of bodily rituals, norms, and taboos practiced and adhered to in a selection of religions. Throughout our study, we will highlight religion's role in constructing and shaping our body. In turn, we will consider the ways that our embodiments themselves contribute to our religious beliefs.

We will employ the category of "Representation of the Body" as we examine a variety of texts and images in which the divine body and the human body are portrayed in narrative, poetry, art, legal, philosophical, and theological discourse. We will explore religious rituals and embodied practices under the category of "Celebrating and Sustaining the Body." These include daily ritual activities, life cycle events, festivals, and healing practices. The third category in our study is "Disciplining the Body," which includes religious rules that define and prescribe body practices related to purity and pollution, gender and sexuality, marriage, reproduction, and modesty. Our fourth category, "Modifying, Liberating, and Honoring the Body," includes traditional and contemporary practices that mark and modify the body, ascetic practices to obtain detachment from the physical body and finally, practices and conceptions of death and the afterlife.

Since the body is ubiquitous in every aspect of religion, there will inevitably be overlaps of topics and categories. Rituals, for instance, can be studied under multiple categories: they represent, discipline, sustain, honor, and celebrate the body. Still, these classifications are convenient in systematizing our exploration of the body across religious traditions. Along with these four categories for studying the body in religion, we also offer brief overviews of a selection of religions, examining their historical origins, philosophical foundations, and sacred texts, as well as highlighting particular beliefs or rituals. The overviews will provide the reader with the fundamentals of each religion, before delving into the core study of the body in historic and contemporary religious contexts. The rationale for this structuring is to enable the reader to have a basic grounding in the primary sources and normative (traditional or orthodox) practices, prior to considering contemporary reforms and theoretical challenges.

Our texts include sacred writings and contemporary theories. We begin examining each topic with references to scriptures and their interpretations, as well as other classical texts. We then review practices and their meanings in their historical context. Finally, we bring into the conversation contemporary changes in attitudes and laws pertaining to the body, as well as ongoing debates on controversial issues within particular religious communities. Some of these issues represent long-standing internal struggles between the orthodox and liberal camps within a particular tradition. Others stem from the rapid development of science and technology that offers us new approaches and choices pertaining to our body. These issues range from food choices to gender and sexuality. These include the following:

- **Food**: Vegetarianism, dietary rules such as Kosher and Halal, impact on health, animal rights, world hunger, environmental sustainability

- **Marriage**: Same-sex marriage, interfaith marriage

- **Hair Covering and Dress codes**: Modesty

- **Drugs**: Legalization and use for religious or medicinal purposes

- **Sexuality**: Purity laws, same-sex relationships, virginity, celibacy

- **Biotechnology**: Reproductive technology, abortion, euthanasia, organ transplantation, life extension

- **Body Modification**: Circumcision, tattooing, FGM, transhumanism

- **Death**: Cremation versus burial

- **Gender**: Gender roles, women's ordination, female infanticide, equal access to education and resources, women's roles in the family and in the public sphere, transgender people

The book chapters follow the cosmic, social, and lived body from the creation of the body to its passing. In Part 1, we move from the divine creation of the world to representations of the divine body in narrative, art, and poetry. In Part 2, we examine how the body is celebrated and sustained in embodied rituals and practices. In Part 3, our focus is on disciplining the lived body in its major life cycles and everyday behavior. In Part 4, we consider spiritual technologies that liberate the body from its desires and attachments, and conceptualizations of the body's temporality and eternal journey.

Part 1 Representing the divine and the human bodies

- Chapter 1 The Body in Creation Myths

  In this chapter, we will first focus on two myths from the ancient Near East and the Eastern Mediterranean: the biblical myth found in the Book of Genesis as interpreted in the Jewish and Christian traditions and one of the Greek myths that is included in Plato's *Symposium*. Analyzing the biblical story from the Jewish and Christian views offers us differing perspectives on a single story. Reading the Greek myth as told in the *Symposium* offers an alternative perspective to both Jewish and Christian views of the body in terms of sexuality, marriage, and gender roles. We will explore Hindu and Zoroastrian creation myths, as well as indigenous myths that offer differing vantage points from which to explore how the cosmos was formed and the origins of humanity. Finally, we will consider how scientific views of evolution complement or conflict with biblical creation myths.

- Chapter 2 Representation of the Divine in Art and Text

  In this chapter, we will review a selection of sacred narratives, doctrines, and artistic depictions of the divine. We will begin with a focus on Christian and Hindu notions of incarnation. We will then consider another view of the divine that is generally placed in contrast with incarnation— that is the belief that God is wholly transcendent and therefore does not have a body. We will examine Jewish and Muslim perspectives on the disembodied God who is nevertheless conceptualized in male terms. In this context, we will consider recent writings by feminist theologians who have critiques theological and legal discourse that indicate patriarchal views in their respective traditions. Finally, we will reflect on how ancient and modern views of the divine and its relationship to the human body continue to shape, and be incorporated into the lives of adherents.

- Chapter 3 Erotic Desire and Divine Love

In this chapter, we will examine the ways that erotic desire has been employed interchangeably with love in representing the human experience of and encounter with the divine. Our selection of texts includes scriptures as well as philosophy, theology, mysticism, and poetry from the Jewish, Christian, Sufi, and Hindu traditions. Some of the texts use explicitly sexual metaphors, while others are subtle and suggestive. Some authors view desire as more embodied and therefore an inferior spiritual state; others conceive of desire as representing a higher spiritual realization. Regardless, the trope of desire is integral to love, whether human or divine. Erotic representations of the divine, whether attributed to a god, a goddess, or to the human encounter with the sacred, illustrate the richness as well as the limits of language to describe the transcendent.

Part 2 Celebrating and sustaining the body

- Chapter 4 The Body in Religious Ritual

In this chapter, we will provide an overview of the ritual body in worship through postures, gestures, and movement. We will examine the ways regularly occurring rituals in Christianity, Islam, Judaism, and Hinduism embody religious beliefs, as well as engage and celebrate the body. We will also highlight rituals such as trance-inducing music and dance in Sufism and African religions, as well as the use of mind-altering drugs in Native American traditions to induce altered states of consciousness. We will discuss how women-based rituals, engendered by the feminist critique of ancient patriarchal and androcentric practices, have been embraced by established religious institutions and grassroots groups alike. We will explore earth-based spiritual practices which, influenced by pagan religions, have also contributed to new religious rituals. Finally, we will ponder the impact of using the internet for spiritual practice.

- Chapter 5 Food: Laws and Practices

In this chapter, we will examine the multiple ways in which food is embodied in religions and cultures. Preparation, consumption, and attitudes related to food are based on notions of health, ethical treatment of animals, religious history and beliefs, and group identity. Applying theories from anthropology, we investigate cross-cultural taboos and prohibitions of food and drink that have guided religious groups and have contributed to their social cohesion and shared values. We explore the symbolism of food, and the ways food has played an integral role in religious rituals and festivals, both in its elaborate preparation and consumption and in its association with divine blessings. We will also address the changes that are taking place as technology and cultural pluralism continue to impact our food habits, our environment, and our spirituality.

- Chapter 6 Sustaining the Body: Breath, Harmony, Health, and Healing

In this chapter, we will investigate views and practices of health and healing, establishing that the religious and philosophical perspectives of the body are integral to their cultures and environments. As we review the function and symbolism of breath as the vital force or energy flow which sustains the body, we highlight its conceptualization and use in Asian healing systems, along with notions of balance, harmony, and the interconnectedness of the elements in the body. We consider biblical narratives of healing as well as ongoing tribal practices that are often linked to supernatural beliefs, whether through deities or spirits that exert influence on the body. We complete our study with a discussion of twentieth- and twenty-first-century perspectives on health, and the gradual acceptance in the West of religious forms of healing, and Eastern practices that promote a holistic approach that integrates the spiritual and physical body in the process of healing.

Part 3 Disciplining the body

- Chapter 7 Purity and Pollution

In this chapter, we consider how purity functions and what it symbolizes. In comparing notions of purity in multiple religions, we ascertain the sources of pollution and the rituals that restore purity. We clarify how purity is different from the notion of holiness, and whether notions of pollution contribute to a denigration of the body. In many cases, gender figures in concepts and laws of purity, suggesting a qualitative difference between the polluting powers of men and women. We examine biblical notions of purity, followed by Zoroastrian, Islamic, and Hindu beliefs and practices. We apply anthropological theories of the function and symbolism of purity to ancient and indigenous codes and rules that define physical boundaries between purity and pollution, as well as focus on practices that define female impurity and purification rituals. Finally, we reflect how notions of purity and pollution continue to shape our religious and cultural practices, albeit in subtle and evolving ways.

- Chapter 8 Gender and Sexuality

  In this chapter, we will begin with a brief consideration of the metaphors of gender as applied to philosophical and religious writings. We will review sexual norms, taboos, and practices in a selection of classical literature from Judaism, Christianity, Islam, and Hinduism. We will also compare traditional and changing views toward gender and sexuality, as these have been and continue to be fervently debated issues. This contemporary debate is accentuated by thinkers such as Judith Butler and Michel Foucault whose study of the discourse about the body informs us about issues of political and religious power and social manipulations of the body in terms of gender and sexuality. We will highlight two important contemporary issues: sexual scandals in religion and views of transgender persons in a variety of traditions, including Buddhism, Sikhism, and Native American religions. Finally, we will consider evolving trends in religion such as the ordination of women, and reflect on gender and sexuality as some of the most dynamic areas in the academic study of religion.

- Chapter 9 Marriage and Reproduction

  In this chapter, we will explore views, rules, and practices of marriage in several religions as these are represented in their history and sacred texts. In this context, we will underscore regulations and procedures pertaining to divorce, and emphasize how views and practices of modesty impact gender roles, and control women's social and religious status in particular. We will highlight the shift that has taken place with the growing acceptance of same-sex relations and the legalization of same-sex marriages in several European countries and the United States. We will consider the growing phenomenon of interfaith marriage in the West, a contemporary trend which influences religious identity. We will then turn our attention to reproduction and reproductive rights, and consider contemporary views and practices related to contraceptives and abortion, and their continued debate within religious communities.

Part 4 Modifying, liberating, and honoring the body

- Chapter 10 Marking and Modifying the Body: From Rituals to Biotechnology

  In this chapter, we will explore body modifications as practiced cross-culturally from ancient times until today. We will address evolving perspectives and practices of ancient rituals such as tattoos and circumcision in the West. Circumcision, originally a religious obligation on Jews and Muslims, shunned by Christians, became a routine hospital procedure performed on newborns since the early twentieth century. Tattoos were employed in ancient Egypt and Polynesian culture as marks of one's social and religious rank, as well as protective amulets. In Chinese culture, they served to mark criminals, and later identified sailors. The recent renaissance of tattoos in the West opens up new ways of looking at tattoos and what they mean. The tattooed body can be understood as challenging the control of religion and culture. The decision to tattoo can be understood as affirming one's personal agency to shape one's body and produce change and transformation. We will raise issues of cultural relativism in the context of controversies such as female circumcision. Finally, we will also review the influence of biotechnology on such procedures as organ transplantation, gender reassignment, and the transhumanist movement as we assess the impact of science and technology on the body.

- Chapter 11 Asceticism: Spiritual Technologies of Detachment

  In this chapter, we will examine the role that ascetic practices have played in Christianity, Jainism, and Buddhism. In our investigation, we will address specific rules, vows, and exercises followed by monks and nuns, with a focus on celibacy, fasting, and poverty as the most common forms of renunciation, as well as various extreme forms of corporal mortification methods. In our study, we will assess the differences between moderate and extreme forms of asceticism, and their link to fundamental views toward the body. We will also highlight social factors, spiritual motives, and religious goals for the ascetic lifestyle, and consider the spiritual and material benefits gained by women renunciants. Contrasting religious views of the ideal of asceticism, we will discuss the negative stance toward extreme forms of asceticism long held by traditions such as Zoroastrianism, Islam, and Judaism.

- Chapter 12 Death and the Afterlife

  In this chapter, we will reevaluate the link between our physical bodies and our spiritual goals in light of the experience of death and our beliefs in the afterlife. We will clarify religious and ethical world views in our examination of burial and cremation practices. These include the sacredness of the body and the environment, notions of purity, as well as beliefs in physical resurrection (as in Zoroastrianism and the Abrahamic religions), or the view that human bodies are temporary vessels for souls

(Hindu, Jain, and Buddhist religions). We will also address indigenous beliefs in the spiritual power that the deceased exert on their families, and the rituals that express awe and veneration for their ancestors. We then turn to other beliefs in the afterlife, exploring notions of heaven and hell as well as notions of reincarnation and the cessation of physical existence. Finally, we will review contemporary issues related to death, such as the controversy and debate regarding assisted suicide and the increasing popularity of cremation around the world.

Brief survey of representative religions of the world

Judaism

Historical origins

Considered by many scholars the first monotheistic religion, the origins of Judaism can be traced to the biblical figure of Abraham who is believed to have migrated from Mesopotamia to Canaan in the beginning of the second millennium BCE. Originating as a nomadic tribe, the Hebrews were later called Israelites, and finally identified by the Romans as "Jews," a name stemming from the land in which they resided—"Judea." Their theological foundation is based on the oneness of God who, despite male pronouns and anthropomorphic references to Him in the Bible, is believed to be transcendent and disembodied. Since idolatry was considered a major sin that contradicted the theological foundation of Judaism, strict rules were instituted against fashioning images and statues that could serve as objects of worship and as religious icons. As adherents of a non-proselyting religion, the Israelites and especially their priests were concerned with the physical continuity of the nation, as much as with all matters related to rituals such as animal and food sacrifices conducted in the Temple in Jerusalem. Once their Temple was destroyed by the Romans in 70 CE, the rabbis became the primary spiritual authorities of the community, replacing the priests, and also replacing the sacrifices with ritualized prayer, learning, and scholarship.

Sacred texts

The primary sacred text of Judaism is the Bible, which consists of the Torah or the five books of Moses, the Nevi'im or "Prophets," which includes the revelations and moral teachings of the prophets who are sent by God to intervene in the political and social life of the people, and the Ketuvim or "Writings," which are additional books of wisdom. The Torah encompasses a variety of topics and literary genres, including creation myths, a record of the life and major events of its patriarchs and matriarchs, historical events of great importance such as migrations to and slavery in Egypt, Moses's leadership and the exodus from slavery to freedom, and the revelation at Sinai when the laws of the Torah were given. It also includes many laws that are designated as "commandments" (*mitzvot*) on the basis of their divine origins and their specific community of recipients. In the academies of learning established by the rabbis in Palestine and in Babylonia, interpretations of the Torah were compiled over the centuries and had become the second most important sacred texts for Jews, known as the Talmud. As an orthopraxy (a religion which emphasizes correct conduct), Judaism is based on the numerous and strict rules of conduct that define and shape the individual and communal life of its members. While the rabbis did not determine general doctrines of faith or theology, they were concerned with maintaining the monotheistic and exclusive character of the religion and their identity as a separate group. Rabbinic literature also includes midrash—the exegetical and homiletical literature that provides commentary and analysis of the Torah.

Although there are mystical elements strewn throughout the Torah and the Talmud, there are distinct Kabbalistic (mystical) texts, the most famous of which is the Zohar, the thirteenth-century book authored by Moses De Leon. The Zohar was written in the form of a commentary on the Torah, but contains distinct theological and cosmological ideas about the nature of God, world, and reincarnation. One of the most distinguished Kabbalistic theories in the Zohar is the *sefirot*, the ten creative forces through which God created and rules the universe.

Jewish denominations

Modern branches of Judaism include Orthodox Judaism, the most traditional expression of Judaism, Reform Judaism which is the most liberal expression of modern Judaism, and Conservative Judaism which is a moderate branch that seeks to avoid the extremes of both Orthodox Judaism and Reform Judaism. There are also other smaller movements including Reconstructionism, which is a small, liberal Jewish movement, and the Jewish Renewal Movement, which offers alternative approaches to traditional Judaism with an emphasis on spirituality.

Christianity

Historical origins

Christianity, like Judaism, is a monotheistic religion. It originated in Roman-ruled Jewish Palestine in the first century on the basis of life and teachings of Jesus and his apostles. Church Fathers later systematized these teachings. Under the harsh occupation by the Romans, Jews who had accepted Jesus as the Messiah and comprised "the early Christians," thought that they were living in the "last days" as prophesied in the Hebrew Bible. Many hoped that the Messiah, in accordance with the belief in the "Kingdom of God," would usher in a new era of peace. Among the early Christians, there was a minority who believed in keeping Jewish laws such as circumcision and the dietary laws while others, especially under Paul's influence, who opted to recruit gentiles, broadened Christian teachings to make it inclusive. For three centuries, Christians were persecuted under Roman rule. Then, in 313 CE, the emperor Constantine converted to Christianity, proclaimed religious freedom for Christians, and sponsored the Council at Nicaea, which created official hierarchy within the Church. From that point forward, the pope became the official and infallible leader of the Church.

The ideal of the religious ascetic, which began with the Essenes (the first-century Jewish group also known as the Dead Sea community), was retained in the Middle Ages and became closely associated with the monastic life. In the third and fourth centuries around the eastern Mediterranean, monasteries were established as monks and nuns built their separate communities to create the most appropriate environment for a life of prayer, devotion, and learning. The monastic communities also performed social services such as caring for the sick and assisting the poor. Celibacy, among other austerities of the body, remained an ideal and holy state for Christian saints. During the Middle Ages, a wave of male and female mystics, consumed by their insatiable hunger and yearning for an "ecstatic union" with God, embraced ascetic practices in their effort to imitate Christ's suffering and experience God's grace. Although bishops and saints were particularly influential for their sermons, letters, and their theological writings, women in the Middle Ages such as Teresa of Avila also gained prominence as saints, teachers, great poets, and visionaries.

Christianity was divided by the Great Schism of 1054, which resulted in the Catholic Church (in the West), headed by the pope, and the Orthodox Church (in the East). The most fundamental schism in the history of Christianity was the Protestant Reformation which began in the sixteenth century with Martin Luther, followed by other reformers, such as John Calvin. The primary impetus behind the Reformation was theological, based on the principle that the Bible alone is the sole infallible rule of faith and practice. Other reasons for the Reformation include the erosion of faith in the papacy and perceived corruption in its administration. Protestant reformers rejected a contingency between the correct performance of sacrament and the gaining of redemption. Faith, not works, offered Christians the gift of grace, through which one gains dominion over sin.

Sacred texts

The sacred text for Christians is the Bible, which includes both the Old Testament (the Hebrew Bible) and the New Testament. The New Testament includes twenty-seven books that were written after the time of Jesus's death and canonized in the fourth century. In the late fourth century, Saint Jerome produced a Latin translation of the Old and New Testaments known as the Vulgate. The books of the New Testament include the Gospels of Matthew, Mark, Luke, and John, the Book of Acts, the Letters of Paul, General Letters, and the Book of Revelation. According to the Gospel of Matthew, Jesus was born to a virgin named Mary. In his 30s, he traveled with his disciples around Palestine, preaching and teaching about the coming Kingdom of God. After about three years, Jesus was arrested during the Jewish holiday of Passover. He was convicted and crucified by the Roman authorities. The Gospels narrate stories of Jesus performing miracles, his teaching in parables, his sermons, and his debates with the Pharisees. In the narratives of his death, Jesus died on a Friday and was buried before the Sabbath. After his resurrection, he taught his followers for forty days. Christians believe that he then ascended to heaven to be with God, and that he will return to usher in a golden age on earth.

Christian denominations

Most Modern Christian denominations have their roots in the Protestant Reformation. The Protestant denominations today are numbered in the thousands; some of the major branches include Lutheran, Presbyterian, Calvinist, Anglican, Baptist, Methodist, Pentecostal, Evangelical, Jehovah Witness, Mormon, Christian Science, and the Seventh-day Adventist Church. Protestant churches generally share three theological principles: (1) The belief in the Bible as the highest source of authority for the church. For many, the Bible is the "inerrant, infallible" Word of God, and is thus read literally. (2) The belief that believers are pardoned for sin, on the basis of faith in Christ rather than a combination of faith and good works. (3) The belief in the right of lay Christians to read the Bible in the vernacular and to participate in the government of the Church.

Islam: historical foundations

Islam is a monotheistic religion with geographic and cultural origins in the Arabian Peninsula in the early seventh century. The Arab population during this time worshipped a multiplicity of deities, including local gods and goddesses, as well as the high god whose name was Allah. The Arabs were divided into tribes and clans who were often in conflict with one another. Many were traders for whom Mecca served as their trading center, which later became the central sacred space of Islam. Other inhabitants in this region were the Jews and Christians, whose influence upon the burgeoning religion was substantial. Islam shares with Judaism an emphasis on correct action (such as the requirement of daily prayers) as well as belief in God and prophets. Muhammad, the founder of the religion of Islam, is believed by Muslims to be the last and perfect prophet. After Muhammad's death, Abu Bakr, the selected Caliph and those who succeeded him expanded Muslim territory to Persia and North Africa. Later, Islam spread to Spain and to the Ottoman Empire.

Sacred texts

When the prophet Muhammad was forty years old, he began having visions and audible revelations, the content of which were communicated and recorded in the Qur'an, the holy book of Islam. The primary message of the revelations is the belief in Allah as the one and only God, the resurrection of the dead, and Allah's Judgment Day. The Qur'an, from the Arabic root word "to recite," is divided into 114 *surahs* (chapters or sections), beginning with the longest and ending with the shortest, and each begins with the refrain "In the name of God, the Merciful, the Compassionate." The themes of the *surahs* include creation, prophecy, political history, laws, and imagery of Judgment Day. Some narratives parallel elements from the Hebrew Bible, such as God's creation of the world in six days, stories about Adam, Abraham, and Ishmael, from whom Muslims believe they descend, as well as Moses and David—all of whom are true prophets. According to the Qur'an, God continues to maintain the world until the Day of Judgment when the dead will be resurrected and judged. The centrality of prophecy is evident as the Qur'an recognizes a series of true prophets (beginning with Adam and including Jesus) sent by God to teach humanity righteousness and faith. Muhammad according to Islam is the final prophet, culminating this tradition of prophecy with the definitive teachings of God as recorded in the Qur'an.

In addition to the Qur'an, Muslims also accept a collection of texts known as Hadith—narratives about the personal life, major events, practices, and sayings attributed to Muhammad and recorded by his companions. Various approaches as to how to read the Qur'an's references to God emerged over the history of Islamic interpretations. Ibn Rushd, one of the greatest Muslim thinkers, held that God articulates His messages in metaphors because only few people have the intellectual capacity to engage in philosophy.

Allah is the Arabic term for God—the Supreme and the Creator of the universe. According to the Hadith, there are ninety-nine names for God. The most common names in the Qur'an that appear in the beginning of almost every *surah* are *Ar-Rahman* (the Compassionate) and *Ar-Rahim* (the Merciful).

Islamic divisions

From its early beginnings, Islam was divided into Sunni and Shi'a denominations, each claiming loyalty and authority to different successors of the prophet. The Shiites claimed that Ali, Muhammad's cousin and son in law, had special spiritual status, whereas the Sunnis do not and instead recognize the authority of the four caliphs who succeeded the prophet. While both factions accept the authority of the Qur'an, the Shiites, who number approximately 10 percent of all Muslims and are concentrated mostly in Iran, have distinct beliefs and practices. In parallel with other traditions, Islam developed not only a well-defined outward religious life and behavior but also an inward, esoteric one—the path of Sufism. This path recognizes the importance of spiritual adepts to guide the individual on their goal toward a unitary experience with the divine. For the followers of the path, the Sufis, like their Christian counterparts, seeking the divine and attaining nearness to God is the essence of their spiritual path. The majority of Sufi orders (*tarikas*) comprised mostly men, who composed Sufi theology and poetry based on love. Prominent Sufi poets were Rumi, Attar, and Hafez and Hallaj. Rabi'a al-Adawiyya (717–801 AD) was one of the greatest women mystics, known for speaking about God as the beloved, and likened for her ecstatic experiences to the Christian mystic St. Teresa.

Hinduism

Hinduism is the largest religion in India and Nepal, encompassing numerous distinct yet interrelated sects with their particular doctrines and practices, but also with common views and spiritual goals. The term Hinduism is derived from the word "Hindu," which is a Persian version of "Sindhu," the ancient name for the River Indus running through northern India. Having originated in the Indian subcontinent, it is also called Sanatana Dharma (the eternal path/law) as it is believed to be the virtuous way of life. A conglomerate of diverse beliefs and traditions, Hinduism has no single founder. Hinduism developed from the ancient texts called Vedas, and spread all over the Indian subcontinent by the fourth century BCE, assimilating elements of all local religious beliefs and practices.

Over the next ten centuries, it evolved further and also absorbed tenets of Buddhism and Jainism, which included the doctrine of nonviolence and an emphasis on vegetarianism. As it has no central religious authority, there are various paths and forms of worship in Hinduism. While all worship one Supreme Being, there are four major denominations based on the god/goddess they worship. Lord Vishnu is worshipped by Vaishnavites; Shiva is the primary deity for Saivites; the goddess Shakti is supreme for Shaktas; and for liberal Hindus or Smartas, the choice of deity is left to the devotee. Each denomination has a multitude of guru lineages, religious leaders, priesthoods, sacred literature, monastic communities, schools, pilgrimage centers, and tens of thousands of temples. Despite the diversity of their deities, spiritual authority, and practices, Hindus share philosophical and religious views of the universal law of cause and effect—karma and the cycle of rebirth—*samsara*. Material goals such as *artha* (wealth) and *kama* (physical pleasure) are appropriate for a joyful and comfortable marriage and family life.

According to traditional Hindu belief, there are four stages of a human life (Ashrama), which include the stage of the celibate student who studies with a teacher in the ashram (Brahmacharya); the second stage is the householder (Grihastha); then there is gradual detachment from the material world in middle age (Vanaprastha); and finally old age is devoted to spiritual aims through adopting an ascetic life (Sannyasa). Also, Hindu society was classified into four classes, called *varnas*: teachers and priests (Brahmins); warriors, nobles, and kings (*Kshatriyas*); farmers, merchants, and businessmen (*Vaishyas*); and the servants and laborers (*Shudras*). This system evolved to extremely rigid castes and an oppressive hierarchy. Reform movements in the nineteenth and early twentieth centuries addressed some of these issues, yet the principles of caste and class still play an important role in marriage, social norms, and politics.

Major Hindu texts

The Vedas are the oldest and primary texts of Hinduism. The four Vedas include the Rig Veda, believed to be the oldest (composed around 1500 B.C.), Sama Veda, Yajur Veda and Atharva Veda. The Upanishads, written between 800 and 400 B.C. elaborate the Vedic philosophy of karma and samsara. The sages who composed these texts, many of whom were ascetics, further expound the idea that the individual soul (Atman) can be united with the abstract, all-encompassing divine reality (Brahman) through contemplation and meditation, a spiritual path known as *jnana* (knowledge), as well as the through one's karma. The goal of this philosophic strand of Hinduism is *moksha,* or liberation from the cycle of birth.

The Puranas are post-Vedic texts that include the history of the universe from creation to destruction, genealogies of the kings, heroes and gods, as well as accounts of cosmology and geography. The laws of Hinduism are compiled in the Laws of Manu, also called Manava-dharma-shastra. The Mahabharata and Ramayana are the national epics of India. A foundational sacred text for Hindus is the Bhagavad Gita (dating from about 400 or 300 B.C.), which is part of the epic Mahabharata, and features a dialogue between Arjuna, a member of the warrior class (*kshatriya*) and Lord Krishna about the paradox of his existential dilemma regarding violence. The Gita, as it is popularly called, synthesizes several strands of Indian thought including karma (actions), *dharma* (duties according to one's social role), and *bakthi* (devotion and service).

Buddhism

Buddhism originated in the fifth century BCE and was developed on the basis of the life and teachings of Siddhartha Gautama. Its name is derived from the term Buddha, which means the Enlightened One. According to tradition, Siddhartha was born a prince who decided to leave the palace and his family. Outside the palace, he encountered sickness, old age, death, and asceticism, referred to as "the four sights." He came to realize that although the first three are inevitable, *avidya* (ignorance) of the impermanence of reality is the true cause of suffering. He set out to discover the solution to the suffering in the world, having left behind his family life and wealth. He began his journey of austerities, contemplation, and meditation which led to his becoming the Buddha.

The Buddha did not teach about an omnipotent deity who either created or ruled the world. The Buddha refused to address questions of metaphysics and therefore some consider Buddhism a philosophy, rather than a religion. At the same time, the Buddha did not rule out the existence of God. The Buddha taught the Four Noble Truths and the Eightfold Path, offering the reasons for human suffering and guidelines to its elimination. The Four Noble Truths are: (1) all existence is *dukkha* (suffering). (2) Suffering is caused by desire. (3) Suffering can end. (4) The eightfold path can lead to the end of suffering. The eightfold path consists of: (1) Right view, (2) Right intention, (3) Right speech, (4) Right action, (5) Right livelihood, (6) Right effort, (7) Right mindfulness , and (8) Right concentration.

Buddhist branches

Soon after the Buddha's death, a devotional element developed, especially in the Mahayana (the Great Vehicle) and the Vajrayana traditions (Tibetan) of Buddhism. Unlike Theravada (Teachings of the Elders), which were the original teachings, Mahayana, that spread throughout Asia, and Vajrayana, incorporated indigenous beliefs, local deities as well as the worship rituals in reverence of the Buddha and their respective deities. In the Mahayana tradition, the Bodhisattva is a central doctrine which valorizes individuals who compassionately refrain from entering nirvana in order to save others. They are consequently worshipped as deities.

Each Buddhist tradition has its own distinct literature consisting of texts called *sutras* (Pali, *suttas*). These include philosophical discourses, poetry, and narratives about the Buddha's life, as well as lay and monastic rules. In Theravada Buddhism, the Pali canon contains the Buddha's teachings in three groups of writings, known as the "Three Baskets" (Tipitaka): 1) Vinaya Pitaka encompasses principles for monks and nuns; 2) Sutta Pitaka comprises the discourses of Buddha; and 3) the Abidhamma Pitaka, which covers Buddhist metaphysics. The Mahayana branch of Buddhism added to the Pali canon over two thousand sutras; the best known among these are the the Lotus Sutra and Heart Sutra. The best known Tibetan text is the Book of the Dead which details the stages of death reflecting a distinctive Tibetan perspective. Buddhism follows the Hindu notions of karma and reincarnation, yet departs from Hinduism in terms of the soul. Given his foundational notion of impermanence, the Buddha taught about the idea of *anatman* (no-soul), namely that there is no permanent essence or soul. Therefore reincarnation in Buddhism is a kind of rebirth, not of a substance but of "stream of consciousness." If there is no substantial entity and reality, all commonly perceived phenomena are in fact *sunyata* (emptiness). Everything is in flux, becoming, or what is called *pratitya samutpada* (interdependent arising).

Jainism

Jainism is an ancient Indian religion that emphasizes complete nonviolence and asceticism. Jainism emerged in sixth century BCE India, at the same time Buddhism was developing. Jainism incorporates the traditional Hindu concepts of karma and reincarnation, but rejects the Veda scriptures, castes, and the idea of a creator god. Karma refers to the principle of cause and effect where intent and actions of an individual influence the future of that individual. One can speak of it as a "residue" imprinted on the soul for actions taken in life by the body or mind, whether positive or negative, and the greater its accumulation, the more firmly the soul is tied to the physical world, and thus, to the body. Since the ordinary person cannot escape the accumulation of karma, the goal is to minimize the amount of karma accumulated, and to strive to accumulate more good karma so that one can be reborn into favorable circumstances in the next life. An abundance of negative karma is believed to earn a soul an existence full of suffering in their next life, whether in a human or a nonhuman body. Jainism is named for the *jinas* (spiritual conquerors) who have achieved liberation. Included among these are the twenty-four spiritual leaders called *tirthankaras*. The last of the *tirthankaras* was Lord Mahavira (sixth century BCE), a contemporary of the Buddha who is generally considered the founder of Jainism. The goal of life in Jainism is to reach liberation by a life of *ahimsa* (nonviolence) and discipline as taught by their masters.

Sikhism

Guru Nanak (1469–1539) is the founder of Sikhism, a religion native to India. Nanak's experience of divine revelation inspired him to eliminate religious divisions, especially between Muslims and Hindus, and to teach about the unity of and devotion to God. Sikh theology ascertains the oneness and transcendence of God, who is nevertheless accessible to human beings through grace. Like Hinduism, Sikhism accepts the notions of *samsara* (cycle of death and rebirth) and karma (one's past actions), but stresses that ultimately it is grace that provides us with liberation from the cycle of existence and the blissful union with God. Sikh scriptures are called the Guru Granth Sahib, which is considered the revealed Word of God as well as the Guru as it contains the teachings of Guru Nanak and his successors. Devotion to God is central and employs meditative practices, especially remembering the name of God through the chanting of mantras and songs of the Gurus.

The Khalsa is the communal body to which orthodox Sikhs are ritually admitted at puberty. Members show their allegiance to the Khalsa by five signs (called the five Ks): *kangha* (comb), *kara* (steel bangle), *kesh* (uncut hair, covered by a turban, and beard), *kirpan* (short sword), and *kuccha* (short trousers, originally for riding). The members of the Khalsa are required to wear the five Ks and abstain from cutting hair and using intoxicants such as alcohol and tobacco.

One of the most auspicious days and rituals in Sikhism is the *Amrit Sanskar*. This is the sacred ceremony for the initiation into the Khalsa. The ritual is done in a quiet place and where the Guru Granth Sahib has been installed. The principles of Sikhism are explained to the initiate who is required to wash and cover their hair and wear clean clothes. *Amrit* (sweet sugar water) is prepared and the initiate drinks it while exclaiming *Waheguru* (victory to God). *Amrit* is then sprinkled on the hair and eyes of the initiate and any leftover is drunk by all present. *Akhand Path* is a ritual consisting of nonstop reading of Guru Granth Sahib, which is done during celebrations such as birth, marriage, death, and Gurpurbs (anniversaries associated with the lives of the Gurus). This nonstop reading takes approximately forty-eight hours and is carried out by family members, or professional readers in the presence of the family. *Karah parshad* (sacred pudding) is also distributed to all present.

The Baha'í faith

The Baha'í Faith is the youngest monotheistic world religion, which began in the mid-nineteenth century in Iran. Baha'u'llah ("glory of God") is considered the founder of the religion, based on an early prediction made by his spiritual leader Siyyid Ali-Muhammad, who was called Bab ("the Gate"). Scholars argue that the religion grew out of Islam, while Baha'ís believe in an authentic divine revelation experienced by Baha'u'llah. His teachings on world peace, democracy, civil rights, and equal rights for women were very progressive for that period.

Baha'ís believe in one God who has sent prophets into the world through whom he has revealed his message. Prophets include Adam, Moses, Krishna, Buddha, Jesus, Muhammad, the Bab, and Baha'u'llah. Considered a heretic by the religious authorities in Iran, Baha'u'llah was imprisoned and exiled to the Ottoman Empire. Under the leadership of his son, *'Abdu'l-Bahá*, the religion gained influence in Europe and America. After the death of 'Abdu'l-Bahá, the leadership of the Bahá'í community evolved from a single individual to an administrative order with both elected bodies and appointed individuals. There are approximately 5 million Bahá'ís around the world in more than 200 countries and territories, but they continue to be persecuted in Iran. The central book of the Bahá'í Faith is the *Kitáb-i-Aqdas*, written by Bahá'u'lláh. The work, written in Arabic, is sometimes also referred to as "the Most Holy Book," "the Book of Laws," or "the Book of Aqdas." The *Aqdas* is referred to as "the Mother-Book" of the Bahá'í teachings, and the "Charter of the Future World Civilization." The *Aqdas* discusses the establishment of the Bahá'í administrative institution, the Universal House of Justice. Additionally, it discusses their religious practices and ethics, while criticizing religious hierarchies, and emphasizing interreligious dialogue and unity.

Shinto

Shinto is the indigenous religion of Japan. This tradition, which has no founder or doctrines, honors and celebrates the *kami,* forces inhabiting the natural world, such as wind and storms, and places such as mountains, waterfalls, and rivers, as well as the spirits of deceased humans. The term Shinto, or "way of the *kami,*" was coined in the sixth century in order to differentiate Japanese traditions from Buddhism, which was introduced in Japan at that time. The kami are believed to reside throughout the Japanese islands, and therefore their numerous shrines are an important locus of Shinto practice.

Shinto is primarily a practice-oriented religion. This religion emphasizes expressing reverence through celebration of festivals such as the new year, and performing pilgrimages to shrines where prayers and offerings are made to the *kami,* who influence various aspects of one's life. Rituals and prayers are also offered for the well-being of deceased ancestors, and to ensure the peace and prosperity of the country.

Shinto holidays include the New Year, Shogatsu Matsuri, which celebrates renewal and fresh beginnings; Hatsumode, is the first shrine visit of the new year during which people exchange last year's amulets for new ones; Hina Matsuri, a festival of dolls that celebrates the daughters in the family; and Obon, the festival of the dead, during which people make offerings to the spirits of the deceased. Traditional Shinto texts include the *Nihonshoki* (Chronicles of Japan, written in 720), and the *Kojiki* (Records of Ancient Matters). Both describe the *kami* as the indigenous gods of Japan. The most important *kami,* the Omikami Amaterasu (Great Heavenly Illuminating Goddess) is believed to be the divine ancestor of the emperor, which justifies the royal line. Both texts also depict Japan as a special place created and guarded by the *kami.*

Daoism

Daoism is a traditional Chinese religion whose origins are usually traced back to the sixth century BCE, and to the sage Lao Tzu, who became concerned with the degeneration of his society and politics, and decided to leave China. Zhuangzi, the other major figure of early Daoism, like Lao Tzu, criticized the social norms through the use of stories that describe the way of the sage, but unlike him, was not concerned with politics.

Daoism became a popular religion in the second century CE, whose organization can be traced to charismatic leaders that appealed to both common people and the political elite throughout China. Daoist holidays include the Chinese New Year (Xin Nian), Tomb Sweeping Day (Qingming) when families visit the graves of their ancestors, Earth God (Tudigong) festival with fireworks and other offerings, Jade Emperor's Birthday, Lao Tzu's birthday, and Ghost Month (Yulan), when the spirits of the dead emerge among the living and are given paper "ghost money" along with food and entertainment.

Daoist literature contains a variety of texts on topics such as histories and genealogies, revelations, codes of conduct, delineations of rituals, hymns and prayers, techniques for alchemy, and numerology. The best known is the classic philosophical text, Dao De Jing (The Book of the Way). The Dao (the Way) is described as a subtle yet vital universal force *(de)* from which all things emerge and are sustained by it. The *Dao* comprises two opposite but complementary polarities, yin and yang. Yin is described in adjectives such as wet, passive, dark, and feminine, while yang is aggressive, dry, active, light, and masculine. These are not diametrically opposed. Rather, each contains elements of the other, and their interaction provides the creative and dynamic force behind the changes that occur in the natural world. The movement of the Dao can be compared to water, which is soft and yielding. When water encounters an object, it flows around rather than resists it. This metaphor captures the Daoist philosophy of "non-action" *(wuwei)*, whereby one gains the wisdom of the Dao by living life harmoniously according to the natural rhythms of the world.

Confucianism

Confucianism is a religion that is based on the philosophy of its founder and sage Confucius, who lived in the fifth century BCE, during a time of social and political turmoil in China. These political circumstances were factors that exerted great effect on his thinking, and led him to devote his concerns to human beings and their social relations with others. Instead of addressing metaphysical topics, he developed a vision of the Way *(Dao)* of the "noble man" *(junzi)*, who embodies the qualities of a truly good human being. While unsuccessful as a political figure, he was a highly respected teacher and scholar. Other thinkers who followed his philosophy included the fourth-century BCE scholar, Mencius. In the second century BCE, the emperor Wu decreed that Confucian classics be adopted as the basis for state examinations. Further acceptance and popularization of Confucianism in China occurred in the tenth century, with the first printing of Confucian classics. Neo-Confucianism, the movement to revive Confucianism, began in the eleventh century and by the fourteenth century, Confucianism was declared state ideology, which remained so until the beginning of the twentieth century.

Confucianism places high regard on rituals and festivals, paying special attention to rituals that embody reverence of ancestors. Both Confucians and Daoists celebrate festivals including the Chinese New Year (Xin Nian), Tomb Sweeping Day, Ghost Month (Yulan), and Jade Emperor's birthday. Confucians also celebrate Confucius's Birthday.

Confucian texts

The Confucian canon includes classics such as the Book of Poetry, the Book of Changes (I Ching), the Book of History, the Book of Rites, and the Spring and Autumn Annals. Additionally, it includes the treatise Lunyu, (the Analects), a collection of aphorisms whose primary focus is the training and character of the *junzi* (noble man), who is restrained, morally upright, and learned.

His philosophy is based on the principle of the *Dao*, which is the natural rhythm or action which he applies to nature as well as to all human societies. Furthermore, Confucius defined a number of virtues that are associated with ethical conduct. These include *li* (propriety) and *ren* (human-heartedness), both of which are manifested in proper attitudes and actions toward others.

Indigenous religions

Indigenous or tribal religions are those practiced by people who have lived in particular regions of the world for thousands of years. Tribal religions have oral traditions, passed from generation to generation. African religions for example, although spread across a great diversity of languages and tribes, usually emphasize the importance of this earthly life. Many also espouse a belief in a Supreme Being in the sky who is the creator of all beings. Religious rituals often focus on specialized local gods, and on ancestral and animal spirits. Their rituals consist of dances, chants, and the use of masks and fetishes. African religions often hold that persons are composed of their ancestral souls, who inhabit all parts of their body, and whose spirits possess them, prompting healing through trances.

Native American religions include hundreds of tribes from North and South Americas. A belief common to all is in the supernatural, which includes both a high god and nature gods. The Mesoamerican Mayan religion for example (flourished between 250 and 900 CE), focused on nature gods, such as the sun, moon, rain, and corn. The Mayans as well as the Aztecs developed a complex calendar and a hieroglyphic form of writing. While numerous ancient civilizations and religions practiced human sacrifice as part of their religious ceremonies intended to appease the gods, the Aztecs in particular placed an emphasis on this ritual. Often offering prisoners but also practicing child sacrifice, they believed that the gods need human blood and hearts to remain strong. Most of the Native American traditions were abolished with the invasion of the Spaniards and their imposition of Roman Catholicism on the conquered people.

Australian Aborigines see themselves as having an overwhelming connection to their land, other humans, and animals. A key aspect of Australian aboriginal belief is the Dreaming, whereby powerful beings arose out of the land, and created or gave birth to people, planted life and animal life. People are believed to possess spirits which originate from the Dreaming. They perform their religious rituals in areas which they consider sacred territory which has the tracks of their ancestors, thus enabling the recreation of the events of the Dreaming. Totemism is also important to the aboriginal religion, whereby representation of mythic or living beings renders access to the spiritual powers of the Dreaming.

Aborigines practice a variety of life cycle rituals including initiation into adulthood. These include practices such as circumcision, sub-incision into the urethra, and bloodletting or tooth pulling for boys. Girls are ritually decorated after their first menstruation. The arrival of Europeans in the eighteenth century devastated the indigenous population through disease, forced labor, and murder. A new ceremony, the *Mulunga*, was recently instituted by some aborigines who believe that by using supernatural powers, they could limit the influence of foreigners in their land.

While our brief survey of some of the world's religions displays fundamental differences in their cosmology, world views, and practices, even so, our focused presentations in the following chapters illustrate the common ground across religions as they represent, mark, discipline, modify, honor, sustain, and celebrate the body.

PART ONE

Representing the Divine and the Human Bodies

In Part 1, our focus is on representation of the body, both the human body and the divine body as conceptualized or precluded in a wide range of traditions. The divine-human relationship, as independent and interdependent beings, is expressed through creation myths, art and poetry, and philosophical discourse. In Chapter 1, "The Body in Creation Myths," we will highlight creation myths where the human and divine bodies are based on the hierarchy of creator and creature, and the human body is subject to rules and commands. In Chapter 2, "Representation of the Divine in Art and Text," we compare theological notions of divine embodiment, such as incarnation, with ideas of divine transcendence. We consider the prevalence of masculine characteristics of the divine in the Abrahamic religions, the feminist critique to patriarchal views of God, and the impact that representations of the divine exert on the religious life of practitioners. In Chapter 3, "Erotic Desire and Divine Love," we examine representations of divine and human love, particularly in mystical literature, poetry and art, wherein their relationship is portrayed as mutual, reciprocal, and passionate. In some traditions where there are multiple deities, the interactions between divine bodies, especially male and female, mirror both hierarchy and mutuality. Thus, divine and human bodies communicate multiple meanings: human bodies, when disobedient to God, are subject to pain and suffering, sin and punishment. When cognizant of, loyal toward and absorbed in the divine body, human bodies become the beloved: they are beautiful, and they enjoy the bliss of divine love.

1

The Body in Creation Myths

The term "myth" comes from the Greek word *muthos*, meaning a tale. Myths are cultural, sacred stories that we tell expressing fundamental "truths" about ourselves in relation to the world around us.

Myths are written or transmitted orally and can be found in most, if not all cultures. Why do we tell these stories? One answer is to create order and meaning in our world. Some of the most profound myths are known as "creation myths," connecting metaphysical and physical reality. They inform through the use of metaphors and symbols how the world (including humans) came to be, and what is or should be our place in it. They can serve as a foundation from which to examine, deconstruct, and interpret beliefs regarding deities in relation to humanity, views of the body and the soul, and social norms regarding sexuality, marriage, and gender roles.

There are several thematic and linguistic resonances among creation myths. These include separation or differentiation of matter from what was originally a unity. Other common themes include flawed humanity, conflict between gods, conflicts between God and humanity, and death. Ancient Near Eastern myths such as the Babylonian epics Enuma Elish, Gilgamesh, and the biblical creation stories in the Book of Genesis share thematic and linguistic similarities, including creation out of chaos, human struggle with the deities, and the search for immortality.

While creation myths describe primordial reality, a central motif and concern is the human body, from whence it came, what was its physical form, and how it was linked to or reflects the cosmic and the divine body. In their description of the drama of the creative process and its aftermath, creation myths also engender dualistic and hierarchical views of spirit and flesh, body and soul, male and female, and life and death. Creation myths and their interpretations also reinforce social roles and rules regarding gender, sexuality, purity, modesty, and the institution of marriage.

Myths from diverse cultures such as Sumerian, Egyptian, Chinese, Incan, and Native American depict humanity as having been formed by the hands of gods from clay, earth, or dust. This image suggests the interconnectedness of humanity and the earth, and the cyclical nature of all life. The plants that humans eat to nourish their bodies get their sustenance from the earth from which they grow, and at the end of human life, the human body is returned to the earth to sustain other life forms.

In this chapter, we will first focus on two myths from the ancient Near East and the Eastern Mediterranean: the biblical myth found in the Book of Genesis as interpreted in the Jewish and Christian traditions and one of the Greek myths that is included in Plato's Symposium. Reading the biblical story from the Jewish and Christian views offers us differing perspectives on a single story. Reading the Greek myth as told in the Symposium presents an alternative perspective to both Jewish and Christian views of the body in terms of sexuality, marriage, and gender roles. We will explore Hindu and Zoroastrian creation myths, as well as indigenous myths that provide differing vantage points from which to explore how the cosmos was formed and the origins of humanity. Finally, we will consider how scientific views of evolution complement or conflict with biblical creation myths.

Creation in Jewish texts

The primary Jewish sacred text is the Bible (Torah, or Tanakh in Hebrew), referred to by Christians as the Old Testament. In Genesis 1, human beings are the pinnacle of God's creation of the cosmos, and the last creation. After every other act of creation God states that it was good, but the creation of human beings, God declares that it was "very good." Furthermore, humans were created in the image of God: "And God created man in His own image, in the image of God created He him; male and female created He them" (1:27). While this statement clearly distinguishes humans from animals and the rest of creation, it begs the question: In what way is the human being "like" God?

The classic Jewish responses have ranged from the dignity and sacredness of the body, to de-emphasizing the physical likeness and focusing on human rationality as being godlike. Rabbi Samson Raphael Hirsch, a modern Jewish thinker, follows the reasoning of the rabbis for whom sexuality is integral to the original human state when he states in his commentary to the creation story that the Torah does not teach us to sanctify the spirit, but to sanctify the body. Our body, with all its urges and forces, was created in the image of God, and therefore we must sanctify the body according to God's will.

On the other hand, Moses Maimonides, one of the most important medieval Jewish philosophers, understood the "image of God" in non-corporeal terms. Since God has no body (a basic principle of the Jewish faith), he theorized that we are godlike insofar as we are able to reason. Another important question in this context is: Did God create two beings, a male and a female, or one androgynous or dual-sexed creature? According to rabbinic midrash (exegesis of the Torah through homiletical stories), the first human was androgynous (Midrash Bereshit Rabbah 8, 1).

The question of whether God created a single androgynous being or two beings—a male and a female, is relevant when considering the second story of creation in Genesis 2, where we are provided with a great deal more detail about the creation of human beings. Here, scholars have proposed that cutting and creating Eve out of Adam can be interpreted as Adam being not male, as is commonly thought, but in fact androgynous.

The second account of the creation of the first human beings is presented in the following verses in Chapter 2 of Genesis:

> Then the Lord God formed man of the dust of the ground, and breathed into his nostrils the breath of life; and man became a living soul. . . . And the Lord God caused a deep sleep to fall upon the man, and he slept; and He took one of his ribs, and closed up the place with flesh instead thereof. And the rib, which the Lord God had taken from the man, made He a woman, and brought her unto the man. And the man said: "This is now bone of my bones, and flesh of my flesh; she shall be called Woman, because she was taken out of Man." Therefore shall a man leave his father and his mother, and shall cleave unto his wife, and they shall be one flesh. And they were both naked, the man and his wife, and were not ashamed.

How is the body portrayed in this story? A literal reading portrays God like a potter who makes Adam out of the earth but then infuses him with breath through which he becomes alive. The human body then is made from the ground. The word "Adam" is close to two other Hebrew words, *adama* which means soil or ground; and *dam* which means blood. Furthermore, this earthly creature comes to life with a divine element-God's own breath.

After their disobedience of eating the forbidden fruit in the Garden of Eden, God punishes the first couple as described in the following verses:

> Unto the woman, He said: "I will greatly multiply your pain and thy travail; in pain, you shall bring forth children; and your desire shall be to your husband, and he shall rule over you." And to Adam He said: "Because you

FIGURE 1.1 *Creation of Adam. Michelangelo. Sistine Chapel, Credit: Michelangelo [Public domain], via Wikimedia Commons.*

have hearkened unto the voice of your wife, and have eaten of the tree, of which I commanded you, saying: You shalt not eat of it; cursed is the ground for your sake; in toil, shall you eat of it all the days of your life."

Read as an etiological story, meaning reading the story as reflecting the prevalent social order at the time of its composition, we learn about normative views of God, human sexuality, gender roles, and marriage. God is a male and acts like a father who sets the rules for his creatures, confronts them after they disobey, and then punishes them. Since men wrote these texts, it is rather easy to discern patriarchal and androcentric values. For example, the woman was created to be Adam's helpmate, and her transgression justifies women's subservience and inferiority. She is the one who was tempted to eat from the forbidden tree and caused the fall. Her punishment specifically states that the man will rule over her.

Feminist reading can liberate Eve to some extent, as biblical scholar Phyllis Trible suggests in *God and the Rhetoric of Sexuality*, by depatriarchalizing or reading the Bible in a non-sexist way, correcting male interpretations that have dominated biblical readings. According to Trible, in no way does the order of the creation of Eve disparage the woman. She draws a parallel with Genesis 1 where humanity is created last and is seen as the crown of God's creation. Eve is not an afterthought; instead, Trible argues that she is the culmination of the creation. By identifying biblical verses such as these that can be interpreted in a way that emphasizes Eve's positive stature, Trible makes a good case for a feminist reading of the story. Still, the fact remains that gender hierarchy was the norm in the biblical period, albeit perhaps not as rigid as in later periods. Even within the context of this reinterpretation of the Genesis text, however, Trible acknowledges that the Hebrew Bible is a patriarchal text, featuring a firmly masculine God who most often communicates directly with men, and not women.

Regarding the institution of marriage, heterosexuality is the norm and marriage is central to the Israelite society depicted in the Bible. In the biblical statement, "It is not good for man to be alone," the ideal human partnerships are envisioned as heterosexual, and clearly within the context of marriage. The very first command in Genesis 1 is *pru urvu*, "be fruitful and multiply." It is no surprise to see the command to reproduce forming the basis of the institution of marriage.

When seeking to determine a general view of the body based on the creation myths in the Hebrew Bible, it is important to consider both creation stories as a unified myth beginning with the androgynous being later split into male and female beings. After the act of disobedience of the forbidden fruit, the body emerges as a problematic site of shame, sin, and punishment. There is a new awareness, a perception and a value judgment about nakedness and the need to cover the body. Adam and Eve hide from God and have to defend their actions. Also, the woman's body is linked to both physical and emotional pain: in childbirth and in sexual desire. Eve's punishment (Gen. 3:16) centers on pregnancy and birth—"I will make most severe your pangs in childbearing; in pain shall you bear children"—and on gender relations: "Yet your urge shall be for your husband, and he shall rule over you."

Biblical and rabbinic views of the soul in relation to the body

The creation stories in Judaism provide the basis for later philosophical thinking on the nature of the body and the soul. The Torah teaches that the body and soul are inseparable.

In contrast with Greek views, the rabbis believed that the body is not the prison of the soul. Rather, the body and soul form a harmonious unity, in which the entire person is a living soul. To them, the body is the medium by which the soul has the opportunities for development and improvement. The rabbis believed that the soul controls our basic two inclinations, the good inclination (*yetzer ha-tov*) and bad inclination (*yetzer ha-ra*), both of which are inherent in us. The soul therefore controls our moral conduct. But whether the soul is an independent entity, capable of existing outside the body after death is unclear from rabbinic sources. Some sources say that the body cannot survive without the soul, nor the soul without the body. On the other hand, we find in other rabbinic sources the view that the soul can have a fully conscious life of its own when disembodied.

One of the metaphors used by the rabbis to describe the relations between the body and the soul is that the soul is a guest in the body here on earth. This means that the body must be respected and well treated for the sake of its honored guest. This rabbinic perspective that the body must be respected for the sake of the soul has weighty implications and, as we will see, will influence many facets of religious practice.

Christian views of the Genesis creation myth

While the New Testament includes the same creation story in the Book of Genesis, Christian thinkers understand and interpret the story quite differently. According to Christian thinking, the story represents the basis of what is known as "the fall" of humanity and the doctrine of "original sin." When the first humans disobeyed, they fundamentally tainted all humans, who are now believed to be born in sin. This view is central to Christian teachings and forms the basis for Christian belief in both the incarnation of Jesus and the sacrificial atoning work of Christ. According to Origen, the first-century Christian thinker, Gen. 1–3 is a double creation or a two-stage creation story where the first one, based on Genesis 1, was a creation of spiritual beings, and therefore it is stated that they were created in the image of God; whereas in the second stage, God created embodied beings and thus we now have sexual differentiation. Following this second stage of creation, things get "messy," driven by desire and become painful to our bodies. Therefore, our goal is to return to our pre-embodied, spiritual state.

Greater culpability is placed on Eve in both Jewish and Christian sources. In the Book of Timothy 1 in the New Testament, we see an attempt to draw harsh consequence for women based on Eve's transgression:

> But I do not allow a woman to teach or exercise authority over a man, but to remain quiet. For it was Adam who was first created, and then Eve. And it was not Adam who was deceived, but the woman being deceived, fell into transgression. But women will be preserved through the bearing of children if they continue in faith and love and sanctity with self-restraint. (1 Tim. 2:15)

St. Paul's remarks in this verse explain his prohibition against women in the ministry in terms of Eve's deception, after which women can be redeemed through childbearing and modest behavior. While Christian theology establishes its doctrine of creation and the fall based on the Genesis story, it should be mentioned that there is an additional account—a creation story that links cosmology to the life of Jesus. This version in the Gospel of John echoes both Genesis 1 and the Greek notion of wisdom, depicted as the "Word" or *Logos*, personified as a distinct agent in creation. Furthermore, in this creation story, there is a direct reference to Jesus Christ and the doctrine of the incarnation of the divine in human form: "And the Word became flesh and dwelt among us."

A Greek creation myth

As mentioned earlier, marriage and procreation are prescribed in the Torah. While homosexuality and homoeroticism are modern constructions and were unknown in the ancient world, homosexuality was tabooed in biblical religion and culture and severely punishable. Considering current debates regarding same-sex marriage, we acknowledge that heterosexuality and marriage have been the norm, not only for Jews, but for other societies as well, for at least two millennia. For other societies such as the Greeks, homosexuality and homoeroticism were more accepted, although scholars continue to debate the extent and nature of sexuality in ancient Greece.

In one of the Greek myths, told by Aristophanes in Plato's Symposium, we find the story of human re-creation by Zeus, where the ideas of erotic love and same-sex relationships are prevalent. According to Aristophanes, human beings originally consisted of three genders: male, female, and androgynous. Males were descended from the sun, females from the earth, and those who were androgynous were descended from the moon. Each person had four hands, four legs, two heads, etc. They could move both forward and backward and would run by spinning themselves around cartwheel-like on all eight limbs. They were powerful and threatened the gods; therefore, Zeus decided to cut each person in two.

Once split in half, they longed and tried to find their other half and reunite with it. When they found their other half, they embraced and did not desire to do anything except remain in perpetual embrace. Eventually, people started dying of hunger and general inactivity. Zeus pitied them and moved their genitals around so that they would be facing frontward. This way, they could have sexual intercourse, and those who were formerly androgynous could reproduce, and even two men and two women who were united could enjoy sexual satisfaction.

This myth explains our desire for others. Those who are interested in members of the opposite sex are halves of formerly androgynous people, while men who desire men and women who desire women were formerly males and females. When we find our other half, we are overcome with concern and love for that person. "Love" is the name that we give to our desire for wholeness, to be restored to our original nature.

When we read the Hebrew and the Greek stories alongside each other, we find some compelling parallels as well as significant differences. To begin with, god(s) and humans are often in struggle against each other. Humans get in trouble with God or Zeus when the gods perceived them as too powerful. The first couple in Genesis gets into trouble, not because they are physically powerful like humans in the Greek myth, but because they are disobedient to God. Despite the notion that they were created in the "image of God," or perhaps because of it, they were threatening to God, which explains why He commanded them against eating from the tree of knowledge of good and evil. At any rate, both the humans in the Genesis story and the humans in the Greek myth were punished for disappointing their creator. A striking element in both myths is the "androgynous" human being. While in the Aristophanes account, the androgynous is the "third" gender, when we read the Genesis story literally, it is only a possibility; however, it is made explicit in rabbinic interpretations that identify the first human as androgynous.

Among the differences between the two myths is that the order of the creation and the transgression in both stories is reversed. In the Greek story, humans are split into two *after* their actions displeased Zeus; in Genesis, their split is part of their original creation and their transgression occurs later. In addition, both stories depict desire but do so rather differently. Whereas the Greek myth is told in more erotic and romantic ways, explaining physical and mental attractions between people and introducing the notion of soul mates, the biblical account of Adam and Eve problematizes desire. Passionate desire for the forbidden fruit leads to sin and punishment. Marriage and procreation are commanded, but male and female unions are hierarchical and conflictual.

Zoroastrian creation myths

The creation myths of Zoroastrianism reflect the importance placed on bodily purity within the religion. In the beginning, there was only light and within this light was the power of the Word and of Nature. The creator, Ahura Mazda, created the world by joining the powers of the Word and of Nature. At first Ahriman, (also called Angra Mainyu) the evil opposing force of Ahura Mazda, was weak, but eventually his powers grew and he had to be contained in hell. Ahriman's powers are seen as polluting, hence the importance of ritual and bodily purity in Zoroastrianism. Eventually, Ahura Mazda decided that the world had become overpopulated with immortal beings and needed to be cleansed.

He warned the faithful king Yima of the flood he intended to send and ordered Yima to take two of every species into his castle atop the mountain. After the flood subsided, Yima and the inhabitants of his castle repopulated the earth.

In one heretical myth, Ahura Mazda and Ahriman were born of the womb of Time, or Zurvan. When Ahriman escaped into the world, Zurvan divided the world into good and evil, until good would eventually prevail at a preordained time in the future. As such, this creation myth also explains how evil entered the world, the eventual destruction of evil, and the world with it. The twelfth-century Zoroastrian text, the Bundahishn, presents yet another creation narrative. In this myth, Ahura Mazda created a spiritual world first rather than a physical world, in order to fool the evil Ahriman. Three thousand years later he created the physical world, which was in complete perfection. Ahriman sought to destroy this perfection and broke through the shell that surrounded the world, creating a disruption that caused the sun, which had formerly been stationary, to begin to rotate. This created days and nights which caused humans to experience a life cycle ending in death. However, the Zoroastrian belief holds that the means to overcome evil are inherent within creation. People can cultivate this goodness through farming the land and giving birth to children. This story is similar to the biblical creation narrative as it explains how evil entered the world that was formerly perfect, which led to death, childbirth, and agriculture.

Hindu creation myths

In Hinduism, there is no single creation myth. Rather, there are many myths of origin throughout the religious texts, with some texts expressing multiple and contradicting myths of creation at once. The earliest known creation narrative is found in the Rig Veda, the first of the four Vedic texts, and is believed to have been composed before 1,000 BCE. One of the myths found in the *Rig Veda* describes the sacrifice of the primeval being, Purusha (cosmic man), who is depicted as having a thousand eyes, heads, and feet. From the sacrifice of Purusha sprang the gods, the sun and the moon, the animals of earth, and the four castes, or *varnas*. From Purusha's mouth came the Brahmins, the priests, from his arms, the Kshatriya, the warriors, from his thighs, the Vaishyas, the merchants, and from his feet, the Shudra, the servants. The structure of the universe and earth emerges from Purusha as well: from his navel, the atmosphere is born; from his ear, the sky; from his head, the heavens; and from his feet, the earth. Unlike the biblical creation myth, the creation stories found in the Rig Veda do not provide a clear chronology of how the universe was created, who created it, and out of what. Rather the Rig Veda states:

Then even nothingness was not, nor existence. There was no air then, nor the heavens beyond it. Who covered it? Where was it? In whose keeping? Was there then cosmic water, in depths unfathomed? But, after all, who knows, and who can say, Whence it all came, and how creation happened? The gods themselves are later than creation, So who knows truly whence it has arisen? (Rig Veda, X, 129).

The Upanishads, one of the central religious texts in Hinduism, likewise conveys multiple myths of origin. In the Brihadaranyaka Upanishad, believed to have been written during the sixth or fifth century BCE, differing creation narratives appear side by side. In the opening myth, creation is the result of the sacrifice of a horse from which all aspects of the universe emerge: its breath is the wind; its body, the sky; its limbs are the seasons while its joints are the months and its feet are the days; its intestines, rivers; its body hairs, vegetation; its urine is the rain; and so forth.

Like the biblical and Greek creation myths discussed, the Upanishads also provide a creation narrative that seeks to explain the creation of man and woman. Brihadaranyaka states that in the beginning there was nothing but a man. Like the story of God creating Eve because it is not good for man to be alone, the Upanishadic myth states that because this primeval man was alone, he found no pleasure and wanted for a companion. He then split his body into two parts, creating husband and wife; male and female were inherent within primeval man, until he split and created the two genders. Afterwards, from their union human beings and all the creatures of earth are born.

While it is important to note that there are many differing creation myths within Hinduism, the accounts presented are particularly revealing of the role that the body plays in the creation of the universe. In the first myth, from the Rig Veda, the universe is created from a primeval man, from which not only the gods, animals, and humans emerge, but the order of the universe. The ordering of society is reflective of the human body, the brahmins, the highest caste, come from Purusha's mouth, while the lowest caste emerges from the feet of Purusha. Since the sky, heavens, earth, and atmosphere arise from Purusha, the human body reflects the order of the universe, or rather, the universe reflects the human body.

The myths that follow the motif of sacrifice leading to the creation of earth illustrate the important role that sacrifice played in early Hinduism. These texts were composed and written by the brahmins, the priestly caste, whose primary role within the community, at that time, was the performance of animal sacrifices. Although the sacrifice passage from the Upanishads describes the sacrifice of a horse, rather than a human, it presents the same idea found in the Rig Veda, of the universe being created from a body, which seems to indicate that early Hindu priests imagined the universe as somehow reflecting

FIGURE 1.2 *A lotus emerging from Vishnu's navel, which gives life to Brahma. Credit: Paul Beinssen via Getty Images.*

the shape and structure of the body. In a sense, these bodies are sacrificed and reused to create something new, which reflects the Hindu understanding of the universe as being in an endless cycle of being created, destroyed, and recreated. Likewise, the pattern of karma and reincarnation also reflects this cosmic cycle.

Australian Aboriginal creation myths

There are nearly 900 different Aboriginal groups in Australia, each with its own language variation and creation, "dreaming," or "dreamtime" stories. Dreamtime can also refer to the realm in which mythical or ancestral beings dwell. However, many of these stories have overlapping themes and are centered upon a Spirit Being's journey, which created "songlines" in the Australian typography. These "songlines" are sacred sites in the Aboriginal tradition. One of the Spirit Beings described in creation myths is the Rainbow Serpent. In these tales, the land was bare, flat, and cold. The Rainbow Serpent remained dormant beneath the barren earth, holding all of the different animals in her belly. Eventually, she shot out of the ground, sending the animals into the world and creating mountains, rivers, and the sun in her wake. The Rainbow Serpent continues to guard the land and water, while also distributing punishment in the form of flooding.

In Australia, young Aboriginal boys take part in *walkabout* (also referred to as vision quest or walking in the Dreamtime), a six-month journey through the Australian wilderness or Outback. In walking alone, the young men are expected to follow the paths of their ancestors by repeating songs and following the "songlines" embedded in the typography of the Outback. In doing so, they not only gather the skills to survive on their own as mature adults, but also build upon spiritual connections between themselves and the spirits present in the landscape. This is especially important because Aboriginal Australians believe that the Dreamtime—where ancestors and spirits dwell—is heavily connected to the physical world. Aborigines also believe that music has been left behind by ancestors, and has become embedded in the Australian geography. By

FIGURE 1.3 *Bark painting depicting three spirit figures, legendary super natural beings of the Aborigine Dreamtime, Australia. Twentieth century. Credit: Werner Forman / Contributor, via Getty Images.*

singing, the ancestors literally brought the world into being; thus, they believe it is possible to follow the "footprints" of ancestors by reciting and singing creation songs, and in doing so, the ancestors will lead the young men back to their homes at the conclusion of their walkabout. By "singing the land," young Aborigines on *walkabout* engage on a spiritual journey that bridges the spirit world with the physical one, and their origins story with the present.

Iroquois creation myth

One version of the Iroquois creation story tells of a Sky Woman who lived on an island that floated above a watery abyss. The woman fell through a hole in the island and was caught by animals that placed her on the back of a turtle whose shell had been covered with mud. The woman remained on the earth, where her body turned into corn, squash, and beans. Eventually, two children, Sapling—who created all that is good—and Flint—who created all that is bad—were born. They are responsible for creating all of the beauty and destruction in the world.

While the details of this story vary, most are unified by the presence of a turtle whose back forms the earth and saves the Sky Woman from falling into the water. Today, North America is still sometimes referred to as "Turtle Island," in recognition of this feature.

Modern views of creation: Theories or myths?

The scientific theory of the Big Bang posits that the universe is approximately 14 billion years old. It began as a point of singularity from which it expanded over time. The Big Bang is problematic for religious fundamentalists, given that it does not require a creator, while those who read the Genesis story metaphorically extrapolate biblical notions of time into the post Big Bang phases of the universe.

Charles Darwin's theory of evolution posits that all of life descended from a common source and developed gradually over time from a simple to a more complex structure. This development is based on his idea of natural selection and the drive to survive. To him, this development entails a gradual process that enables species to evolve over time. This theory contradicts not only the biblical story of a divine being creating the universe out of nothing, but also the origins of humans. For religious persons who understand the biblical stories of creation metaphorically, Darwinism does not pose any issues.

This is not the case for religious fundamentalists, who read the Genesis story literally and espouse creationism. Creationists object to several claims in the evolution theory, including the element of randomness, the human's brain having evolved from an earlier and much smaller brain, and the lack of reference to souls.

Questions for review and discussion

1   Is Eve the pinnacle of creation because she was fashioned from living flesh and not from the dust of the earth, or is her body inferior to Adam's because it was derived from his?

2   How do Jewish and Christian interpretations of the creation myth differ in terms of their fundamental views of the body and the soul?

3   How are gender and sexuality represented in the biblical and Greek myths?

4   How do creation myths depict their distinct topography and relationship to their environment?

5   What are the dynamics of human and divine interactions in these myths, and what do these reveal about the human notion of selfhood?

6   How and why did the rabbis interpret the first human to have been an androgynous person?

7   Given global overpopulation, what should we do with *pru urvu* (the commandment to be fruitful and multiply)?

8   If humans are intended to mirror the divine image, how do transgender bodies complicate our understanding of the embodiment or vestige of God?

9   How is the notion of evil portrayed and interpreted within the Zoroastrian, Christian, and Jewish creation myths?

10   What do narratives of punishment in the creation myths reflect about the relationship between adherents and their god(s)?

11   How have creation myths been used to reinforce patriarchal structures?

Glossary

Androcentric-emphasizing masculine interests or points of view.

Androgynous-having the characteristics of both male and female.

Caste-hereditary classes in Hinduism.

Creationism-the belief in a creator god who brought the world into existence out of nothing.

Depatriarchalizing-a feminist approach of reading the Bible in a non-sexist way by divesting it of patriarchal views.

Dreamtime-an Australian aborigine myth of creation of the first ancestors in a period of Golden Age.

Etiological story-a story that explains the origin of a cultural, social, or a religious norm.

Indigenous-tribal peoples, first peoples, and native peoples.

Karma-the law of nature according to which actions determine rebirth.

Midrash-exegesis of the Torah through homiletical stories.

Zoroastrianism-an Iranian, pre-Islamic monotheistic religion founded by the prophet Zoroaster in the sixth century BCE.

1, 4, 5, 8, 10

2

Representation of the Divine in Art and Text

Studying the body in religion encompasses not only notions of the human body, but also the ways in which theologians and artists conceptualize and envision the divine. This topic raises questions such as: Is there a correlation between the ways the divine's body and the human body are viewed? If the religion's deity is believed to be incarnated, does it translate to a positive view of the human body? If God is portrayed exclusively as male, and if there are powerful goddesses in the pantheon of a religion, do these impact social and gender roles? In sacred texts such as scriptures, creeds, and mystical writings, there is a diversity of notions regarding the nature of the divine, and dogmas regarding the correct way of speaking of the divine. Practitioners as well as scholars of religion agree that cross-culturally the divine is transcendent, and therefore beyond a limited form or body; some religions even prohibit and denounce any physical imagery of God. At the same time, numerous traditions have produced literary and artistic masterpieces that represent the divine in an embodied form. The physical forms attributed to the divine in text as in art encompass a wide range of qualities, such as male or female, fierceness or compassion, and creation or dissolution. These forms permeate sophisticated and awe-inspiring sacred artistic traditions, including the fine arts, the performing arts, and poetry.

In this chapter, we will review a selection of sacred narratives, doctrines, and artistic depictions of the divine. We will begin with a focus on Christian and Hindu notions of incarnation. We will then consider another view of the divine that is generally placed in contrast with incarnation—that is the belief that God is wholly transcendent and therefore does not have a body. We will examine Jewish and Muslim perspectives on the disembodied God who is nevertheless conceptualized in male terms. In this context, we will consider recent writings by feminist theologians who have critiqued theological and legal discourse that indicate patriarchal views in their respective traditions. Finally, we will reflect on how ancient and modern views of the divine and its relationship to the human body continue to shape and be incorporated into the lives of adherents.

Transcendence and immanence

Two pivotal concepts that have been advanced by theologians and philosophers and applied to the interpretation of the divine are transcendence and immanence. Transcendence can be said to be otherness, whereas immanence suggests closeness of relationship, producing unity or identity. The divine as transcendent means that God is a Being beyond the limits of human knowledge. Furthermore, God is distinct from humanity and the world. In contrast, the divine conceptualized as immanent means that God is partially or wholly identical with humanity or the cosmos. Additionally, immanence also suggests that God is present to and closely associated with believers.

Euhemerism

Most often human beings imagine their deities in anthropomorphic ways. The Greek mythographer Euhemerus theorized that the gods had originally been highly gifted humans who upon their death were worshipped by the local population. This theory is plausible when applied to kings, such as the Egyptian pharaohs. Furthermore, this theory of gods as superhuman, called Euhemerism, is particularly applicable to polytheistic religions, but may also be relevant in other traditions.

The notion of incarnation in Hinduism and Christianity

Incarnation literally means embodied in flesh or taking on flesh. It refers to the conception and birth of a sentient being who is the material manifestation of an entity, god, or force whose original nature is immaterial. In this section, we will examine representations of the divine and the meaning of incarnation in two traditions—Christianity and Hinduism. What are the implications of notions of incarnation for religious views of the human body? To answer this question, it is important to examine the rationale for incarnation. Is it to enable a direct pathway of communication between the divine and the human person? How does the gender of the incarnated deity impact the social status of men and women in a specific religion and culture?

In Christianity, a well-developed doctrine of incarnation states that Jesus, while remaining fully God, became fully man. Jesus became fully human by taking on human flesh. Jesus was conceived in the womb and was born (Lk. 2:7), he experienced normal aging (Lk. 2:40), he had natural physical needs (Jn. 19:28) and human emotions (Mt. 26:38), he learned (Lk. 2:52), he died a physical death (Lk. 23:46), and he was resurrected with a physical body (Lk. 24:39). Moreover, according to Heb. 4:15, while Jesus was human in every way, he lived a completely sinless life.

In Hinduism, the equivalent idea of incarnation is the Sanskrit term "avatar," which means "descent," and refers to the descent of the divine from heaven to earth. Incarnations of Vishnu or God can be either as animal or human form. Examples of avatars or manifestations of immortal beings include Buddha and Krishna. These are two of the ten avatars delineated in the Puranas (religious texts from ancient times) that are attributed to Lord Vishnu. There are also avatars of other Hindu deities in the Puranas, including avatars of Lord Shiva and avatars of Devi (or Divine Mother). Krishna explains the notion of the avatar in the Bhagavad Gita in this way: "Whenever righteousness wanes and unrighteousness increases I send myself forth. For the protection of the good and for the destruction of evil, and for the establishment of righteousness, I come into being age after age" (Bhagavad Gita 4:7-8).

In both traditions, the notion of incarnation must also be appreciated in the context of artistic representations of the divine. We will now turn to sacred texts and sacred art in both traditions to deepen our knowledge of the divine as the subject of contemplation and worship cross-culturally.

Representations of the Divine in Hindu text and art

Notions and representations of the divine in Hinduism include both Brahman—the formless and the Supreme, Universal Soul—and a myriad of gods and goddesses. The so-called Hindu *trimurti* (trinity) comprises the Creator God or Brahma, Vishnu the Preserver, and Shiva the Destroyer. Hindu deities are frequently portrayed with multiple heads and arms, emphasizing the omnipresence and omnipotence of the deity.

Brahma is the creator of the universe and of all beings and is believed to be the creator of the Vedas. According to the Puranas, Brahma is the son of God, having been born of the Supreme Being Brahman and the female energy *Maya*. He is represented as having four heads, four arms, and red skin. Brahma sits on a lotus and moves around on a white swan. Brahma is often depicted as having a long white beard, with each of his heads reciting the four Vedas.

Vishnu maintains the order and harmony of the universe and is usually worshipped in the form of an avatar. Vishnu's ten avatars (incarnations of God on earth in bodily form) include Rama and Krishna. Rama is an ideal king, son, and husband and is the hero of the Hindu epic, the Ramayana, where he is a young prince exiled from his kingdom. Lord Krishna is one of the best known of the gods in Hinduism. Krishna is portrayed as both a cowherd who charms his devotees and the wise lord who instructs and guides his disciples.

The third deity of this trinity is Shiva, the destroyer of the universe. Shiva destroys in order to create, since death is the medium for rebirth into a new life. Both life and death, creation and destruction, are embodied in him. One of the best known forms is Shiva Nataraja (Lord of the Dance), or Shiva's cosmic dance. Through his dance movements, Shiva creates and sustains the diverse phenomena of the universe. The raised leg shows the freedom of his dance, the drum raised by the right hand symbolizes the sounds of creation,

FIGURE 2.1 *Shiva Nataraja, Credit: Vassil, via Wikimedia.*

FIGURE 2.2 *Image of the Shiva linga. Credit: Raquel Maria Carbonell Pagola / Contributor, via Getty Images.*

the flame in the left hand represents the change brought about by destruction, and the right hand grants protection and assures the maintenance of life.

Shiva is often worshipped in temples as the *linga*, an abstract phallic form, enclosed in a *yoni*, a vaginal form, showing the equal, yet opposing forces of the Universe. Sometimes he is depicted riding a bull called Nandi decked in garlands. Another image of Shiva is one where he is sitting on a tiger skin, his hair piled high and the river Ganges dropping from his hairs. A serpent is coiled around his neck representing the *Kundalini* (spiritual energy coiled at the base of the spine until awakened) and his whole body is covered with ash.deities

Among the goddesses are Saraswati, the consort of Brahma. She is the goddess of wisdom and learning, as well as music. Lakshmi, the consort of Vishnu, is the goddess of good fortune, wealth, and well-being. Durga is a goddess who is terrifying to her adversaries as she fights to restore the *dharma* (conformity to one's duty). These are some of the more popularly known deities.

Hindus venerate deities in the form of the *murti* (idol). Hindu idols of gods and goddesses are kept in shrines in temples. Once bathed, dressed, and adorned with garlands of flowers in an elaborate puja (ritual showing reverence to a deity), priests then invoke the spirit of the deity. During this ceremony, the image is believed to embody the divine being's presence. When invited to inhabit the image, the deity represented becomes the locus of worship. Hindus place great importance in the act of seeing an image of a deity, termed *darshan* (seeing and being seen by the deity) as a reciprocal act between the worshipper and the deity that brings blessings to the worshipper.

FIGURE 2.3 *Hindu goddess Durga. Credit: Godong, via Getty Images.*

The Guru

The guru ("dispeller [*ru*] of darkness [*gu*]") is a spiritual leader who guides devotees toward the truth, and is acknowledged in classical Hindu texts as a god to his or her disciples. He or she is a realized being, one who attains a spiritual state that merits great reverence. The process of becoming a guru is different from that of monks, nuns, and priests insofar as it is the result of cultivating a spiritual path under the tutelage of another guru. Gurus are grounded in a lineage of teachers and serve as transmitters of the sacred teachings in Hinduism, Buddhism, Jainism, and Sikhism. Traditionally, gurus have been men whose spiritual path demanded a profound relationship with their disciples for whom they serve as ultimate authorities. Such training and bonds require the disciple to cultivate deep trust in and reverence for the guru. Intimate love also characterizes the disciple's relationship with the guru, who is described as a mother, father, and god. After receiving initiation and years of living and learning with the guru, the disciple may well become a guru who in turn serves others. In classical Hinduism, most gurus were married men; in modern Hinduism, most gurus are ascetic, and there is also an increase of Hindu female gurus as well. The experience of *darshan* (the sight of a deity or a holy person, such as a guru) is understood as an auspicious experience which imparts merit on the believer and the disciple.

FIGURE 2.4 *Sri Mata Amritanandamayi Devi, known as Guru Amma, the Hugging Saint. Credit: Miquel Benitez / Contributor, via Getty Images.*

Representations of the Divine in Christianity

Christian theology is rooted in three fundamental beliefs: original sin, the divinity of Jesus, and Jesus's death as the atonement for human sins. Although God created a perfectly good world, the doctrine of "original sin" purports that all humans are born morally and spiritually tainted, based on the Christian interpretation of the sins of Adam and Eve. Jesus was incarnated and is therefore both human and divine. The rationale for the incarnation of the divine as a human is the fallen state of humanity and Jesus's role as the savior. Jesus's death and resurrection is based on the task of atoning for and redeeming human sin. Several official meetings of the Church Fathers were held to define and proclaim Church doctrines, which are also integral to the liturgy of many churches. The fourth-century Apostles' Creed and Nicene Creed represent Catholic beliefs of incarnation and resurrection that are at the heart of Christianity. In the Nicene Creed, it is stated that "Lord Jesus Christ, the Only Begotten Son of God, born of the Father before all ages. God from God, Light from Light, true God from true God, begotten, not made, consubstantial with the Father." The Nicene Creed defines the doctrine of the Trinity of the coincidence of God, Son, and the Holy Spirit. Jesus, Son of God is "of one substance" with God. The Holy Spirit "proceeds from the Father," and together the three are "worshipped and glorified."

The affirmation of these creeds by Christians attests to their orthodox and correct faith. According to these creeds, Christians must believe in both the human and the divine natures of Christ, as well as the Holy Trinity. While scriptures do not contain the term "Trinity," Christian theologians referenced concepts from the Bible to support their doctrine. Statements such as the one found in the Gospel of Mt. 28:19 were influential for the Church Fathers' formulation of the belief in the three consubstantial persons or expressions of the divine. "Therefore, go and make disciples of all nations, baptizing them in the name of the Father and of the Son and of the Holy Spirit." The three expressions of the divine according to Christian theology are distinct, yet one substance.

The two foundational texts for Christian representations of the divine are the Bible and the Creeds. Christians believe in God as the Creator, as portrayed in the Book of Genesis. At the same time, Christians also believe that God was incarnated in the person of Jesus. What is the Christian notion of Jesus's body?

In Christian theology, Jesus had a physical body. He was born and he died. His life before the crucifixion, and his resurrection, were physical, as Luke recalls: "'Touch me and see,' says the risen Christ; 'for a ghost does not have flesh and bones'" (Lk. 24:39). As the theologian Origen states: "the whole human person would not have been saved unless the Lord had taken upon him the whole human person" (Dialogue with Heraclides).

Why did God need to be incarnated? The answer is, so that He could die for human sin. Adam and Eve's disobedience and rebellion brought on original sin and the concept of fallen man as the plight of all future generations (Gen. 3:14-19). Without Adam and Eve's sin, or what became the doctrine of "original sin," Christianity's salvation story and the central story of Jesus would have no foundation. Adam and Eve's story provides the lens through which all human failings can be viewed. Shame, self-doubt, self-loathing, pain, and suffering prove to be the consequence of human disobedience. For Christians, the quest to save oneself from sin and death finds its full expression in the story of Jesus, the Incarnate Christ, whose mission was to "take away the sin of the world" (Jn 1:29).

Christians acknowledge Jesus as "the Word made flesh" (Jn 1:14), and hold that those who believe he is the Son of God can be assured of salvation (Jn 3:16, 17). To know Jesus is to know the Father—to know God (Jn 14:1-2, 6-7) and those who know Jesus are guaranteed eternal life (Jn 8:32; 3:16), those who do not, await a very different fate; they shall be "thrown away like a branch" to wither and die, and then be "thrown into the fire and burned" (Jn 15: 6). According to the Gospel of John, the way to God demands obedience, even to the point of being willing to lay down one's life for the cause of Christ; this is what it means to "love one another" as Christ loves his own (Jn 15:12-13).

For Christians, Jesus's death by crucifixion serves as a "ransom" paid for man's sin, and through "obedience to the truth," Christians believe they will be purified, and hence reborn of "imperishable seed" (1 Pet. 1:18, 22-23). It is in this motif of death, resurrection, and the rebirth of the Spirit that he gains dominion over the mortal body and its passions (Rom. 6:12). Paul writes in his letter to the Romans, "If, because of the one man's (Adam's) trespass, death exercised dominion through that one, much more surely will those who receive the abundance of grace and the free gift of righteousness exercise dominion in life through the one-man Jesus Christ. Therefore, just as one man's trespass led to condemnation for all, so one man's act of righteousness leads to justification and life for all" (Rom. 5:17, 18).

The Divine in Christian Art

Roman Catholics and Eastern Orthodox Catholics have created countless images of Jesus Christ. The patriarchal church structure accentuated the masculine view of Jesus Christ, who was often envisioned as a knightly figure and the embodiment of masculine perfection. Perhaps influenced by compelling female mystical poets, such as Julian of Norwich and Saint Catherine of Sienna, exceptions to the predominant masculine image of Christ are found in paintings such as Francesco Vanni's *Saint Catherine Drinks the Blood of Christ* (1594), in which the act of the Eucharist is reimagined as a maternal experience, where humanity is transformed into a child suckling from the breast of her divine mother. From a patriarchal and androcentric perspective, this may have been a subversive message, yet such artistic images must have fulfilled the spiritual needs of parishioners, for whom the image of a compassionate, maternal Christ was a welcomed change.

FIGURE 2.5 *Francesco Vanni, Saint Catherine Drinks the Blood of Christ. Sailko via Wikimedia.*

Catholic and Protestant Christians disagree on artistic representations of God. Images representing God the Father in human bodily form, such as those in Michelangelo's Sistine Chapel ceiling paintings, are considered acceptable in Catholicism. However, Protestants accuse Catholics of flouting the commandment prohibiting idolatry, contending that Catholics worship these images. This opposition to religious iconography was so strong that some Protestants engaged in iconoclasm during the Reformation, attacking and destroying Catholic religious artwork in their effort to "cleanse" churches of idols. Protestant churches are typically more austere than Catholic churches, using simple symbols, such as the cross for decoration, but mostly lacking figurative artwork and refraining from depicting God the Father or Jesus in bodily form.

Catholics defend themselves against this charge of idolatry using several arguments. The first argument is that the images themselves are not the object of worship, but instead it is the divinity that the images represent that is the object of worship. Catholics also explain that the use of images is

FIGURE 2.6 *Baroque Crucifix of unknown Central European woodcarver. Credit: Beata Zawrzel / Contributor, via Getty Images.*

traditional and dates to the earliest days of Christianity, when, as a persecuted sect, Christians hid in Roman catacombs, which they decorated with paintings depicting Christ as the Good Shepherd, among other themes. Later, when Christianity was legalized in the Roman Empire and churches could be built, images were used in churches to depict scenes from the Bible to transmit biblical teachings to a largely illiterate populace. Finally, Catholics point out that when God spoke to Moses at Sinai, He did not reveal himself to the Israelites physically, so any depiction of God would be erroneous from the perspective of the Hebrew Bible. However, Catholics believe that since God did reveal himself bodily in the form of Jesus Christ, a depiction of Jesus cannot be idolatrous because it is not a work of imagination, but is instead based upon the image of the actual divine person. Images of Jesus range from Middle Eastern, which is the more realistic representation of the culture from which he came, to white European, which became the standard portrait. Protestants generally do not accept these arguments, claiming that Catholics worship idols when they bow or kneel before iconic representations of the divine, in exactly the way the Hebrew Bible prohibits.

FIGURE 2.7 *Madonna and Child. Credit: Leonardo da Vinci [Public domain], via Wikimedia*

In other religious traditions, however, most notably in Judaism and Islam, the creation of images of God, prophets, people, or animals as religious icons is strictly forbidden. This prohibition, known as aniconism, is based on the notion of idolatry in the Hebrew Bible as well as in the Qur'an. There has been debate about the parameters of the prohibition; some believe that it applies only to three-dimensional sculpture, and then only in worship spaces, while others believe that all naturalistic visual representation of God, humans or animals, is forbidden, regardless of the medium or context. The concern is that an image, particularly of a human or an animal, may inspire worship and thus distract the viewer from undivided devotion to the Transcendent God. Despite the taboo against figurative representation of the divine, both religious traditions have highly sophisticated artwork, but no visual representation of the divine itself.

Representations of the Divine in Judaism

Notions of God in Judaism can be classified under both "transcendence" and "immanence." In the Bible, the underlying belief is that God is transcendent—without form or body. One passage is quite explicit on this matter: "The Lord spoke to you out of the fire; you heard the sound of words but perceived no shape—nothing but a voice. . . . Take care not to make for yourselves a sculptured image in any likeness" (Deut. 4:12-24). Still, there are references to prophetic experiences of seeing or at least imagining the divine form in the Bible. Furthermore, the Bible states that humans were created in the image of God. Yet, if God does not have a body, and the divine and the human are different due to their embodiment or lack thereof, then in what sense were humans created in the "image of God?" A common rabbinic and philosophical answer is that humans and the divine share common qualities such as intellect, free will, and conscience.

Anthropomorphic representations of the divine in the Bible are pervasive. Besides God's voice, God's hands and feet are common in these descriptions. In Exod. 33:23, God says to Moses "I will put you in a cleft of the rock and shield you with my hand . . . you will see my back but my face must not be seen." Another reference to God's physical form appears in the Book of Ezekiel—who sees "a semblance of the human form. From what appears as his loins up, I saw a gleam as of amber . . . and from what appeared as his loins down, I saw what looked like fire. There was a radiance all about him" (Ezek. 1:26-28). Some prophets saw or at least imagined the divine in some human form, which suggests that the form of the human body can be godlike.

Moses Maimonides, the most influential medieval Jewish philosopher and codifier of the laws, addressed biblical anthropomorphic references to God, and warned against idolatry in our notions of the divine. His stance is that we should read descriptions of God's hands, feet, and voice allegorically. He explains that biblical images of an angry God or a God who loves us are meant for the uneducated masses, in order to help them maintain their faith. According to Maimonides, since God is not physical, we cannot attribute any physical qualities to him. He concludes that God can only be described in negative terms, or what is called "negative theology." This means that we can only state what God is not (i.e., God is not bound by time), rather than what God is. Maimonides formulates a faith-claim of the incorporeality of God, and asserts that any deviation from it is heretical.

Representation of the Divine in Jewish Mysticism

Although Judaism prohibits depictions of the divine in art, there is nonetheless significant discourse on the form of the divine in Jewish mystical writings. This view of God is found in writings beginning in the rabbinic period. Based on the biblical vision of Ezekiel, Merkavah (the heavenly chariot, after) Shi'ur Komah, written between the first and fourth centuries CE literally "the measure of the heights," describes in divine throne and the divine body. The extreme form of anthropomorphism in Shiur Komah was criticized by Maimonides as idolatry. Still, kabbalists view the text not as describing the appearance of God, but rather as a description of a visionary spiritual experience. The medieval mystical text, the Zohar, develops the theory of the sefirot (divine emanations), as a further adaptation of the description of the divine body as found in the Shiur Komah.

The sefirot are ten creative forces that emanate from the infinite, unknowable God—the *Ein Sof* (literally, without end or the infinite). Emanation then is the extension of a spiritual entity into a substance that does not separate itself from its source. According to such a view, the infinite, the Ein Sof, underwent a process of development that produced a realm of ten divine powers which together constitute the divine. The names of the *sefirot* include qualities such as wisdom, understanding, splendor, grace, and presence. They are usually portrayed on a vertical line with the higher *sefirot* being closer to the divine source. Their diagram is sometimes imposed upon a male figure, signifying *Adam Kadmon* (primordial man). Symbolically, the *sefirot* are associated with biblical personalities, male or female, values such as justice and benevolence, organs of the body, colors, etc. In some respects, they resemble the Indian chakra system. The lowest *sefira*, called Malchut or Shekhinah is the female divine potency which is a symbol of the divine presence in the world, and receives the forces from the higher *sefirot*.

According to the Kabbalah, the perfection and unification of the divine world (which influences the fate of God and therefore of humans) depends on the harmonious balance between individual *sefirot* as well as harmonious interrelationships among all the *sefirot*. The mystic is one who attempts to perform the necessary steps that will preserve the harmony of the divine realm. His work begins with the Shekhinah (or Malkhut) but affects the rest of the *sefirot*. The holy union of Tiferet (a "masculine" *sefirah*) and Shekhinah (a "feminine" *sefirah*) is the most important task that the mystic assumes in his quest; human action can therefore reunite the *sefirot* and restore harmony to the world. One of the implications of the Kabbalistic view of the divine is the sacredness of human sexuality, which can affect the rewards of earthly and divine union.

Representations of the Divine in Islam

Islam can be characterized as aniconic, in other words, opposed to the use of idols or images. There is a strong condemnation of *shirk* (idolatry) in the Qur'an, particularly against the statues worshipped by Arab pagans. Even images of Muhammad or members of his family are prohibited from any artistic creations in Islam. This has led to Islamic art being dominated by geometric patterns and calligraphy of Quranic verses as reflected and embodied in spaces such as mosques, and objects like the Qur'an, neither of which incorporates any figurative images.

FIGURE 2.8 *A calligrapher copies pages of the Qur'an on sheets of paper, August 30, 2010. Credit: MAHMOUD ZAYAT / Stringer, via Getty Images.*

Similar to Judaism, the proscription against idolatry has resulted in an absence of images of living beings in art. Like the Torah, the Qur'an refers to God in anthropomorphic terms. Numerous verses mention the hands (5:64, 48:10) or eyes (20:39, 52:48) of God, or state that God has mercy on believers (11:119, 12:53) and is wrathful toward those who are evil and idolatrous (4:93, 48:6). Symbolic and esoteric interpretations of God in the Qur'an include image of light: "Allah is the Light of the heavens and the earth. The example of His light is like a niche within which is a lamp, the lamp is within glass, the glass as if it were a pearly [white] star lit from [the oil of] a blessed olive tree, neither of the east nor of the west, whose oil would almost glow even if untouched by fire. Light upon light. Allah guides to His light whom He wills" (Qur'an 24:35).

Representations of the Divine in Buddhist philosophy and cultures

Buddhism denies the existence of an eternal, omnipotent God or godhead who is the creator and controller of the world. The falsehood of the idea of god is explained in Buddhist literature as an expression of *sassata ditthi* or eternalism, which affirms the notion of permanence. Since nothing is permanent, there cannot be an entity that exists forever. Therefore, the Buddha rejects the belief in God along with other metaphysical concepts, such as the soul.

Nonetheless, as Buddhism integrated into indigenous traditions, deities such as Avalokiteshvara (literally, the Lord who gazes down toward the world) were developed in different Buddhist cultures as either gods or goddesses who embody the compassion of the Buddha. According to Mahayana doctrine as expressed in such texts as the Lotus Sutra, Avalokiteshvara is the *bodhisattva*, the one who postpones his own Buddhahood or enlightenment, until he has assisted every sentient being in achieving nirvana or the ultimate state of liberation from *samsara* (the cycle of death and rebirth). A Buddhist story tells of Avalokiteshvara who realizes that there are still many unhappy beings that need to be saved. As he tried to comprehend this, his head splits into eleven pieces. He is then given eleven heads with which to hear the cries of the suffering. Upon hearing the cries, Avalokiteshvara attempts to reach out to all those who needed aid, but found that his two arms could not handle such an enormous task and shattered into pieces. He is then provided with a thousand arms with which to aid the suffering multitudes.

FIGURE 2.9 *Bodhisattva Avalokiteshvara. Credit: Gavin Heller / via Getty image.*

In Tibetan Buddhism, a form of Mahayana Buddhism, also called *vajrayana* or *tantra*, one of the most common practices is experiencing oneself as a deity, as well as through identification with deities who are archetypes of enlightenment. Buddhist deities are often used as devotional images helping the practitioners to visualize and concentrate on their spiritual path.

Contemporary Issues and Trends

Feminist theology and contemporary visions of the divine feminine

Feminist theologians strive to liberate religion from the dominance of patriarchal traditions, correcting gender imbalance and providing a religious world view where women are equal in matters related to doctrines, beliefs, and practices. Feminists have shown that representation of the divine matters to considerations of body, gender, and sexuality. The main concern of most feminist theologians is that the divine is usually represented in masculine terms. Even religions that have multiple gods and goddesses generally have a male Supreme God, to which all other gods and goddesses submit. The supremacy of the male god and the traditions that this divine hierarchy promulgates can be seen reflected in societies and the daily lives of their believers. Yet the presence of goddesses in religions such as Hinduism has not always correlated to gender and social balance for women. The order in the divine realm as conceived by spiritual leaders and theologians has been used by them as a justification for maintaining the social structure in which gender inequality has persisted.

Christian feminist theology

Since the second half of the twentieth century, numerous Christian theologians have been prominent in their commitment to gender equality in Christian life and thought. Theologians such as Mary Daly have objected to the phallocentric language used in both the Hebrew Bible and the New Testament, because, as she phrases it, "Since God is male, the male is God." Although the use of the male pronoun "He" and male form of the noun "God" has been traditionally accepted as inclusive of women, it underscores the view that "male" is the norm and "female" is "other." This "otherness" has been bolstered by language itself, reinforcing the view of women as an addendum to men. Considering the occasional representations of a feminine aspect of God in the Bible in such texts as Isa. 66:7-13 where God is represented as female, giving birth, feeding and comforting her children, some feminist theologians have proposed the rejection of overtly misogynist passages of the Bible, and embracing those with a more egalitarian view, recognizing that the books that comprise the Bible were chosen exclusively by men.

While Mary Daly has rejected Roman Catholicism and mainstream Christianity, Sallie McFague is a feminist reformer who remains within Christianity. McFague promotes Christian "ecofeminism," urging people to equate the body of God with the earth, and also suggesting a new model of God as mother, lover, and friend. Theologian Rosemary Radford Ruether also has an ecofeminist thrust to her writing, as well as a demonstrated concern for the impact of phallocentric language on Christian thought. Ruether replaces the word "God" with "God/dess" and extends her concern beyond Christianity to embrace the truths of other religious traditions. Ruether suggests that the focus of Christian goals and rituals should turn from the sole worship of "God the Father" to concern for Gaia, which represents the ecology of the earth. The concern for liberating traditional male-centered Christian theology, and the aim to gain equality for all women has led to the development of new voices within the Christian feminist movement, including the scholarship of Womanist theology, whose focus is to empower and liberate African American women, Asian feminist theology, and mujerista theology, the theology from the perspectives of Latinas.

Jewish, Muslim, and Buddhist feminist theology

Jewish feminist thinkers began with questions of gender inequality, but have since extended the parameters of their work to all areas of Jewish life and thought that pertain to gender, sexuality, and ethics. Both theological and halakhic scholarship have informed and shaped new perspectives and methodologies in interpreting, constructing, and democratizing an inclusive Judaism. Scholars such as Judith Plaskow, Ellen Umansky, Marcia Falk, and Rebecca Alpert have centered their work around the critique of traditional male god-language, and advocated for changes of rules and views that subordinate women, the creation of egalitarian liturgy, and new and innovative rituals for women. One example is Rachel Adler's ethical commitment contract—*brit ahuvim* (lovers' covenant), based on the principle of mutuality, replacing the traditional marriage contract (*Ketubah*) and its language of acquisition.

Feminist theology provides a theoretical framework for re-envisioning the three pillars of traditional Judaism—Torah, God, and Israel, and aims to apply the moral imperative for inclusivity and equality, not only for women, but also to all aspects of life. Judith Plaskow's scholarship was the first systematic feminist Jewish theology that focuses on recovering women's history and redefining women's relationship with the sacred. One of the most important questions that Plaskow raises is whether feminism is in fact transforming Judaism, or it is only attaining equal rights while social and religious structures remain unchanged. She challenges women and men to embrace the notion of Jewish transformation, and is adamant that women must see themselves "standing again at Sinai" as recipients and partners of the covenant. This entails critiquing deeply embedded notions of hierarchy and exclusivity as these exist in the Torah, in liturgy, and in Halakha. Furthermore, as partners of the covenant, feminist theologians must redefine the Jewish community's ethics of inclusivity, ameliorate what they characterize as imbalanced god-language, and create new midrashim and liturgy that reflect women's experiences and sensibilities.

Along with Jewish and Christian theologians, feminist scholarship in traditions such as Islam and Buddhism has been actively contributing to critiques of patriarchal authorities in their religions. Islamic feminism is a more recent movement of women which draws on the Qur'anic concept of equality of all human beings, and promotes the application of this theology to Islamic law. Muslim feminists argue that while some Islamic countries violate the true teachings of Islam, the Qur'an is in fact compatible with the ideas of gender equality. Feminist scholars such as Amina Wadud and others quote verses from the Qur'an that express the equality between men and women, and explain the subordination of women in the religion on the basis of patriarchal interpretations by conservative clergy and legal scholars.

Buddhist feminism is also in its early stage of development. Like feminists in other religious traditions, they work to advance gender equality in areas such as the spiritual status of women, the treatment of women in Buddhist societies, and the role of women in the history of Buddhism. Feminist scholars such as Rita Gross and Miranda Shaw acknowledge a misogynist strand in early Buddhist texts, but argue that the core teachings of Buddhism promote gender equity. One of the causes that Buddhist feminists have undertaken is advancing the availability of ordination to women, particularly in societies that denied women such spiritual roles, due to the ancient belief that women cannot reach enlightenment.

Thealogy, Neo-Paganism, and female vision of the Divine

Countering and correcting the patriarchal theology of the Abrahamic religions is "thealogy," the discourse of the female divine (thea) in contrast to the male God (theo), providing a framework for giving voice for representations of the divine in a female form. Naomi Goldenberg first used this term in her book, *Changing of the Gods* (1979). Thealogy has become widely known as a provocative term denoting a shift away from the androcentric (male-centered) theological paradigm. Like Christian and Jewish feminist theology, thealogy developed from radical feminist criticism of religion as the glorification of masculinity, and from feminist reflection on women's experience and the sacral power of femaleness.

While thealogy is not associated with any one religious or spiritual tradition, it shares valuing the power of femaleness with Neo-Paganism. Neo-Paganism, earth-based spirituality, and goddess-centered traditions are decentralized, possessing no clergy, holy books, or geographical centers. These traditions can also be characterized as pantheistic, promoting the idea that the divine is immanent in the world. Since the divine permeates all, this creative life force is typically identified with nature, and thus with Gaia or "Mother Earth." Mother Earth, also revered as a goddess, provides the gifts of the earth that sustains all living things.

Questions for review and discussion

1   What role does the body play in understanding our view of God?

2　How do the notions of God as transcendent (separate from the material world) and God as immanent (embodied) differ in terms of the essence of God?

3　Can God interact with the world without a body?

4　Is the God described in the New Testament gospels the same as the God of Abraham, Isaac, and Jacob, described in the Hebrew Bible?

5　How does theology contribute to our comprehension and appreciation of the divine?

6　Discuss feminist critiques of masculine god-language. How strong and valid are their arguments?

7　How does the commandment against idolatry—that is the making and worshipping of images of the deity—affect how we think of God?

8　How does the notion of the world as a process and consequence of divine emanations different from the belief in a Creator God—the divine as separate being who creates the world "*creatio ex nihilo*"?

9　What does it mean for a religion to have a "positive view of the body"? What are some examples of positive and negative perspectives of the body that are engendered from religions?

10　Can the term "God" be employed in a positive way in facilitating interfaith and cross-cultural dialogue? And if so, how?

11　Do Neo-pagan views of the divine help to correct issues of gender and sexuality engendered by patriarchal religions? And if so, how?

1, 2, 3, 6, 7, 9, 11

Glossary

Aniconism-opposition to the use of idols or images for worship; the absence of material representations of the supernatural, particularly in the monotheistic Abrahamic religions.

Anthropomorphism-Attributing human characteristics to God.

Eternalism-the belief in eternal life or eternal things such as soul which according to Buddhist philosophy is false.

Euhemerism-theory named after the Greek mythographer Euhemerus who conceived the view that the ancient gods were superhuman.

Gaia-Greek goddess personifying the earth; Gaia in contemporary Neo-pagan spirituality is identifying Mother Earth as the divine feminine.

Guru-a spiritual master in Buddhism, Hinduism, and Jainism.

Halacha-the collection of Jewish laws derived from the Oral and Written Torah.

Idolatry-the worship of a physical object as a god.

Immanence-divine presence dwelling in the world.

Incarnation-the embodiment of a deity in an earthly form.

Patriarchy-social system where men hold primary power.

Thealogy-a study of the meaning of the Goddess (thea)—the feminine divine in distinction from God (theo).

Neo-paganism-modern religious movements influenced by historical pagan traditions based on fertility and the worship of nature.

Transcendence-divine presence beyond the material world.

Trinity-derived from the Latin number three or triad; the Christian belief that God comprises three beings: Father, Son, and Holy Spirit.

3

Erotic Desire and Divine love

Eros is named after the Greek god of fertility, and represents the idea of sexual passion and desire. Eros is associated or identified with feelings of attraction to and longing for people, things, and ideals, including God. Eros and desire are often used colloquially to express romantic feelings, and desire is often interchangeable and entwined with love. For the Greeks and later religious thinkers, eros is viewed as an irrational and dangerous form of love.

When we speak about the body in religion, we refer not only to the physical body, but also to human consciousness, emotions, and behaviors. Love and desire are among the most profound states of the human experience, and religions have rigorously attempted to control these and channel them toward the divine. We will address the subjects of sexual desire and sexual pleasure in Chapters 8 and 9, where we will examine views and rules pertaining to sex and sexuality, gender, marriage, and reproduction. In this chapter, our attention will be directed toward a religious phenomenon which appears cross-culturally, where mystics, saints, and other spiritual adepts express their experience of loving God in erotic terms. These men and women have left us a rich body of literature, including poetry and philosophy, which has been accepted by many devotees and followers as sacred writings. For our study of the body in religion, the subject of love and desire offers a unique opportunity to revisit the popular use of erotic terms, which are often directed to physical sexual experiences, but in their original definition were intended to represent a transcendent state. Considering our present study, the notion of the erotic in religious contexts engenders a more expansive perspective, which enables us to diffuse rigid binaries such as mind versus body, spirituality versus sexuality, and transcendence versus immanence.

We will examine the ways that erotic desire has been employed interchangeably with love in representing the human experience of and encounter with the divine. Our selection of texts includes scriptures as well as philosophy, theology, mysticism, and poetry from the Jewish, Christian, Sufi, and Hindu traditions. Some of the texts use explicitly sexual metaphors, while others are subtle and suggestive. Some authors view desire as more embodied and therefore an inferior spiritual state; others conceive of desire as representing a higher spiritual realization. Regardless, the trope of desire is integral to love, whether human or divine. Erotic representations of the divine, whether attributed to a god, a goddess, or to the human encounter with the sacred, illustrate the richness as well as the limits of language to describe the transcendent.

Erotic desire and love figure prominently in the ways that religious individuals and communities cross-culturally represent and relate to the divine. Yet, dualistic and hierarchical thinking that pit the mind against the body, male versus female, reason in contrast to emotion, and spirituality as opposed to sexuality have shaped and continue to inform religious discourse. Worldly desire has been perceived as a hindrance to spiritual progress, and at the same time, if directed toward spiritual goals, as a profound state through which one can transcend carnality. Erotic language in sacred literature accentuates the paradoxical phenomenon of religions' perception of the sexual drive as a threat to authority and tradition, while at the same time employing erotic and sexual symbolism to convey the human relationship to the transcendent.

Erotic desire is a feature of the metaphysical imaginary; that is, the way religions conceive the nexus of the human and the divine, whether a tradition considers celibacy to be the ideal path to the divine, or endorses fertility and sexual pleasure as positive and suitable for spiritual growth. In recent scholarship of sexuality and religion, the phenomenon of the erotic in mystical and spiritual experiences has been theorized, among other ways, in terms of how the biological body and mating behavior might influence religious symbols, or explaining a celibate's erotic spiritual experience psychologically, in terms of sexual sublimation.

While eros in everyday parlance conveys an explicit sexual desire, erotic desire can be broadly understood as the quest to abandon and transcend ourselves for an experience of "otherness." Religious traditions often speak of human desire for intimacy with an "Other," such as a god or a goddess. In some traditions, erotic figuring of the divine is integral to the concepts and images of gods and goddesses who are depicted as erotic beings embodying and symbolizing the fecundity of love. Sexual passion personified as a god or a goddess is a common feature in ancient religions. In Greek mythology, for example, Eros and Aphrodite are god and goddess of sexual desire and fertility; in Hinduism, Kama and Rati are god and goddess of erotic love, respectively, while Lord Shiva alternates between eros and asceticism. In numerous mythological writings, divine couples are depicted as sexually passionate, active, and promiscuous, qualities that contribute to the expansion of the divine family.

In theistic traditions where God is either conceived of in an embodied form or imagined as disembodied and transcendent, we find accounts by religious adepts of their personal experiences of a mutuality of erotic love for and with the divine. The theology undergirding such religious views is the belief that God loves us. Such divine love in turn elicits our devotion and attachment. This notion of the divine can engender a variety of relational models, such as parent-child or lover-beloved. In romantic relationships, a dynamic of separation and union is common, and is illustrated in emotions such as joy and ecstasy, as well as frustration and longing for the other. As we shall see in our selection of sacred poetry, human-divine love often follows this dynamic, and embodies passionate desire in similar, albeit culturally distinct metaphors.

"Desire" and "Love" in Western philosophical writings

The earliest thinking in the West on the notion of desire is found in the philosophies of Plato and Aristotle. For Plato, eros is neither purely human nor purely divine: it is something intermediate which he calls a *daimon*. In the Symposium, Aristophanes narrates a myth of human origins that explains sexuality and the yearning for a soulmate. Later in the Symposium, Diotima teaches Socrates about the ascent of eros from earthly to heavenly forms of love. She delineates the steps on the ladder of love from love of an individual body which is love that is subject to pain; moving up the ladder, one shifts from the body to the inner qualities of the individual. Continuing the ascent, one reaches the ultimate love—love for the Good and the Beautiful.

Aristotle in De Anima says: "It is manifest, therefore, that what is called desire is the sort of faculty in the soul which initiates movement" (De Anima, iii 10, 433a31–b1). The soul is the essence of every living thing, and desire is the soul in motion—animals desire things, and in their desire acquire locomotion. Yet desire implies incompletion and inferiority, even when it is a necessary means toward the Form of the Good. Aristotle also identified *philia*—meaning love in the context of friendship based on loyalty and sacrifice. In his Rhetoric, he defines *philia* as "wanting for someone what one thinks is good, for his sake and not for one's own, and being inclined, so far as one can, to do such things for him" (1380b36–1381a2).

[handwritten annotation: archetype cards]

Another Greek term for love is *agape*—which is passionate, selfless, and without the necessity of reciprocity. Such love requires absolute devotion and sacrifice. While in the New Testament, *agape* is the highest form of love, usually associated with God's love for humanity, for Aristotle, imperfect mortal beings desire and love God, yet God, the Unmoved Mover, has no desire for humans. For Plato as well, the gods do not love because they do not experience desires, inasmuch as their desires are all satisfied. They can thus only be an object of love, not a subject of love (Symposium, 200–1). Eros leads humans to divinity, but not vice versa.

The late-fifth-century Christian Neoplatonist, (Pseudo-) Dionysius synthesizes Neoplatonism and Christian ideas of love. In his Divine Names, he describes eros as a cosmic, unifying force of all relationships, human and divine. Dionysius further explains the concept of "yearning" for union with the Good and the Beautiful. He locates the dynamics of love in a Christian context when he describes St. Paul's possession by divine love as Christ living in him. For Dionysius then, eros as an ecstatic passionate love is a most appropriate term for comprehending Christian divine love.

The distinction between desire and love

In the writings of the Neoplatonist Renaissance philosopher, Judah Abrabanel, better known as Leone Ebreo, desire and love are highlighted as distinct emotions. In his magnum opus, *Dialoghi d'Amore*, he describes love as the principal source and goal of the universe, as love strives toward the union of the beautiful and the good in the beloved. While he discusses human love, his main emphasis is metaphysical love. Abrabanel makes the distinction between desire and love. As modes of being and becoming, love is the state for which we strive—to be with the object of our desire and thus the fulfillment of desire. Love then is a state which is dependent upon desire. Abrabanel maintains a transcendental conception of the Godhead, and with it the notion of divine love as the urge to come nearer to God.

Erotic desire and Divine love in Jewish Writings

The Torah offers us multiple notions of eros and love. These include explicit terms for desire, allusions to the human inclination toward sexuality, commandments to love, and an imagery of God in union with the nation of Israel.

Taavah and *teshukah*, Hebrew terms for eros, occur in the story of Adam and Eve: "The woman saw that the tree was good for food, and that it was a delight (*taavah*) to the eyes"; Once she disobeys, desire is part of her punishment, "And your desire (*tshukatech*) shall be for your man."

According to rabbinic thought, all human beings possess the *yetzer ha-tov* (good inclination) and *yetzer ha-ra* (evil inclination). The Torah offers the path to increase the *yetzer ha-tov*, our desire for the highest good, through the fulfillment of all the commandments. Among these is the injunction to love God:

> Hear, O Israel! The LORD is our God, the LORD is one! "You shall love the LORD your God with all your heart and with all your soul and with all your might." These words, which I am commanding you today, shall be on your heart. (Deut. 6:5).

The medieval Torah commentator, Rashi (eleventh century) explained that the way to express love of God is to perform God's commandments out of love, rather than out of fear.

The Hebrew prophets further expanded the biblical imagery of divine love in their conception of the union of the nation of Israel (female) and God (male), derived from the historic event of *b'rit* (covenant) and encompassing mutual promises and obligations. Their rhetoric highlights the hierarchical nature of this relationship, shaped by gender roles that advance male authority and female subservience. Jeremiah speaks of God as the faithful and jealous husband/king who demands of his preferred wife absolute fidelity.

An alternative relational model for the bond between God and his chosen nation is provided in Song of Songs, which depicts sensuous love between young lovers. Scholars of the ancient Near East show parallels in themes and metaphors between the Song and Egyptian love poetry. Rabbi Akiva ben Yosef (50–135 CE) establishes the status of the Song proclaiming its holiness based on conceptualizing the "lover" as God and the "beloved" as the community of Israel. He therefore justified its inclusion in the Bible by stating that while all of the Torah is holy, the Song of Songs is holy of holies.

Since its inclusion in the Bible, Song of Songs has become a base-text for spiritual contemplation among Jews and Christians. The love depicted in the Song is contextualized in a romantic relationship, and celebrates a series of spontaneous and passionate moments that produce joy and ecstasy, however fleeting. Fulfillment of this love relationship is yearned for, yet never fully obtained. For centuries, rabbis, philosophers, theologians, and mystics commented upon and explicated verses of the Song employing allegorical exegesis to convey the intimate relationship between God and the community of Israel, and between Christ and the Church.

Erotic desire and the vicissitudes of separation and union permeate the Song's poetry. The separation of the two lovers and their longing for the consummation of their love is a recurring theme. The suspense of the lover's whereabouts increases the passionate desire for him: "Swear to me, daughters of Jerusalem! If you find him now, you must tell him I am in the fever of love" (Song of Songs, 5:8). Their passionate desire for each other is given the following profound expression about the nature of love: "Love is as fierce as death, its jealousy bitter as the grave. Even its sparks are a raging fire, a devouring flame" (Song of Songs, 8:6). The lovers' frequent separation generates the longing for sustained intimacy: "Bind me as a seal upon your heart, a sign upon your arm. . . . Great seas cannot extinguish love, no river can sweep it away" (Song of Songs, 8:7).

In contemporary scholarship of the Song that draws upon the categories of gender and sexuality, the binary of human and divine love that results from traditional interpretations has been questioned. Scholars have underscored the amplification of the woman's voice that is stifled in the majority of biblical texts. Some even speculate that a woman or a group of women may have composed this collection of poems, given the first-person voice and pivotal role of the female in the Song. For feminist thinkers, the Song has engendered notions of positive sexuality and an egalitarian relationship, focusing especially on the portrayal of the woman lover who asserts her emotions and desires.

Erotic desire and Divine love in Christian writings

Love is identified with God in Christian scriptures, narrated not only as a story of love but also as a fundamental theological doctrine—(God is love). "Beloved, let us love one another, for love is from God, and whoever loves has been born of God and knows God. Anyone who does not love does not know God, because God is love" (1 Jn 4:7-8).

Christian theologians and saints, like their rabbinic counterparts, offered their insights into God's love through the allegorical interpretation of the Song of Songs or Canticle. Among the first Christian thinkers to compose a commentary to the Song is Origen (ca. 185–254 CE). Two primary Christian views on reading the Song suggest that (1) the male lover is Christ and the female beloved is the Church, and (2) the more mystical one according to which the Song describes the relationship of an individual soul to Christ as bridegroom.

For the early Christian theologian St. Augustine, desire is the emotion which is the manifestation of love. Like Plato, he distinguishes between lower and higher desires. He also sharply discerns between love or desire for God and the desire or love of self. Augustine believes that because humans are creatures of desires, divine grace can infuse and direct human desires toward the good, which is God.

Both Origen and the Neoplatonic mystic, Plotinus, can be said to have initiated what has become known as "bridal theology," which reached its climax in the writings and sermons of Bernard of Clairvaux (ca. 1090–1153). Another mystic, Gregory of Nyssa, offers a commentary on the Song of Songs which emphasizes this erotic dimension of lover and beloved. Though the Greek text of the Song of Songs uses *agape* for "love" and for being in love, in Gregory's commentary, *eros* and not *agape*, best describes love of God as intense yearning, at once painful and blissful, which leads one to union with God. At one point in his commentary, Gregory notes: "For heightened *agape* is called *eros*."

This rhetoric of divine love persists among mystics and theologians throughout the Middle Ages. Erotic desire for God becomes an important trope, especially for women contemplatives. Mechthild of Magdeburg (1207–c. 1282/94), a beguine and mystic, speaks in her autobiography *Flowing light of the Godhead* about the divine lover in profoundly erotic terms:

you are my softest pillow,
my most lovely bed,
my most intimate rest,
my deepest longing,
a stream for my passion.

St. Teresa of Avila, Spanish nun, mystic and writer (founder of the Discalced Carmelite Order, 1515–82; canonized 1622), authored numerous books, including *Life*, a personal autobiography, the *Way of Perfection*, a handbook for her nuns, and *Interior Mansions*, in which she describes the many different steps on the path to mystical union with God. She mediates the spiritual and the sensual in her well-known autobiography where she describes her ecstatic experience of sweet pain and pleasure in the midst of her great vision in chapter XXIX:

It pleased our Lord that I should see the following vision a number of times. I saw an angel near me, on the left side, in bodily form. This I am not won't to see, save very rarely. . . . In this vision it pleased the Lord that I should see it thus. He was not tall, but short, marvelously beautiful, with a face which shone as though he were one of the highest of the angels, who seem to be all of fire: they must be those whom we call Seraphim. . . . I saw in his hands a long golden spear, and at the point of the iron there seemed to be a little fire. This I thought that he thrust several times into my heart, and that it penetrated to my entrails. When he drew out the spear he seemed to be

FIGURE 3.1 *(a) Bernini's Ecstasy of St. Theresa. Credit: Bettmann / Contributor, via Getty Images; (b) Full statue. Credit: By Miguel Hermoso Cuesta (own work), via Wikimedia Commons.*

drawing them with it, leaving me all on fire with a wondrous love for God. The pain was so great that it caused me to utter several moans; and yet so exceeding sweet is this greatest of pains that it is impossible to desire to be rid of it, or for the soul to be content with less than God.

The intersection of aesthetics, sexuality, and spirituality is profoundly embodied in one singular experience. The physical piercing of her heart that St. Teresa describes has been labeled transverberation—a spiritual wounding of the heart. The references to the beautiful form of the angel, her moaning during his continuous thrusting the spear into her heart, and the experience of sweet pain is an outstanding portrait of an erotic spiritual moment. The Italian sculptor Gian Lorenzo Bernini's famous masterpiece, "the Ecstasy of St. Teresa" located in the Coronado Chapel in Rome follows her own admission that "the body doesn't fail to share in some of it (the erotic pain of desiring God), and even a great deal." Bernini's sensual artistic rendition of her experience further challenges the distinction between inner and outer senses, and blurs the conceptual binary between physical and spiritual love.

Teresa's experience of the wound culminates in her union with and marriage to God. Analogously to the Song of Songs, which stirred hearts and minds and engendered numerous new poetic and theological works, the ecstasy of St.

Theresa, whether read or gazed at in Bernini's creation out of stone, inspires the reader and the spectator—stimulating and recreating ecstatic experiences through the engagement with the erotic aesthetic. Despite Christian theological doctrines that distinguish between divine *agape* and human eros, visionary experiences by Christian nuns such as Teresa blur such views and further illustrate the complex phenomenon of erotic representations of the divine.

Love and Eros in Sufi Writings

Sufis derive their notion of love from this verse: "God will love them as they will love him" (Qur'an 5:54). Scholars interpret this verse to mean that human love for God stems from God's love for humans. In Sufi writings, ecstasy and joy, as well as pain and loneliness, characterize the spiritual path. Sufis underscore the dynamic of separation from and the longing for the Beloved divine. In the poetry of Rabiah al-Basri (717–801), who is regarded as the first female Sufi, yearning for God is expressed in the language of lover and beloved:

Brothers, my peace is in my aloneness.
My Beloved is alone with me there, always.
I have found nothing in all the worlds
That could match His love,
This love that harrows the sands of my desert.
If I come to die of desire
And my Beloved is still not satisfied,
I would live in eternal despair.
To abandon all that He has fashioned
And hold in the palm of my hand
Certain proof that He loves me
That is the name and the goal of my search.

The greatest and best known Sufi poet was Mewlana Jalaluddin Rumi, a theologian and mystic (1207–73). Born in Balkh, Afghanistan, Rumi spent time traveling throughout the surrounding countries before eventually settling in what is present-day Turkey. Like many other mystics, he conveys his sense of the ineffable nature of the divine in what he describes in his poetry as the "hidden treasure." Employing erotic imagery and sensuous language, he depicts his mystical experiences of intimacy with God as well as his longing for Him, by referring to God in terms of endearment, such as "Beauty," "O Love," and "Beloved."

Rumi points out that separation is the crux of love in the very first line of his love epic, the *Mathnawi*: "Listen to this reed as it complains, telling the tale of separation." In conveying the vicissitudes of love and the rhythm of separation and union, Sufis employ *ishq*, a term that denotes passionate love. Like eros, *ishq* is an obsessive yearning of the lover that is often understood as an illness. This state of longing is described as a fire which God ignites in the hearts of His friends in order to burn in them all worldly preoccupation and egocentric desires.

Such an uncompromising longing for the Beloved culminates in a mystical state Sufis term *fana fillah*, or annihilation in God, conveying the elimination of the ego. The projected union with God is sometime referred to as *baqa*, in which the Sufi reaches balance and stability. This is shown in the Persian story of Layla and Majnun, where the lover is in perpetual state of *ishq* for his beloved, but ultimately transforms his madness for his woman beloved into the bliss of the divine Beloved.

The notion of beauty plays a prominent role both in the theoretical writings and in the poetic Sufi tradition. Rumi declares that his *yar* (beloved) has come in the human form as the holy man, Shams-i Tabriz:

> My sick heart, it's time for your medicine.
> Take a deep refreshing breath! The time has come.
> The Beloved who heals the sick hearts of lovers,
> Has come to our world in human form.

In addition to celebrating beauty in general and the human form in particular, a frequent metaphor in Sufi poetry refers to wine and the intoxicating experience of mystical love. Wine in Sufi verse is a depiction of an overwhelming state of love. Just as the quality and taste of wine depends on its degree of fermentation, so is the degree of the state of love. Clarifying that this "wine" is not alcoholic wine, Rumi says:

> You'll wake up from the drunkenness of this world
> After a good night's sleep
> But the drunkenness from God's wine
> Will last until the grave.

In Sufi literature, the ultimate mystical state is where there is no longer a distinction between love, lover, and beloved. Here we find references to love for the divine couched in so-called profane language and behavior that would be perceived as transgressive in orthodox Islam. This trend parallels mystical writings in other traditions that once again problematize the dichotomy of sacred and profane, human and divine love.

Deities, love, and desire in classical Hindu literature

In the Puranas (Hindu texts that include narratives of gods and kings), it is told that Lord Shiva, known as an ascetic, veered away from asceticism once *Kama* shot arrows into his heart that caused him to develop a desire for Parvati whom he then marries. Shiva manifests his dual nature as an ascetic who combines the heat of *tapas* (yogic practices) with the heat of erotic desire. Shiva is often represented in the form of a *linga*, a phallic symbol of creative energy, encircled in a *yoni*, a symbol of the womb as well as his consort, the goddess Devi or Shakti.

Desire in Hindu texts and worship is also spiritualized and contextualized in *bhakti* Hindu theology. According to *bhakti* (devotional love for a deity) thought, as the devotee cultivates a personal relationship with a deity, desire and love for one's deity is integral to the path and its goals. Thus, in the Bhagavad Gita, Lord Krishna, an incarnation of Vishnu, states "Fill your mind with me, Love me, Serve me, Worship me always. Seeking me in your heart, you will at last be united with me" (9:33-34).

In *bhakti* philosophy, we find a systematic approach to cultivating an intimate relationship with the divine. Bhakti aesthetics classifies emotions, moods, and tastes that comprise phenomenon of love. A primary example of such a systematic approach to love is the theory of erotic *rasa* (essence; denoting a mood or an emotion) which dominates Sanskrit drama and poetry. The theory of erotic *rasa*, while couched in worldly terms of passionate sexual metaphors, is nevertheless a spiritual experience that is integral to the path of devotion.

A central theme in the erotic *rasa* theory is the designation of *viraha* (absence or separation) or the phenomenon of "love in separation," particularly applicable to imagining Krishna as a lover. Erotic *rasa* dominates the twelfth-century Sanskrit poem, the Gitagovinda. This is one of the most important works in Hindu poetry and a source of religious inspiration in both medieval and contemporary Vaishnavism. This poem offers a paradigm of the rhythm of the intensification of desire—both Lord Krishna and his beloved Radha are depicted in intense states of desire during their separations from each other.

In contrast with the Song of Songs which lacks references to God (despite its canonization in the Bible), and where God is only invoked in its allegorical interpretations, the Gitagovinda explicitly describes the divinity of Krishna. Jayadeva, as its narrator, initiates his readers in the complex and multilayered meanings of the poem by instructing them of the celestial identity of the protagonist lovers. The challenge here, as with other erotic poetry written by

FIGURE 3.2 *"Radha and Krishna in a Bower: A folio from the Gita Govinda" dated 1780. Credit: Historical Picture Archive / Contributor.*

spiritual adepts, is negotiating the nexus of the metaphysics and physics of love. As in the Song of Songs, each appellation and metaphor is contextually meaningful at the level of both human and divine love.

Cross-cultural parallels

In reviewing our selection of texts from the traditions of Judaism, Christianity, Islam, and Hinduism that depict and celebrate erotic representations of, and encounter with the divine, significant cross-cultural parallels can be drawn. Philosophers and poets alike allude to and at times clearly distinguish between a passionate desire that is highly sensuous and a more stable and enduring love for God. There are terms that signify desire and accentuate its distinction from the more general notion of love. The Hebrew term *teshukah* or the Arabic *ishq* in Sufism for example are akin to the Greek term *eros* and connote erotic passion. In some cases, such as the theology of bridal mysticism, the adherent's erotic depiction of the encounter with the divine is framed in a normative context such as marriage; at other times these texts refer to antinomian behavior such as intoxication or sexual promiscuity. Theologically, however, an additional interpretive layer transforms what appears to be transgressive behavior, spiritualizing and transforming eros into allegory.

The writings of rabbis, Kabbalists, Sufis, Christian saints, and Krishna devotees testify to the reality that spiritual adepts from diverse theistic traditions contemplate the divine through notions of human embodiment. Such contemplations depict an intense intimacy of lover and beloved. As lovers of God, they are certainly susceptible to erotic engagement with the subject of their ultimate desire. Thus, they succeed in unraveling the dialectical relationship of eros and *agape*, spirituality and sexuality, and in establishing a harmonious model for integrating human and divine love.

Questions for review and discussion

1 Is desire necessary in order to love?

2 Is it a contradiction to command love?

3 Why do the rabbis, Church Fathers, and philosophers insist on the allegorical interpretation of the Song of Songs and other erotically infused sacred literature?

4 Does erotic desire as portrayed in the Song of Songs, St. Teresa's vision, the Gitagovinda, and Rumi's poetry validate sexual love?

5 Why do you think some thinkers espouse desiring God as the highest spiritual state, while others believe that loving God is the most sublime experience?

6 How do religions differ in the ways they manifest divine love?

7 Is divine love universal, or historically and culturally derived?

8 Is divine love still a relevant idea in our lives today?

Glossary

Agape-Greek: passionate, selfless love.

Allegory-literary device that conveys hidden meanings through symbolic figures, actions, imagery, and/or events, which together create the spiritual meaning of the text.

Eros-Greek god of fertility; a state of strong physical and emotional attraction to another person.

Fana fillah-Arabic: annihilation of the self in Sufism.

Godhead-the essential being of God or the Supreme Being.

Ishq-Arabic: passionate love.

Neoplatonism-a philosophical school (third to seventh century CE), espousing the priority of mind over matter, or consciousness as the supreme form of reality, and the belief of a single divine cause.

Otherness-the state of being different or distinct.

Philia-friendship or brotherly love.

Sufism-the Muslim mystical path.

Teshukah-Hebrew: passionate desire.

Transverberation-a spiritual wounding of the heart.

Theism-belief in the existence of a god or gods, especially the belief in a personal God as creator and ruler of the world.

Viraha-Sanskrit: absence or separation.

3,4

PART TWO

Celebrating and Sustaining the Body

Having examined the foundational beliefs in religion, particularly the notion of a relationship between the divine and the human, we are now ready to consider the embodiments of religious beliefs and doctrines in everyday life, in major life cycles, and in festivals. Many of these events take place with other members within our community, and our individual bodies are now seen as part of the "social body." In Chapter 4, "The Body in Religious Ritual," we employ the term "celebrating the body," to convey the ways we honor and praise the divine body. We focus on rituals that enable us to sustain our own bodies and rejoice in the pleasures they provide us.

In Chapter 5, "Food: Laws and Practices," we provide an overview of laws and teachings that guide our dietary practices. Not only does food provide us with nourishment and health, but food as integral to religious rituals, holidays, and festivals has rich symbolism in commemorating historic events associated with our religious stories. In Chapter 6, "Sustaining the Body: Breath,

Harmony, Health, and Healing," we turn our attention to notions and practices that sustain us through life. We begin with conceptualization and practices of breath and breath control and their relevance for health and healing. We review traditional beliefs as found in scriptures and other sources that often link a person's state of health or disease to notion of harmony and balance. Additionally, notions of health and disease are seem in some traditions and cultures as derived from the influence of supernatural powers, and employ magical or miraculous techniques in their healing practices. We then consider modern Western views of health based on science and technology, and examine how traditional healing modalities that were integral to religious systems are influencing contemporary healthcare practices.

4

The Body in Religious Ritual

Ritual is an act or a series of acts that are regularly repeated. Ritual must fit into four categories: it must be a repetitive social practice, it must be set off from the routines of day to day life, it must follow some sort of ritual schema, and it must be encoded in myth. (*Cultural Anthropology: A Perspective on the Human Condition*, by Emily Shultz and Robert Lavenda)

In this chapter, we will provide an overview of the ritual body in worship through postures, gestures, and movement. We will examine the ways regularly occurring rituals in Christianity, Islam, Judaism, and Hinduism embody religious beliefs, as well as engage and celebrate the body. We will also highlight rituals such as trance-inducing music and dance in Sufism and African religions, as well as the use of mind-altering drugs in Native American traditions to produce altered states of consciousness. We will discuss how women-based rituals, engendered by the feminist critique of ancient patriarchal and androcentric practices, have been embraced by established religious institutions and grassroots groups alike. We will explore earth-based spiritual practices which, influenced by pagan religions, have also contributed to new religious rituals. Finally, we will ponder the impact of using the internet for spiritual practice.

The body is often celebrated through the performance of rituals. At times, our lived bodies and the social body (the community) are celebrated; at other times, the divine body is celebrated. Celebrations of the body in ritual include reenactment of historic events; life cycle events such as birth, coming of age, and marriage; prayers and blessings for physical and spiritual well-being, and the plentitude of food; and the joys and beauty of communal song and dance. At the same time, not all religious rituals emphasize the pleasures and celebrations of the body. As we shall see in Chapter 11, some rituals, aimed at cultivating self-control and moral virtues incorporate extreme technologies that inflict pain and suffering upon the adepts. Practices such as lengthy and frequent fasting, sleep deprivation, and self-flagellation often represent dualistic views that demand subduing natural desires for the sake of spiritual liberation and redemption.

In recent decades, the study of religion and ritual has incorporated methodologies and theories from sociology and anthropology. Expanding our understanding of ritual beyond textual and historical studies, ethnographic research has provided data and case studies that complement and enrich our understanding of ritual cross-culturally. Current theorists of ritual advance various approaches to explaining how and why rituals work and what they mean. In attempting to break down mind-body dualism, the embodiment theory applied to religious ritual clarifies the primacy of the body in participating in and experiencing the process of ritualization. Ritual acts are also identified as practices and performances that empower the participants. Scholar of religion, Manuel Vasquez argues that rituals are not a matter of belief, but rather of practices that engender religious experiences. The sacred, then, is created and embodied, and is integral to a holistic view of life.

Sociologist Pierre Bourdieu's notions of *Habitus* and *Hexis* (*Outline of a Theory of Practice*) illuminate the meaning of bodily disposition in social systems, including religious rituals. Our dispositions for certain postures, such as speech, eating, and thinking, are habits that are imprinted on our body. His notion of the habituated body can also be applied to religious rituals, where repetitive postures, movements, and speech embody and perform sacred myths at regular sequences in space and time.

Ritual theorist Ronald Grimes describes the quality of naturalness of our embodied rituals. "Deep ritual knowledge, like inspired music or choreographic knowledge, feels like the most natural thing in the world" (Grimes 1995, *Deeply into the Bone*, 144). Rituals not only celebrate the body, but also, as spiritual technologies, employ the body (and mind) in the performance of beliefs. Our embodied participation in rituals influences our physical bodies by which we create spiritual meaning.

Posture, gesture, and movement: Engaging the body in worship

Worship incorporates ritual postures, hand gestures, and body movement, setting the performance apart from ordinary activities, and centering the worshipper's mind on communion with the divine. These postures and movements implicate the body in the ritual activity, signifying the sacredness of the action, demarcating it from ordinary or mundane behavior. These postures and gestures are frequently as simple as bowing the head for the ubiquitous "moment of silence."

Perhaps the most universal of postures is either the hands folded together, held palm-to-palm, or even one or both hands covering the face. Combined with bowing the head and kneeling, this posture engages the body in a state of humility, underscoring respect, deference, devotion, and awe. The degree of bowing varies in different religious contexts. An intensification of prostration is found in Islamic prayer, where the worshipper touches the forehead to the floor while facing in the direction of the Ka'ba in Mecca. Another common prayer posture in many religions is the palms-up hands, either cupped together or spread wide, in an attitude of supplication and receptivity to the divine.

Hand postures called *mudras* (seals or postures) are integral to yoga traditions in Hinduism and other Indian religions. Buddhist prostration, known as "five-point veneration," involves hand posture called *anjali mudra* (palms together, fingers flat out and pointed upward), raised to the forehead and then lowered to the ground along with the forehead. Full body prostration is commonly performed by pilgrims as well as devotees in the presence of their guru (spiritual master).

Hand gestures in Jewish households can be seen when the woman of the house lights the Shabbat candles and then waves the light toward herself three times using a circular motion, before covering her eyes and reciting the blessing. Roman Catholicism has a repertoire of hand gestures, the most well known is the "sign of the cross," in which the worshipper gestures with their right hand to the forehead, then the heart, left then right shoulders, ending with hands in the palms together prayer position. This gesture is used in simple daily prayers as well as formal church services. There are other hand gestures that are performed at various times during the Catholic Mass, and these hand gestures, combined with the changing position of the body—sitting, standing, and kneeling—involve the worshipper in the church service, engaging the worshipper as an active participant, not just a spectator.

Ritual movement in worship service is a common practice as well. During a regular church service, Roman Catholics are expected to dip a finger into holy water and make the "sign of the cross" upon entering the sanctuary, and then men are expected to genuflect before entering the pew. Later in the service, Catholics will shake hands with their neighbors to exchange the "sign of peace." Finally, Catholics and other Christians leave their seat and journey to the altar to receive the Eucharist.

Processions are another way that worshippers engage their bodies in worship. An example of an elaborate ritual is the performance of the "stations of the cross," in which worshippers reenact the journey Jesus took while carrying the cross on the day of his crucifixion as they physically move from one marker to the next in the progression of Christ's Passion. Another significant ritual of body movement is circumambulation, the act of moving around a sacred object or idol. Circumambulation of temples or deity images is an integral part of Hindu and Buddhist devotional practice as is the circumambulation of Islamic pilgrims around the Ka'ba in Mecca during the Hajj. Jewish prayer services for the holiday of *Simchat Torah* involve *hakkafot*, circumambulation of the synagogue while carrying the Torah scrolls.

The body in Christian ritual

The Eucharist

No ritual has more significance for Christians than the Eucharist. Sometimes referred to as Holy Communion, or the Lord's Supper, this sacred ritual celebrates Jesus's life and death, specifically acknowledging that through his suffering, death, and resurrection believers are granted life in God's kingdom (Mt. 26:29). During the ritual of the Eucharist, participants consume consecrated bread and wine.

We can view the Eucharist as a case study of the centrality of the body in religion. As a ritual that is practiced regularly, that reenacts a significant historic moment, and is comprised of taking the divine body into the body of the believer, the Eucharist is the paradigm of the embodiment of religious belief. We will examine the textual sources and historic development of this ritual from its biblical origins to modernity, illuminating how despite the evolution of its practice and its diverse interpretations over time and across denominations, the Eucharist retains its significance. The Eucharist offers a most revealing representation of a ritualized religious practice that unites the divine and human bodies.

There is no clear evidence that Jesus intended to establish a distinctly new ritual. The traditional Passover meal celebrated by Jews can be found in Paul's first letter to the Corinthians as well as in each of the synoptic gospels (Mt. 26:17-30; Mk 14:22-25; Lk. 22:8-9). The apostle Paul offers the earliest record of this event, an occasion that eventually established the Eucharist as the central liturgical rite of the church:

> For I received from the Lord what I also handed onto you, that the Lord Jesus on the night when he was betrayed took a loaf of bread, and when he had given thanks, he broke it and said, "this is my body that is for you. Do this in remembrance of me." In the same way he took the cup also, after supper, saying, "This cup is the new covenant in my blood. Do this, as often as you drink it, in remembrance of me." For as often as you eat this bread and drink the cup, you proclaim the Lord's death until he comes (Cor. 11:23-26).

Matthew, Mark, and Luke each offer similar accounts of the Lord's last supper, but the emphasis on remembrance is omitted in Matthew's account, which instead recognizes the pouring out of Jesus's blood for the forgiveness of sin (Mt. 26:28). Each account includes a blessing, a thanksgiving for the body and blood of Jesus, while anticipating his Father's kingdom. The Johannine gospel makes no mention of a ritual meal, but suggests as much in these words attributed to Jesus, "I am the bread of life, whoever comes to me will never hunger, and whoever believes in me will never be thirsty. . . . Those who eat my flesh and drink my blood abide in me and I in them" (Jn 6:35, 56). Thus, in its earliest tradition, remembrance and thanksgiving were the central themes of the sacred meal that ultimately united a body of believers in Christ.

Evidence for the Eucharist as a liturgical rite or sacrament begins to appear as early as 96 CE, when First Clement, Bishop of Rome, writes in a letter to the Corinthians that "the conduct of public services should not be haphazard or irregular, but should take place at fixed times and hours." In a letter to the Philadelphians, Ignatius advises believers to be certain that they "observe one common Eucharist; for there is but one Body of Lord Jesus Christ, and but one cup of union with His blood" (Early Christians Writings, 94). Justin Martyr's *First Apology*, written in the middle of the second century, records an order of service for the Eucharist that proceeds in a very similar way to the one still practiced today, requiring affirmation of belief along with baptism as

FIGURE 4.1 *Pope Francis gives the Holy Communion during the Easter Vigil at the St Peter's basilica on March 26, 2016 in the Vatican. Credit: ALBERTO PIZZOLI / Staff, via Getty Images.*

prerequisites for communicants, who seeking mystical union with God join in commensality of bread and wine—the body and blood of Jesus.

Just how Christ could be present in the bread and wine posed no problem for early Christians; they simply accepted Jesus's word and that of the Church Fathers. By the beginning of the thirteenth century (1215 CE), however, debate over the exact meaning of those words spoken by Jesus on the night before his crucifixion resulted in this proclamation by the Fourth Lateran Council:

> There is one universal church of the faithful, outside which no one at all is saved. In this church, Jesus Christ himself is both priest and sacrifice, and his body and blood are really contained in the sacrament of the altar under the species of bread and wine, the bread being transubstantiated into the body and the wine being into the blood by the power of God, so that to carry out the mystery of unity we ourselves receive from him the body he himself receives from us.

This interpretation of Jesus's words raised another consideration for some: Exactly when did the bread and wine become the body and blood of Christ? Since the very beginning, communicants had recognized the consecration of the host by the priest was the moment of transubstantiation, but by the late medieval period, adoration of the host, simply viewing the bread and wine, gained prominence as a holy rite, and therein distinguished itself from the communal meal as a means of encountering Christ and entering God's kingdom. This had several implications for the faithful—since only the priesthood could consecrate the host, their power and influence grew exponentially with this development, along with the sense of awe their role inspired. This, in turn, increased the divide between priests and lay persons, causing a deep ambivalence regarding the Eucharist. Some became fearful of receiving communion because they felt unworthy, while others were encouraged to abstain from frequent communion out of awe for the sacredness of the ritual. By the late medieval period, participating in the Eucharist evolved to include all the senses, offering an inward as well as outward encounter with Christ's suffering, along with a vision of his glorified triumph over sin and death, and it was this prospect of victory over the darkness of this world that brought comfort to the faithful.

Now one could be fully present with Christ, fully participate in his suffering and death and be accorded salvation, not just by receiving the elements, but also by viewing them. Mystics longed for what they called a "showing," whereby they might imitate Christ and thereby realize a full redemption for themselves and others. Julian of Norwich, writing in 1373, describes one such showing in her *Revelations of the Divine*:

Suddenly I saw the red blood trickle down from under the crown of thorns—hot and fresh and flooding out, as it did at the time of his Passion when the crown of thorns was pressed into his blessed head—he who was both God and man who suffered for me. And I knew in my heart that he showed me this without any go-between. . . . This sight of the blessed Passion, with the knowledge of God I felt in my mind, I knew was strength enough for me—yes, and for all living creatures—to conquer all the fiends of hell and spiritual temptation.

By the late medieval period, "passion piety" evolved to include not just a way to change and repair the soul and in turn ransom it from the devil; it gave rise to a penitential theology that maintained that while the cross satisfied humanity's guilt of sin, it did not satisfy the penalty due for sin. This, argued Church Fathers, could be achieved by participating spiritually in Christ's suffering, and more importantly, imitating it. As we will examine in greater detail in Chapter 11, during this period, a wave of mystics, beguines (ascetic women who entered a convent but did not take any permanent vows), and nuns, consumed by their insatiable hunger and yearning for an ecstatic union with God, embraced extreme ascetic practices in their effort to imitate the cross and, like Christ, experience God's grace.

Beliefs in the efficacy of the Eucharist and other rituals instituted by the Church however, did not go unchallenged. While the Eucharist remained central to Christian life, Protestant reformers rejected a contingency between the correct performance of this sacrament and redemption, as well as veneration of the sacramental elements and divine favor. In the sixteenth century, Martin Luther maintained that sin causes suffering, and through suffering faith is tested, sin is rectified, and empathy for fellow sufferers created, thereby conforming sinners to Christ. Christians, like Jesus, were destined to encounter the darkness of this world, and their duty was simply to endure the suffering it brought; this was bearing the cross of Christ (Lk. 14:27). Faith, not *works* (in this case the sacrament of the Eucharist), afforded men the gift of grace. Through faith one gained dominion over sin, and by grace man would be saved (Eph. 2:8).

Luther's Swiss counterpart, John Calvin, shared his objection to the reenactment of the Last Supper as a means of atoning for sin and thereby realizing the gift of grace. Calvin maintained that since the body and blood of Christ dwells in heaven it is only accessible to communicants through the power of the Holy Spirit. He, likewise, shared Luther's conviction that it was through faith that believers received the gift of grace, emphasizing that the main role of the Lord's Supper is to establish a bond of love among believers.

Today almost all Christians observe the Eucharist, albeit in various forms and with varying frequency. Roman Catholics continue to embrace the belief in transubstantiation, the real presence of Christ in the bread and wine, and understand this sacrament as a conduit of grace, as do Eastern Orthodox Christians. Anglicans vary regarding transubstantiation, some believing in a literal presence while others in a spiritual presence. Lutherans view the real presence of Christ as a sacramental union, whereby Christ is present in, with, and under the sacramental elements, but remains distinct from them. Presbyterians and Methodists reject the idea of transubstantiation, but recognize Christ's presence at the communion table through the gift of the Holy Spirit, maintaining that it is an experience of grace open to all as a gift of God's unconditional love. Baptists interpret the Lord's Supper as a call for remembrance, whereby the bread and cup serve as symbols of Christ's body and blood, shed as an act of love for humankind. Quakers do not observe the Lord's Supper, but believe communion with the Holy Spirit is a personal experience requiring no rite. Although numerous other less well-known Christian denominations observe the Eucharist in a variety of ways and degrees, it is safe to say that all recall Jesus's Last Supper with his disciples and thus commemorate his life and death, and more importantly, his mission and message.

The Easter holiday

For Christians, the celebration of the Easter Feast is a joyous occasion emphasizing Christ's resurrection as proof of God's eternal, living presence in the world and the promise of new life in Christ. Easter officially begins at sundown on Holy Saturday. Worshippers gather in darkness; the Paschal candle is lit and then blessed by the priest to symbolize the light of Christ. The light of the Paschal candle is subsequently passed along—with each recipient offering light to his neighbor. It is a moving ceremony intended to dispel the darkness, sin, and despair of the world. The sacraments of baptism and confirmation, as well as the Eucharist, are subsequently celebrated, commencing the season of Eastertide, which lasts for fifty days and ends with Pentecost Sunday, a celebration of the descent of the Holy Spirit upon the Apostles.

Many customs associated with Easter have pagan origins; even the word "Easter" is derived from the term *Estre*, which refers to the pagan goddess of sunrise and spring, illustrating how Christians came to associate their Easter feast with the Risen Christ—*the light of the world*—and the gift of a new life in Christ (Jn. 8:12). The egg, one of the oldest pagan symbols of evolving life and spring, undoubtedly gained its prominent place in Easter tradition from a very early custom that forbids eating eggs during Lent, but with Easter's arrival, eggs colored red were brought to the table to symbolize Easter joy—new life, light, and hope.

FIGURE 4.2 *The head of the Greek Orthodox Church in Bethlehem, Bishop Theofilactos (C), leads the "Holy Fire" ceremony in Bethlehem on April 30, 2016, during the Orthodox Easter. Credit: MUSA AL SHAER / Stringer, via Getty Images.*

Charismatic Christianity

Charismatic Christians are a group that believes that the healing practices and charismatic miracles of the first-century Christian Church can and should be practiced in modern times. While Charismatics are often confused with Pentecostals, they are different in a few ways:

They do not place the same importance on speaking in tongues as Pentecostal churches may; and

Charismatics may still identify with other Christian denominations, such as Catholicism or Episcopalianism.

Pentecost and speaking in tongues

The Christian holiday of Pentecost is a festival during which Christians commemorate the Holy Spirit's enlivening the church as a spiritual movement. Its biblical origin was a miracle believed to have occurred in a gathering of followers of Jesus in which the Holy Spirit entered their bodies and they began to speak in a variety of languages. The Acts of the Apostles, Chapter 2 narrates:

and when the day of Pentecost had come, [the first followers of Jesus] were all together in one place. Suddenly, a sound came from heaven, like a strong wind, filling the house where the people had gathered. Something like tongues of fire rested on their heads. And they were all filled with the Holy Spirit and began to speak in other languages as the Spirit gave them the ability to speak.

The Bible does not fully describe this miracle; thus, it is impossible to know what speaking in tongues sounded like or how it affected the behavior of the early Christians who experienced it. Speaking in tongues, then, is a phenomenon where an individual is said to channel the Holy Spirit and speak a language that she does not know or is not human. Speaking in tongues continues to be practiced and encouraged among subgroups of Evangelical Christian denominations, including Pentecostals and the Charismatic movement.

Those who actively practice speaking in tongues view it as a way to edify the presence of God, perpetuate the message of the Gospel, and draw closer connections between humans and the divine. They fully believe that this miracle is a holy sign of the presence of God and is in no way associated with demonic possession as others may suggest.

Some denominations believe that only those who can speak in tongues have received the blessing and grace of the Holy Spirit and are thus saved. Many Christians who acknowledge, but do not practice speaking in tongues view it as a natural gift that cannot be taught; for these Christians, speaking in tongues has no impact on whether an individual can be, or has been, saved.

Scientists at the University of Pennsylvania have shown that a person who is actively speaking in tongues experiences a noticeable shift in brain activity, which creates loss of control over their language centers and diminished activity in the frontal cortex, which decreases a person's ability to control voluntary actions. This provides evidence that speaking in tongues has both spiritual and psycho-physical components. We will consider neuroscientific research on religious and spiritual practice more broadly in Chapter 6 where we discuss notions and practices of healing and their positive health and well-being effects.

The body in Jewish ritual

Celebrating the body in Judaism can be linked to commandments through which the body is honored and cared for. Among the positive *mitzvot* (commandments) is the commandment to observe the Sabbath. While the Sabbath is commonly perceived to be a day of serving and celebrating God,

God is served with mind, soul, and body. Serving God with the body can be interpreted in two ways: (1) that the body is engaged in the performance of the *mitzvot* and (2) that physical acts, while neutral in themselves, become vehicles for reaching the divine through proper intention and proper performance.

Jewish life is shaped by observance of the 613 *mitzvot* (commandments) in the Torah, which have been divided into negative and positive commandments. In the Talmud, the negative commandments, "Thou shalt not," whose number is 365, is a number the rabbis attribute to the number of days in the solar year, and the positive commandments or the "Thou shalt," number 248, a number which the rabbis describe as the number of bones and main organs in the human body. Thus, we can view the commandments as the spiritual acts that Jews must observe every day and with every part of their body.

While the biblical injunction of Sabbath observance is to refrain from work, there are references both in the Bible and the Talmud to the joyful satisfaction of the body. For example, Isa. 58:13 renders it a duty to call the Sabbath a delight. The idea and practices of the Sabbath suggest that the body is meant not only for work, but also for pleasure—enjoyment of the gifts of this world: good food, fine wine, marital bliss, and rest. "And God blessed the seventh day and declared it holy, because on it God ceased from all the work of creation that He had done" (Gen. 2:2). The day is sanctified through all these bodily pleasures. Jews should not forget that they are also obligated to acknowledge and praise the divine source of all that they enjoy on the Sabbath as on any other day.

Another idea that reinforces the significance of pleasure in Judaism is the one echoed in Abraham Joshua Heschel's *The Sabbath*, namely that the Sabbath is the climax of the week. Jews do not rest in order to resume work in the following week; rather, they work so that we can rest and enjoy the pleasures of the body and the spirit that are embodied in the Sabbath rituals.

Jews are concerned with "correct action," which on the Sabbath means refraining from thirty-nine types of creative work (and their rabbinic interpretations) that were employed in the building of the holy Temple in Jerusalem. They are also inspired by the belief that God has a covenantal relationship with them, that is described by prophets and poets in the simile of lover and beloved, of husband and wife. The rabbis and kabbalists speak of welcoming the Sabbath as a groom welcomes his bride. The Sabbath is seen not only as a day of rest, but also as a holy day celebrating the love between God and the Jewish community. On Friday afternoon, many recite the biblical text Song of Songs, a revered poem depicting the erotic love and desire of a shepherd and a shepherdess. The commentaries on this text are extensive and often allegorize the lovers as God and the community of Israel. The rabbis taught that the marital relation on the Sabbath is a special mitzvah; the kabbalists espouse it on Friday night as a sacred ritual which mirrors the union of the godhead and the Shekinah (female aspect of the divine).

Jews and Christians both use wine and bread as part of their rituals, albeit in different ways. In Judaism, wine is a symbol of joy. Blessings are said in the home and synagogue before drinking wine on the Sabbath, most Jewish holidays, and at life cycle celebrations. A special braided egg bread called *challah* is eaten at the beginning of the Sabbath meal. For Christians, wine (some churches use grape juice) and bread or a wafer are used as part of the Eucharist ritual, symbolizing the body and blood of Jesus.

Prayer (*tefillah*) is a daily requirement for Jews and must be fulfilled three times per day: morning, afternoon, and evening. Public prayer in a synagogue with recitations from the prayer book (*siddur*) is particularly efficacious for strengthening one's relationship with God and one's community. Some prayers (such as the *kaddish*) can only be recited in a minyan, a quorum of ten over the age of thirteen that is required for traditional Jewish public worship. In Orthodox communities, only men count for the minyan, while modern Conservative and Reform communities practice an egalitarian minyan, counting men and women. During the morning prayer, a religious garment called *tallit* (prayer shawl) is worn, at the four corners of which are tassels (*tzitzit*), based on the commandment to wear "fringes" on the four-square corners of garments. In addition, traditional Jews wear a garment that is specifically made to have four corners with fringes known as the *tallit katan* or *tzitzit*, and is worn under the shirt at all times.

A ritual which represents the notion of serving God with the body is the morning practice of putting on *tefillin*. This ritual is practiced each weekday, as specified in the Book of Deuteronomy in the context of the commandment to love God. This practice involves wrapping black leather straps attached to small boxes containing hand-printed scriptural verses, consisting of the four sets of biblical passages in which *tefillin* are commanded. The straps are wrapped around the arm seven times with the box placed near the heart, and around the head with the box resting at the top of the forehead. Separate blessings are said during the placement of each box. The arm strap is wrapped around the hand and fingers to create the shape of the Hebrew letters, *shin, dalet,* and *yod* comprising the word *Shadai,* one of the names of God. The *tefillin* are worn for the duration of the morning prayer.

Inspired by Ps. 35:10 which states: "All my limbs shall say 'Who is like You, O Lord?'" it is common to see Jews expressing devotion to God through body movements. Standing is the most important physical position of Jewish prayer. The *Amidah* or the "Standing Prayer," which is one of the most important prayers, is recited while standing in silent devotion. When beginning the *Amidah,* it is also customary to take three steps back and three steps forward, enacting the idea of approaching God with respect and humility. Standing is also required during *Neilah,* the final prayers and the culmination of the holiest day of the year—Yom Kippur, or the Day of Atonement.

Biblical narratives describe devotion to God in the posture of kneeling, such as Daniel, who "kneeled upon his knees three times a day, and prayed, and gave thanks before his God"(Dan. 6:11). While full prostration was common in prayer in ancient Israel, bowing came to replace it and bending of the knees and upper body is now the common practice. The one exception where some Jews perform full prostration is on Yom Kippur.

In addition to standing and bowing, which are required, other movements that express passionate devotion in Jewish worship are swaying (in Yiddish, *shocklen).* Swaying in prayer has been interpreted as improving one's spiritual intention and connection with God. Another body movement in Jewish prayer is the gentle beating of one's breast with a closed fist as a symbol of contrition when reciting certain confessional prayers.

The body in Muslim ritual

In addition to holidays such as the month-long daytime fast, Ramadan, which we will discuss in Chapter 5, the ritualized form of prayer, *salat,* constitutes one of the five pillars of Islam. Prayer is ubiquitous in the Qur'an. Done with proper intention and purity, it is believed to be the most essential act of devotion to God. In one verse, the requirement of daily prayer is stated in this way: "Recite what has been revealed to you of the Book; perform the prayer; verily the prayer forbids indecency and wrong; God's remembrance is greater; and God knows the things you work" (Qur'an 29:45). The great Sufi thinker and Qur'anic exegete, Ibn Arabi, understood this verse to mean that prayer prevents the practitioner from sins, vices, excesses, negligence, disobedience, and egoism.

Prior to prayer, Muslims are required to ensure that their body, clothes, and the place of prayer are clean and free of impurities. As we will discuss in Chapter 7, a purification regimen washing the hands and feet precedes prayer.

FIGURE 4.3 *Indonesians attend the last Friday prayers before Ramadan begins. Credit: Barcroft Media / Contributor, via Getty Images.*

Performing *salat* does not require a specially designated sanctuary. Muslims may pray wherever they happen to be at the time of prayer.

While the practice of ritualized prayer is a universal and pivotal expression of faith cross-culturally, prostrations comprise a distinctive element in Islamic prayer. Prostrations were practiced in the ancient Near East before the time of Muhammad; it is told in a Hadith that Abraham and Moses served as advisers to Muhammad regarding prostration. The Arabic word for prostrations, *sujud*, appears numerous times in the Qur'an, including in the title of *sura* 32:1 As-Sajdah (The Prostration). Another reference to prostration in the Qur'an is about Mary, mother of Jesus, who is revered as a woman of the highest purity, faith, holiness, obedience, and humility. Mary is called *sajidah*—"she who prostrates to God in worship" (Qur'an 3:43). It is believed that *sujud* derives from Mary's sajidah—an act of sublime humility where the hands, knees, and forehead simultaneously touch the ground.

The significance of prostration in Islam can also be seen in the term for mosque (*masjid*) which denotes the "place of sujud," which further reinforces the significance of the notion of prostration. The tradition provides elaborate guidance as to how prayer is to be performed both individually and collectively. Each of the five daily prayers consists of a fixed sequence of movements (standing, prostrating, kneeling, sitting), accompanied by fixed Arabic recitations and prayer-cycles. Sujud is specifically the position in the prayer when one drops on the knees, places the palms of one's hands on the ground, and puts nose and forehead on the ground. In Hadith traditions, sujud is the part of prayer when the practitioners are closest to God.

It is also important to note that in Islam, prostration to anyone but Allah is absolutely forbidden. Muhammad strictly prohibited Muslims from prostrating before him, because prostration should not be performed to any humans. Prostrations are aimed to express praise and humble oneself before God (Allah), whether the prayers are performed alone or as a congregation. Prostrations in Islamic prayer can therefore be said to endow the body with the capacity to express qualities such as humility, as well as servitude and surrender to God.

The body in Hindu ritual

Hindu worship is centered around the *puja*, the ritual involving prayers to the divine. The *puja* engages all of the senses, rendering the body a central element in Hindu worship. In *puja*, a consecrated image (*murti*) representing a deity serves as the focus of the practice, inviting, honoring, and creating an embodied bridge between the devotee and the divine. Once the deity has been placed in its designated place, the following actions are performed: bathing of the deity in liquids such as milk, curds, honey, butter, and water; dressing them in special clothes and jewelry; anointing with sandalwood; and offering them flowers, food, and water. The ritual also involves the scents of incense; the sound of music, bells, and chants; and the light of lamps. At the end of the *puja*, the food offered to the deity is distributed to the devotees to consume as *prasad* (sacred food).

FIGURE 4.4 *Tamil Hindu priests perform special prayers honoring the Goddess Sri Meenakshi Amman, Credit: NurPhoto / Contributor, via Getty Images.*

Puja can be an elaborate ritual performed by priests in a *mandir* (temple) or practiced in a family home on a small scale. In inviting the deities and honoring them, their presence can now be accessed through *darshan*, the vision of the divine. In *darshan*, it is also believed that not only does the devotee come to see the divine, but she or he themselves are seen by the deity as well. The receiving of the gaze of the deity and the returning of that gaze is a reciprocal performative process and the culmination of Hindu devotion, whether done in public or in private. This reciprocity is experienced in giving the deity honor and reverence, while receiving grace and blessings. *Darshan* enables devotees direct contact with the deity.

Dance is one of many offerings to the deity and constitutes an embodied practice in the Hindu tradition. This performative mode is one way the sacred becomes meaningful in Hindu practice. Dancers perform the themes and narratives of Hindu deities, often Krishna or Shiva, as told in the Ramayana and Mahabharata, enacting the experience of devotion (*bhakti*) to the gods through movements and gestures. Through their dance, they create an aesthetic-religious emotional state and mood (*rasa*) to be experienced by their audience. The focused gaze of the eyes of the dancer, the facial expressions, and hand gestures are integrally linked with the audience and enable them to experience the presence of the deities who are personified in the dance. Historically, it was performed by temple dancers or *devadasis*–women who dedicated their lives to the temple and were considered married to the temple deity. Scottish anthropologist James Frazer is among scholars who viewed this practice as integral to Mother Goddess worship, which was an ancient custom in civilizations such as Mesopotamia, Egypt, and Greece. In the modern period, artists have recreated the dance into a stage performance known as *Bharatanatyam*, based on the 108 positions of Shiva's dance and the *rasa* theory which delineates 8 distinct moods as described in the Natya Shastra, a second-century text focused on the art of performance and aesthetics. *Bharatanatyam* can be understood as a spiritual technology, which through its performance and especially the personal devotional experience, creates the "devotional body."

The body in masks, trance, dance, and music

The body serves as a medium that can be transformed into something new during religious rituals. This is particularly evident in the use of masks and costumes in healing ceremonies, initiation rites, and the performance of mythic narratives in dance. One of the most corporeal ways of transforming oneself is using masks, as they cover the face without changing the body.

Shamans, indigenous spiritual adepts for example, invite spirits or ancestors into their bodies using a mask during a state of trance.

Trance can be defined in a variety of ways, mainly as a state of semi- or half-consciousness in which the individual is either partially or entirely unaware of themselves, their actions, and/or their surroundings. This altered state can be induced by hypnosis, physical rituals such as the ceremonial ingestion of drugs and performance of ritual dances, or it may arise spontaneously through mental exercises like prayer and meditation. In many cases, trance is associated with religious ecstasy. Trance states are practiced and experienced in wide and varied ways throughout spiritual traditions across the globe.

Trance dance is often associated with *Thaipusam*, an annual Tamil Hindu festival dedicated to Murugan, Lord Shiva's son. Devotees who watch the procession of the deity and become possessed enter a trance dance state, while other spectators treat them as (temporarily) divine, seeking to touch their feet or actively seeking out their gaze (*darshan*) as they would with one of the gods.

Sufis, Native American tribes, and African religions use dance and music as a way to induce a hypnotic state, aimed at bringing the individual closer to a higher power. The Order of Mevlevi—also known as the "Whirling Dervishes"—are a sect of Islamic Sufism in Turkey that utilizes music, dance, and prayer (*sema*) to transition the dancer into a trance-like state. In doing so, the dancers use their bodies to create a bridge between the physical and spiritual worlds, unifying the two through ecstatic movement.

FIGURE 4.5 *A Sufi in trance. Credit: logosstock, via Getty Images.*

Various African religions use trance-inducing dance and music as a form of healing and heightening of religious experience. The god Shango, also known as "Chango" or "Xango," is recognized among the Yoruba in Nigeria and throughout Afro-Caribbean religious traditions, especially in Trinidad. The yearly four-day ceremony honoring this god of fire, thunder, and lightning involves a series of dances and drum-based music. During the dance, one devotee is said to become possessed by Shango's spirit for a period of time. Though the entire community engages in dance, the movements of the one entranced by the god are said to be noticeably different from the rest, obviously differentiating who has and has not been touched by the god.

Some Native American tribes and other indigenous groups use plant-based drugs in order to induce a state of altered consciousness. In Brazil, Ayahuasca was originally ingested in a strictly ritual setting, allowing for the participant to safely consume the *Banisteriosis caapi* vine and the *Psychotria viridis* leaf and experience the effects of the naturally occurring DMT (psychoactive chemical that causes intense visions). With guidance from a "Godmother/father," the individual would embark on a spiritual journey, brought upon by DMT's psychoactive properties, in order to unlock the gateway into the mind and soul. Today, the drug has become largely divorced from its indigenous roots as "Ayahuasca tourism" has drawn larger numbers of outsiders into Central and South America to pay for participation in this spiritual experience.

Peyote, a small cactus plant grown largely in Mexico, has grown in infamy for its hallucinogenic properties. Among the Huichol, the process of gathering, preparing, and ingesting Peyote is long and complex, and includes a "hunt" for the plant in the wilderness and a series of ritual purifications, confessions, prayers, and chants, which culminates in a distribution ritual. It was believed that this hunt and subsequent rituals brought members of the tribe closer to *Wirikuta*, or Paradise. Eventually, the plant spread out of Mexico and into the United States, where some Native American groups of the Great Plains, including the Kiowa and Comanche, began using it. It is deified for acting as a messenger between the consumer and God as well as having medicinal properties. These ceremonies are practiced sparingly today.

Contemporary trends and practices

New women's rituals

With the growth of feminism in the 1960s and 1970s, women across a variety of religions began to create their own women-centered rituals and ceremonies. These rituals and celebrations are an attempt to better reflect the embodied experiences of women. Many of these ceremonies are related to the life cycle rituals that only women experience; for example, celebrations such as Red Tents that center around a woman's menstrual cycle.

Neo-Paganism has become a spiritual movement in which women have developed their own space and rituals. "Neo-pagan" widely refers to a group of practices that seeks to elevate the gods and goddesses of pre-Christian religious practices. Many pagans reject the term "Neo-pagan," as they see their religion as a continuation of an ancient religious practice that pre-dates Christianity. Nonetheless, this term is useful in the sense that it provides an umbrella for a variety of related practices and movements that includes, but is not limited to, Wicca, Asatru, and Heathenism. Although most Neo-pagans acknowledge gods and goddesses, the male and female energy, practitioners tend to place a larger focus on the Goddess, as they believe that after centuries of domination by patriarchal religions, it is appropriate for the Goddess to be elevated once again. Many women have come to Neo-paganism to celebrate their womanhood in a way that they have not found to be possible in other religious traditions. Unsurprisingly, the focus on femininity and the Goddess has led to rituals that empower womanhood and celebrate the power inherent in the female body.

Wicca tradition

While Wicca is the most commonly known Neo-pagan tradition, it is not an all-inclusive term that includes all pagan practices. Wicca is its own separate branch of Paganism, founded by Gerald Gardner when he was initiated into what he calls, "The Old Religion," in 1939. Wicca is a pagan tradition; however not all pagans are Wiccan. Wicca is defined as an independent practice based on two criteria: a practitioner must practice magic and must follow the "Wiccan Rede," a poem that defines the major holidays and ideas of the Wiccan religion. The Rede often appears in the shortened form that summarizes the rules of the religion, "And ye harm none, do what ye will."

While Wicca seems to be the most common organized pagan tradition in the United States, many practitioners simply consider themselves pagans without any specific affiliation with one branch or pantheon, and many do not choose to participate in witchcraft. Other common traditions fall into the category of "Ancestral Religions," in which the practitioner attempts to follow the religion of their ancestors, believing that religion is not a choice, but rather something inherent in one's DNA. Asatru, Heathenism, and Slavic Paganism fall into this category.

FIGURE 4.6 *Pagan ritual in Stonehenge in England. Credit: Matt Cardy / Stringer, via Getty Images.*

Many rituals and ceremonies that began, or gained traction as a part of Neo-pagan practice have gained popularity across religious traditions. "First moon celebrations," are one such ritual. The first moon celebrations, or first menstruation parties, are an opportunity for girls to feel that their entrance into womanhood is celebrated, rather than shamed. Women are invited to a young girl's first moon party to share their experiences of womanhood and wisdom. Passages to Womanhood "ceremonial kits" can be purchased online and have been designed to be used within any religious tradition. These parties may include a circle for women to sit and share their wisdom with the young girl, a red cake to celebrate the first moon, music, and prayer.

FIGURE 4.7 *Druid order's spring equinox celebration, London. Credit: Mike Kemp / Contributor, via Getty Images.*

Similarly, in the past few decades the Red Tent Temple Movement has developed across the world. The Red Tent is a place where women of all ages can meet once a month, usually on the new moon. These gatherings serve as a sacred space to honor women and their journey, as well as a place where women may share their wisdom with the younger generation. In keeping with ancient practice, some birthing centers, Red Tent groups, and women's groups will encourage women to camp during their menstrual cycle. While the women are on their cycle or "moontime" as it is often called, other women in the community will take up the menstruating woman's chores and bring her food while she is camping, helping to foster a sense of connection and sisterhood.

Jewish women also hold new moon gatherings to celebrate *Rosh Chodesh*, a minor holiday that corresponds to each new moon. According to Jewish tradition, women were given *Rosh Chodesh* to celebrate as a reward for refusing to participate in the creation of the Golden Calf. Of course, there is also the correlation between the movements of the moon and a woman's menstrual cycle, lending additional significance to *Rosh Chodesh* as a woman's holiday.

FIGURE 4.8 *Members of the liberal Jewish religious group* Women of the Wall, *carry a Torah scroll during prayers in the women's section of the Western Wall, in the Old city of Jerusalem. Credit: MENAHEM KAHANA / Staff, via Getty Images.*

Another realm in which women's rituals of one religious practice have gained popularity within the larger women's movement is in Native American traditions. Native American medicine women have begun holding wise women circles for women both of their own heritage and beyond, in order to create a sacred space for sisterhood and to pass on the teachings of their ancestral mothers. Like the Jewish *Rosh Chodesh* meetings, the Native American women's circles begin with calling together the circle in which the women assemble and the medicine woman lights the fire and smudges both the space and each woman. Next, the intention for the meeting is set and the "speaking stick" is passed around so each woman may introduce herself and share her individual intention. During this time, the medicine woman may lead a guided meditation to help ground the women and transition into the teaching phase of the circle. The teaching includes anything needed to carry on the path of the ways of the wise women, including herbal medicine. Finally, the circle is closed by paying homage to the ancestors, the earth, and the four cardinal directions.

As the alternative birth movement has grown, some Native American birthing traditions have also gained popularity, specifically the "undisturbed birth." The idea of the undisturbed birth comes from the tradition of Native American women isolating themselves during labor and giving birth to the baby alone. Today, this practice has regained some popularity as women seek an environment that is more comforting and natural than a hospital. A medicine woman or midwife trains the expectant mother, and sometimes her partner, on how to deliver a baby. Midwives who support this method of delivery argue that since they were not present for the conception of the child, they should not be there for the birth. On the other hand, some Native American women who have decided to give birth in a hospital have found that their spiritual needs have not been accommodated in modern hospital environments. Rituals important to their labor, such as the burning of sage and drum circles, have not been welcomed or permitted. To combat this problem in New Mexico, a Navajo midwife, Nicolle Gonzalez, has decided to open the first Native American-specific birth center, where Native American women from different tribes across New Mexico can feel comfortable performing their religious and cultural rituals. Gonzalez is unfortunately one of only fourteen registered Native American midwives in the United States, which makes it difficult for Native American women to have their spiritual and medical needs simultaneously accommodated.

New women's rituals are gradually transforming women's sense of self, particularly within patriarchal religions, whose rituals and liturgical life have been shaped and defined by androcentric beliefs. As our study shows, women's voices have been silenced or ignored in many religions. In Chapter 7 for example, we will focus on the common tendency to identify women's bodies with states of impurity. One of the consequences of such a perspective is that women's bodily experiences have not been celebrated. New women's rituals correct this imbalance by celebrating events or life cycles such as the onset of menstruation, pregnancy, and birthing. In this way, women's bodies and selves are sustained and honored.

Liturgical use of the internet

As the internet and social media allow us to live part of our lives in a virtual reality, some of the body-centered rituals that have traditionally required a physical space, such as a sanctuary and physical acts, are now being performed online. Even the Pope has finally made his way to the internet, marking the larger trend of utilizing the internet for liturgical and prayerful uses across faiths. In January 2016, Pope Francis began a monthly video blog prayer series, in which he will pray for a different world issue each month, such as interfaith peace and better treatment for women. While some people believe that the use of the internet, cell phones, and apps as part of religious practice is distracting, materialistic, and unnecessary, others find that it helps connect those who share their beliefs.

For homebound seniors and the disabled, the internet provides a way for them to participate in religious services, as churches and temples across the world are beginning to live stream services. Apps and social media can also help foster a sense of community. The prayer app Instapray allows you to follow groups and individuals, request prayers from your followers, and notify others when you have prayed for them. Sister Catherine Wybourne, a Benedictine nun in Hereford, UK, is an active twitter personality, @Digitalnun. With over 16,000 followers, Sister Catherine uses twitter to broadcast daily prayer intention and share inspirational quotes, often retweeted from rabbis and other leaders of different faiths. For less mainstream religious traditions like Neo-Paganism and Wicca, the internet is a vital source of connection to other believers. Websites like witchvox. com help Wiccans and Pagans to find covens in their area, while some choose to form online covens instead. There is even a popular pagan dating website, Pagan Partners.

Although one of the goals of religion has always been to transcend the body in order to reach the divine, it remains to be seen how transcending the body through virtual reality enabled by technology, complements or contradicts the search for the divine.

Questions for review and discussion

1 What is the relationship between belief and ritual?

2 Is it important to engage the body in religious worship through ritual posture, hand gesture, and/or movement? Why or why not?

3 How is ritual a relationship between the human being and the divine?

4 In what ways is the Eucharist a "celebration" of the body?

5 How would you explain the different Christian (such as Catholic versus Protestant) approaches to the Eucharist?

6 How is speaking in tongues an embodied ritual?

7 How is the Sabbath a celebration of both the body and our relationship with God?

8 What are the meaning(s) that rituals such as the Sabbath or the Eucharist communicate about the worshipper and her/his relationship to the divine?

9 How does trance exhibit a human desire to be close to, or one with, the divine?

10 Should drug-induced experiences be considered "religious"?

11 What are the benefits of rituals that require an inward turn such as silent prayer or meditation, and those rituals that are outwardly such as singing and dancing?

12 What are the benefits of communal and private worship?

13 What are some potential detriments to liturgical use of the internet? Benefits?

14 Does the internet enhance interfaith dialogue?

Glossary

Charismatic movement-a movement within some Christian Churches emphasizing spiritual abilities such as speaking in tongues and healing of the sick.

Circumambulation-circling or moving around a sacred object.

Consecrated-sanctifying, making something sacred, dedicating the object for worship of a deity.

Darshan-ritual process of seeing and being seen by a Hindu deity or a guru.

Equinox-twice each year when the sun crosses the equator and day and night are of equal length. Pagan celebrations of spring and fall equinox.

Habitus-Pierre Bourdieu's notion signifying deeply ingrained habits, skills, and dispositions that we possess due to our life experiences.

Hexis-Pierre Bourdieu's notion of stable arrangement or disposition of the person; the tendency to hold and use one's body in certain ways, such as posture.

Pagan-religions that have more than one deity; beliefs and practices that are nature oriented.

Practice-habitual doing or carrying out of something; usual or customary action of performance.

Puja-act of worship in Hinduism through invocations, prayers, songs, and rituals.

Rosh Chodesh-Jewish celebration of the new moon.

Salat-Muslim prayer required to be performed five times daily.

Solstice-occurs twice a year. June 21, signaling the beginning of summer and December 21, the beginning of winter in the northern hemisphere. Pagan celebrations of winter and summer solstice.

Tefillin-phylacteries; small black leather boxes containing scrolls of parchment inscribed with verses from the Torah. They are worn in the Jewish morning prayer.

Trance-an altered state of consciousness; a state of ecstasy.

Transubstantiation-Catholic belief that the bread and wine of the Eucharist become the flesh and blood of Christ.

Veneration-act of worship or respect for wise beings, such as saints.

5

Food: Laws and Practices

In this chapter, we will examine the multiple ways in which food is embodied in religions and cultures. Preparation, consumption, and attitudes related to food are based on notions of health, ethical treatment of animals, religious history and beliefs, and group identity. Applying theories from anthropology, we investigate cross-cultural taboos and prohibitions of food and drink that have guided religious groups and have contributed to their social cohesion and shared values. We explore the symbolism of food, and the ways food has played an integral role in religious rituals and festivals, both in its elaborate preparation and consumption and in its association with divine blessings. We will also address the changes that are taking place as technology and cultural pluralism continue to impact our food habits, our environment, and our spirituality.

We consume food not only to survive and maintain our health, but also as a material way in which we express our religious and social identity. Food passes through the boundaries of the body and becomes part of the person. While many bodily practices serve as important means of asserting the distinctiveness of religious bodies (in both the individual and the communal senses), food in particular fulfills this goal. Social and religious groups are marked by distinctive diets and religious occasions, as food moves from one person's hand to another's plate and then into the body, and individuals sharing food practices become part of a community.

Food plays a fundamental role in religion cross-culturally. Food is represented in religious myths, symbolizing the divine gift of nurturing, and linked to blessings and curses. Religious holidays often coincide with agricultural cycles of planting and harvesting. Special food is assigned religious meaning and is prepared, consumed, and celebrated in ritual practices. Food as sacrifice celebrates the relations between humans and the divine. Religions often have food rules and taboos that shape group identity, and serve as safeguards for health, and as a means of disciplining the mind and the body. Food is also integral to religions' teachings of ethical stewardship of the environment and treatment of animals. Additionally, food practices reflect and shape gender roles and social roles among and between religious groups and cultures.

Food taboos exist in one form or another in every society. Food taboos involve plants as well as animals, solids as well as liquids, hot as well as cold, and wet and dry items. Social anthropologists explain taboos in multiple ways, providing utilitarian (conserving resources as well as a person's health) as well as spiritual reasons. Abundance of food is traditionally understood as a divine blessing; simultaneously, religious teachings also view it as a passion which must be controlled and regulated. Food taboos divide types of foods into prohibited and permitted, pure and impure as well as prohibiting gluttony or excessive eating or drinking. There are food taboos such as the prohibition against eating pork for Jews and Muslims, and beef for Hindus. Laws of proper slaughtering of animals with the purpose of minimizing their pain, also dictate Jewish and Muslim practices. While wine is used as a substance for religious celebrations in Judaism and Christianity, the prohibition against consuming alcohol is prevalent in Islam, Baha'ísm, Jainism, Sikhism, Mormonism, and Seventh-day Adventism. Religions such as Hinduism and Jainism that promote vegetarianism base their teachings on *ahimsa* (Sanskrit, nonviolence), karma, and reincarnation.

The eating habits of society have changed drastically over the last century and especially in the last few decades. The influx of technology, advertising, images in the media, and changes with modern cultural and family values play a major role in food consumption. Whereas historically, "eating out" at inns was only for travelers, restaurants have become a normative practice for the middle class. The "foodie" industry has become a cultural focal point of life for millions, who are now preoccupied with food preparation and presentation. With the zeal of religious sectarians, people now search for the perfect food, hunting down restaurants and seeking the latest dietary fads. Meanwhile, overeating and obesity are now part of the wider cultural problem of consumption and materialism.

Food practices and habits have also undergone transformation in the life of individuals and religious communities. This transformation is often due to the openness to the religious "other" engendered by cultural and religious pluralism. "Mindful Eating" has become a rule for food consumption for Westerners who have adopted Buddhist and other Eastern spiritual practices, enjoying the pleasures of food while maintaining self-control. Incorporating Eastern views of food into Western food habits, especially those from Hinduism and Buddhism, has also resulted in the increased consumption of a vegetarian diet among Westerners. With the establishment and spread of the interfaith dialogue movement, faith leaders and activists have become role models of interreligious coexistence by breaking bread together in their meetings. A related trend among liberal religious practitioners is embodying inclusivity in holiday celebrations; whereas these were traditionally practiced in their separate communities, ritual meals such as Passover, Diwali, and Iftar have become occasions for inviting friends from other traditions to one's table. Furthermore, as interfaith marriages become more prevalent today, couples of mixed heritages use food as a way to both observe their religious paths and transmit them to their children. Ecological activism is another important project taken up by religious practitioners in an effort to implement socially just food practices, including advocating for clean air and water, animal rights, vegetarianism, and eating locally grown food.

Foods and religious festivals

Food and its symbolism are integral to religious celebrations, festivals, and holy days in every society. For example, the pomegranate is prevalent cross-culturally as a symbol of women's fertility, prosperity, eternal life, marriage, abundance, life, and rebirth. Scholars believe that it was a pomegranate, rather than the apple with which Eve tempted Adam. In Christian art, the Virgin Mary is often painted with a pomegranate in her hand, which is supposed to symbolize the resurrection of Jesus Christ and eternal life. The Qur'an mentions the pomegranate multiple times as a blessed and superior fruit, along with the olive, fig, date, and banana. In China, Buddhist couples on their wedding day often receive an image of an open pomegranate or multiple open pomegranates as a symbol of prosperity, children, wealth, and abundance.

Apples and honey are a staple of Rosh Hashanah celebrations, and the combination is symbolic of wishes for a sweet new year. Potato pancakes and jam-filled doughnuts, both fried in oil, are eaten on Hanukkah, to commemorate the miracle of the oil that kept the lamp in the Jerusalem Temple lit for eight days. At the Passover meal (*seder*), several foods symbolize the experience of the Jewish people as slaves and their departure from Egypt: *matza* (unleavened bread) is eaten to symbolize the haste of the Jews' departure which did not permit their dough to rise; *maror*—is bitter herb, usually horseradish, symbolizes the bitterness of slavery in Egypt; and *charoset*—a sweet paste, representing the mortar made by the Jews in slavery.

At the end of the fast of Ramadan, it is a custom to eat three dates following the example of Muhammad. After the fast, Baklava, a sweet pastry made of layers of filo filled with chopped nuts and sweetened and held together with syrup or honey, is also eaten. In Turkey and other countries, on the first anniversary following death, it is a religious custom for relatives of the deceased to offer halva, a dense confection of semolina, ghee, and sugar, to visitors.

In Chinese culture and religion, the egg symbolizes fertility, while the duck is a symbol of wedded bliss. Noodles symbolize longevity and are consumed on Chinese New Year. Foods such as sweet green rice balls are offered in honor of the ancestors whose families visit their tombs during the annual spring Qingming Festival in China. In Spain, Portugal, and Peru, twelve grapes are consumed in celebration of the new year symbolizing twelve sweet months. Bread, often unleavened representing Christ's body and wine representing his blood are the two elements consumed in the sacrament of the Eucharist. Hot cross buns are traditionally eaten on Good Friday to break the fast required of Christians on that day. Eggs on Easter symbolize rejuvenation, resurrection, and immortality.

During the Hindu festival of Diwali—the Festival of Lights— there is a custom of exchanging sweets with friends and neighbors. *Ladoos*, ball-shaped sweets are one of the most liked Indian sweets. On festive occasions or any *puja* at home, a happy time is incomplete without a *ladoo*. On Diwali, *ladoo* is of special significance because it is considered auspicious to offer *ladoo* to Lord Ganesha at the Lakshmi-Ganesh *Puja*. Another favorite during this time is *Badam Phirni*, made of almond, rice flour, and milk.

Food in the Hebrew Bible and in Jewish practice

In the biblical creation narrative, we encounter many references to food that offer guidance, restrictions, and temptation as well as curses. In Genesis 1, after the creation of humanity, God instructs them to "rule the fish of the sea, the birds of the sky, and every creature that crawls on the earth . . . every seed-bearing plant on the surface of the entire earth and every tree whose fruit contains seed. This food will be for you" (Gen. 1:28-29). The first prohibition by God involves food: "And the Lord God commanded the man, 'You are free to eat from any tree of the garden, but you must not eat from the tree of the knowledge of good and evil, for on the day you eat from it, you will certainly die.'" (Gen. 2:16-17). The first sin then involves food as is the divine punishment of Adam: "You will eat bread by the sweat of your brow until you return to the ground" (Gen. 3:19).

The theme of food is also represented in the Genesis story of the first fratricide which resulted from jealousy regarding God's favorable response to Abel's animal sacrifice, and in contrast, God's rejection of Cain's plant sacrifice. Other stories with the theme of food in the Book of Genesis include Abraham's instruction to Sarah to prepare food for their three visitors; famine in the land of Israel and Abraham's subsequent departure to Egypt;

Jacob's preparation of food as a foil for stealing Esau's birthright; and Joseph's successful management of the food crisis in Egypt.

There are numerous stories and rituals in the Bible that convey the significance of agricultural cycles of planting and harvesting which were the basis for the holidays along with the commemoration of historic events. These include pilgrimages and the offering of sacrifices at the Jerusalem Temple. The connection of food and its divine source is expressed not only in the special foods that are designated for holidays, but also in the required recitation of blessings prior to any intake of food (even if it is only water), as well as the lengthy prayers of thanks after meals.

In addition, certain foods take on religious symbolism to mark historic events, such as the exodus from Egypt and the celebration of Passover.

> This is a day you are to commemorate; for the generations to come you shall celebrate it as a festival to the Lord—a lasting ordinance. For seven days, you are to eat bread made without yeast. On the first day remove the yeast from your houses, for whoever eats anything with yeast in it from the first day through the seventh must be cut off from Israel. On the first day hold a sacred assembly, and another one on the seventh day. Do no work at all on these days, except to prepare food for everyone to eat; that is all you may do (Exod. 12:14-16).

Passover, also called the "holiday of unleavened bread," commemorates the escape of the Israelites from Egypt: the *matzah* is in remembrance of the bread which did not have time to rise during their hasty departure.

The dietary laws in the Book of Leviticus define the foods that are kosher, or permissible. These include properly slaughtered, domesticated animals that have cloven hooves and which chew their cud. Kosher fish must have fins and scales. Leviticus 11 specifically enumerates prohibitions against eating pork, shrimp, shellfish and many types of seafood, most insects, scavenger birds, and various other animals.

In addition to avoiding the proscribed animals, slaughter of permitted animals must be done in a quick, deep stroke across the throat, windpipe, and jugular veins with a perfectly sharp blade with no nicks or unevenness. This is followed by total drainage of blood; one must consume only permitted animal parts: the sciatic nerve and surrounding blood vessels are prohibited, as is the *chelev*, fat surrounding vital organs and the liver. Another Jewish dietary law is derived from the biblical injunction against "boiling a kid in its mother's milk" (Exod. 23:19). Rabbinic laws inferred and extended the law of eating milk and meat together by instituting the law that a certain number of hours must be allowed between eating meat and dairy. Furthermore, utensils, pots, and pans for dairy and meat must be kept separate. Additional dietary

FIGURE 5.1 *Passover* Seder *plate. Dror Avi via the PikiWiki—Israel free image collection project, via Wikimedia.*

laws include that fruits and vegetables must be carefully washed to ensure that no insects are ingested.

Some scholars use medical theory to explain food taboos. Could avoiding pork be explained through health reasons like outbreaks of *Trichinosis*? Is shellfish prohibited because of the perils of food spoilage? Many anthropologists reject this theory, including Mary Douglas, who claims that most food taboos cannot be explained in terms of medical concerns. Douglas theorizes that dietary laws advance the metaphor of holiness. She makes the argument that the foods prohibited in the Book of Leviticus had to do with animals that cross boundaries that seemed unnatural. For instance, fish without scales. These are considered "not clean," not because there was some plausible biological basis for ingesting shark (no scales) and getting sick. Instead, they were "dirty," because they did not fit into a neat creation scheme. Another explanation for the dietary laws of Leviticus, especially the pig, could be its association with pagan rituals, and the need for safeguarding group cohesion and identity.

Food in the New Testament and in Christian practice

Food is a prominent theme in the New Testament, demonstrating the continuity with the Jewish tradition from which Jesus came, as illustrated in his celebration of the Passover meal. The nexus of food and faith is depicted in the miracles performed by Jesus. In a compassionate and prayerful act, Jesus divides five loaves of bread and two fish and feeds thousands of people. (See for example Mt. 14:13-21). Another narrative in which food plays a pivotal role is the Passover meal that later became known as the Last Supper, which Jesus shared with his followers just before his arrest and death. The ritual entails the blessing and consuming of bread and wine which he designated to be his flesh and blood. Whereas Protestants understand this ritual symbolically in remembrance of the death and resurrection of Jesus, Catholics view the process of ingesting the wine and the bread or wafer as a mystery, calling its process "transubstantiation"— believing that the flesh and blood of Christ are physically present in the bread and wine and are then transferred into the body of the believer. Catholics and other liturgical Churches conduct the Eucharist weekly (and some perform it daily) while Protestants have monthly communions.

Jesus is portrayed gathered with his twelve disciples:

> While they were eating, Jesus took bread, and when he had given thanks, he broke it and gave it to his disciples, saying, "Take and eat; this is my body." Then he took a cup, and when he had given thanks, he gave it to them, saying, "Drink from it, all of you. This is my blood of the covenant, which is poured out for many for the forgiveness of sins. I tell you, I will not drink from this fruit of the vine from now on until that day when I drink it new with you in my Father's kingdom" (Mt. 26:26-29).

Sensing his death, he transforms this occasion from a traditional Passover celebration to a ceremony which is to become the foundation for the central ritual of the Eucharist.

Food is also employed symbolically in the internal critique of political/ religious power and hierarchy in the New Testament. For example, in Jesus's polemic against the Pharisees, he makes the point that dietary laws, specifically impure food that is meant to maintain the purity of the group is not as important as impure words which come out of people's mouths: "It is not what enters the mouth that defiles the man, but what proceeds out of the mouth, this defiles the man" (Mt. 15:11). Food is a topic of debate among his followers and serves as a reminder of the ambiguity of the status of the laws especially during and following the ministry of St. Paul. Therefore, Christian teachings absolve adherents from the observance of the food prohibitions as dictated in the Old Testament. However, Christian Seventh-day Adventists have adopted many of the Jewish/biblical dietary laws but unlike Jews, prohibit the drinking of alcohol.

Fasting was a common practice among the Essenes, a Jewish sect during the time of Jesus. In the Middle Ages, women saints practiced fasting as a tool to control and shape their spiritual identity vis-à-vis the male-dominated Church. Christian food restrictions are integral to the preparation for the holiday of Easter. This is called a Lenten period; it begins forty days before Easter on what is known as Ash Wednesday. During Lent, Catholics are required to give up meat on Fridays. The final week of Lent is known as Holy Week and commences with Palm Sunday, the Sunday prior to Easter. Fasting is a part of many Christians' observance of Good Friday. For Catholics in some dioceses, meat is prohibited on all Fridays. Animal products such as fat, eggs, dairy, and broth are permissible, as is fish. These acts of self-denial and penance are done to purify the body prior to receiving communion; furthermore, fasting and other food restriction are encouraged to be undertaken as acts of repentance for one's sins. Whereas self-denial is understood as a significant value for observant Christians during Lent, the daily practice of reciting grace before a meal serve as a strong reminder of one's continuous connection with the divine.

Food in the Qur'an and in Islamic practice

The Qur'an makes numerous references to food and delineates dietary laws under the category of foods that are *halal* (allowed) and those that are *haram* (forbidden). Alcohol is also forbidden in Islam, as it is stated: "intoxicants and games of chance and (sacrificing to) stones set up and (dividing by) arrows are only an uncleanness, the shaitan's work; shun it therefore that you may be successful" (Qur'an 5:90). Seafood is permitted, but pork or pork products, birds of prey, carnivorous animals, blood, and meat that is not slaughtered in the name of Allah are considered *haram*: "He hath forbidden you only carrion, and blood, and swine flesh, and that which hath been immolated to (the name of) any other than Allah" (Qur'an 2:173). Islamic slaughter laws follow Jewish practice: the slaughterer must be Muslim; Allah's name must be invoked at the time of slaughter; and the throat, windpipe, and jugular veins are cut with a sharp blade.

Fasting on Ramadan, the ninth month of the Islamic year, is mandatory and is one of the five pillars of Islam. "Ramadan is the (month) in which the Qur'an was sent down, as a guide to mankind and a clear guidance and judgment (so that mankind will distinguish from right and wrong). Oh you who believe! Fasting is prescribed to you as it was prescribed to those before you, that

FIGURE 5.2 *Muslims taking* Iftar *to break their fast. Credit: Hindustan Times /
Contributor, via Getty Images.*

you many learn piety and righteousness" (Qur'an 2:183). It is a month-long
fast; literally defined, fasting during Ramadan requires complete abstention
from foods, drinks, intimate intercourse, and smoking from the break of dawn
until sunset during the entire month. Many of the activities that take place
during this month tend to heighten a feeling of solidarity among Muslims.
The evening meals during Ramadan, called *Iftar,* are occasions for family and
community get-togethers. As one of Islam's pillars, the purpose of Ramadan
is to inculcate and nurture piety, self-discipline, patience, humility, compassion
for the poor, and a sense of service to others.

Controversy in Europe over ritual slaughtering of animals in the Jewish and Muslim community

Shechita (ritual slaughter of animals) is facing opposition across
Europe by politicians who view it either as a foreign element to their
culture or as those who believe it is inhumane. Ironically, most Islamic
and Jewish scholars argue that their ritual slaughtering requirement that
the throat, windpipe, and jugular vein must be cut with a single stroke
specifically, is to minimize suffering for the animal. Religious laws in Islam
and Judaism require that animals be conscious when their necks are slit.
Several Western European countries such as Denmark recently banned
this ancient practice, insisting that the animals must be stunned first.

Food in Hindu sacred texts and practice

While Hindu beliefs emphasize the importance of living in harmony with nature, and having mercy, respect, and compassion for all creatures, the cow is revered as a source of food (dairy) and symbol of life and may never be killed. In ancient India, oxen and bulls were sacrificed to the gods and their meat was eaten. But even then, the slaughter of milk-producing cows was prohibited. Verses of the Atharva Veda refer to the cow as a *devi* (goddess): "Oh Goddess cow you make a weak person strong, you make a glow—less person beautiful and not only that you; you with your auspicious sounds make our homes auspicious" (4.21).

For Hindus, one's bodily state is constantly subject to accumulation of impurities depending upon the choices one makes. As *ahimsa* (nonviolence) is one of the spiritual principles of Hinduism, vegetarianism is the ideal diet, considered *satvic* (pure) and is widely practiced among Hindus. Certain special religious festival days (including Gandhi Jayanthi, marking the anniversary of Mahatma Gandhi's birth) are declared by the Indian Government as "Meatless Days" when no meat is sold anywhere. Specific foods are also important based on whether they enhance or hinder physical and spiritual development. According to Ayurveda, there are three categories of food: (1) *Tamasic* foods are considered heavy, dull, and depressive and include meat, heavy cheese, onions, garlic, and mushrooms among others. The category also includes old and stale food. (2) *Rajasic* foods are hot, spicy, and salty and said to irritate and stimulate, often to a state of high agitation, anger, and hate. And (3) *Sattvic* foods, like many fruits, fresh yogurt, and leafy greens, are supposed to bring clarity and perception and help unfold love and compassion in the consumer.

The Bhagavad Gita describes the effects of different kinds of food:

Foods in the mode of goodness increase the duration of life, purify one's existence and give strength, health, happiness and satisfaction. Such nourishing foods are sweet, juicy, fattening, and palatable. Foods that are too bitter, too sour, salty and pungent, dry and hot, are liked by people in the modes of passion. Such foods cause pain, distress, and disease. Food cooked more than three hours before being eaten, which is tasteless, stale, putrid, decomposed and unclean, is food liked by people in the mode of ignorance (Chapter 17, 8–10).

Food also plays an important role in Hindu worship, and *prasad* (the food offered to the deities) is thought to bestow religious merit, purifying the body, mind, and spirit. *Prasad* that has been on the altar is especially sacred as it is believed that the deity consumes it. It is then handed out to worshippers by the priest at the shrine or as worshippers leave the *mandir* (temple). *Prasad* is also served in the form of a full meal, especially on festival days. Many Hindus have an altar at home and offer their food before eating their meals. This practice follows the teachings of Krishna in the Bhagavad Gita: "If one offers Me with love and devotion a leaf, a flower, fruit, or water, I will accept it" and "All that you do, all that you eat, all that you offer and give away as well as austerities that you may perform, should be done as an offering unto Me" (9:26-27).

Langar

Langar is the Sikh practice of the free kitchen—a revolutionary concept which was established in the sixteenth century. The Sikh gurus rejected the inequality that existed in the caste system in India at that time by inviting all visitors to eat at the Sikh *gurdwaras*—Sikh places of worship; at the *langar*, only vegetarian food is served, although in general Sikhs have the option to consume Jhatka meat (an animal that was not ritualistically killed) meat if they wish. *Langar* embodies the principle of equality among all people regardless of religion, caste, color, creed, age, gender, or social status. This tradition promotes not only the values of sharing and community, but also the significance of oneness. The tradition was not intended to be a symbolic gesture of charity, but to fully involve all who came to the gurdwara in the cultivation and provision of food.

FIGURE 5.3 *Yudit Greenberg at* langar *at the Golden Temple Complex, Amritsar, 2013. Courtesy of David Greenberg.*

Preparing *langar* is said to be of great merit and is an important part of the life of the Sikh community where men, women, and children all participate in it. After the *ardas* (blessings for the food) are recited, the servers circulate among the people who sit on the floor on long rows of rugs in the *langar* hall, as they provide them with fresh food. The atmosphere in the *langar* hall is joyful with a warm sense of community. At the Golden Temple in Amritsar in India, *langar* is offered to approximately 50,000–100,000 people every day.

Food in Buddhism

Buddhists, like Jains and Hindus, believe in reincarnation and that the soul may at some point inhabit an animal. Thus, they abstain from killing living creatures. In Theravada Buddhism, there is no prohibition on eating meat, if the monk or nun has not seen, heard, or suspected that the animal was slaughtered specifically on his or her behalf. An important principle underlying Buddhist monasticism is that monks should be dependent upon the laity for alms and should go out daily into the local community to beg for food. The general principle is that monks should accept with gratitude whatever they are given and not be selective in preferring or rejecting foods.

Under the influence of Mahayana Buddhism, which stressed the virtue of compassionate concern for all sentient beings, vegetarianism came to be regarded as the most appropriate diet. Consumption of the "five pungent spices" (onions, garlic, scallions, chives, and leeks) is also discouraged, as when cooked they are said to intensify sexual desire, and when raw increase anger. Following the principle of mindful eating, the practice of the "Five Contemplations" while eating is advised by Vietnamese Buddhist monk, Thich Nhat Hanh:

1   Consider where the food came from including the work required by those who grew it.

2   Ask yourself: Have I been virtuous to deserve the blessing of this meal?

3   Be aware of the tendency toward gluttony and guard against it.

4   Contemplate the way that food can be used to heal various physical ailments.

5   The reason for eating is to provide the needed energy and nutrition to be able to continue on the path toward enlightenment.

While these rules and attitudes represent ideal behavior for Buddhists, especially for those on the monastic path, lay Buddhists in most of Asia do not practice strict vegetarianism, while still maintaining their religious observance.

Food in Jainism

Vegetarianism is the most significant hallmark of Jain identity. Vegetarianism is a way of life for all Jains who practice nonviolence (*ahimsa*, literally "non-injuring") and peaceful coexistence with all living beings. Jains consider nonviolence to be the most essential religious duty. It is an indispensable condition for liberation from the cycle of reincarnation, which is the goal of all Jain practices. Jains share this goal with Hindus and Buddhists, but their approach is particularly strict, especially among monks and nuns.

An example of the comprehensiveness of dietary practices followed by Jains is the rule against eating root vegetables, such as potatoes, onions, and garlic, because small life forms are injured when the plant is plucked and because the bulb is seen as a living being, as it is able to sprout. Also, consumption of most root vegetables involves uprooting and killing the entire plant whereas consumption of most terrestrial vegetables does not kill the plant. Beansprouts are prohibited because they are living, and eating them kills the whole plant. Mushrooms, fungus, and yeasts are forbidden because they are parasites, grow in unhygienic environments and may harbor other life forms. Eggs are forbidden as they are offspring of five-sensed beings. Cheese and yogurt are permissible but must be freshly prepared on the day they are eaten and no animal rennet (curdled milk from the stomach of an un-weaned calf) may be used to make them. Vegetable and microbial rennet is acceptable but in strict practice only acid coagulated fresh cheese will fit the same day rule. Vinegar is forbidden, as it is a product of fermentation (yeast to alcohol then bacteria to vinegar).

Honey is forbidden, since its production results in violence against the bees. Jains do not consume fermented foods (beer, wine, and other alcohols) to avoid killing of many microorganisms associated with the fermenting process. Alcohol is also forbidden because it may destroy the power of discrimination, create delusions and result in ill health. Water must be filtered before use for cooking or drinking. Food must be prepared fresh daily. Keeping cooked food overnight is forbidden. Strict Jains, especially monks and nuns take the vow of not eating after sunset to prevent accidental harming of insects.

One might think that being a guest in a Jain household would be a dull gastronomical experience, but quite the opposite is true, as Jains have developed a delightful cuisine within the strictures of their religious rules.

Food in the Baha'í religion

Many followers of the Baha'í faith adhere to a vegetarian diet, due to 'Abdu'l-Bahá's views that a vegetarian diet is what is most natural for humans.

'Abdu'l-Bah'a, the son of the prophet of their faith, Baha'u'llah taught that the food of the future will be fruit and grains and that in the future, meat will no longer be eaten. For Baha'u'llah, the focus is not just on compassion for animals, but also on proper care for the human body.

Every nineteen days, Baha'ís host "feasts"—celebratory gatherings that are centered on an aspect of spiritual development. These meetings, which may be held in individual homes or in public gathering spaces, are meant to bring members of the community together once every Baha'í month to read prayers, discuss national and local affairs, and build comradeship through dialogue, spiritual growth, music, and prayer.

The formal portion of readings and prayers lasts approximately one hour and concludes with an informal period of discussion and socializing over food. The meal shared at feasts changes depending on the location of the practitioners, and may range from light snacks to a full meal. Since the Baha'í faith was founded in Iran, common dishes at feasts often reflect their Persian roots. Despite the name, the focus of a feast is not necessarily on the food portion; in fact, Bahá'u'lláh stated that practitioners should gather monthly, even if "only water be served." His successor 'Abdu'l-Bahá later said that the importance of the monthly feasts is in coming together as a community to find spiritual nourishment and sustenance in the context of a regular, communal religious, intellectual, and social experience.

Food in Native American traditions

The Zuni, located in the American Southwest, celebrate the harvest during August. During this harvest festival members of the community (pueblo) come together to share in the success of the season's crops. Dances are part of the ceremonies and serve as a way to share Zuni culture and celebrate the end of the growing season. Those who are selected to participate (historically young boys) each receive a gourd rattle, which is decorated with pieces of coral and turquoise and filled with seeds. The gourd not only signals the dancer's part in the ceremony, but also indicates his/her place as a respectful and obedient community member. Today, the dance also signals a return to recognizing the importance of traditional foods (such as corn, beans, and squash) within Zuni diets, and a return to sustainable agriculture among Zuni pueblos.

In spring, first-salmon ceremonies are central to native tribes in the Pacific Northwest who believe that the salmon is a gift from the immortal salmon king. After undergoing a purification ritual, the man selected by the chief would catch the first salmon. Once caught, the salmon would be carefully prepared, cooked, and distributed to members of the tribe. The ceremony is

FIGURE 5.4 *Native American fishing for salmon. Credit: Natalie B. Fobes / Contributor, via Getty Images.*

filled with awe and respect for the salmon: returning the carcass of the fish to the river with blessings of thanks is believed to help the salmon continue its journey and return the following year.

Food in Paganism

Paganism preceded Christianity in Europe as the dominant religion. As Christianity came to replace it, most pagan rituals disappeared. The contemporary neo-pagan movement aims to revive many of its ancient rituals. Food in pagan life and ritual symbolizes the blessings from the womb of the Goddess, as well as the complex and interrelated relationship between humans and the earth. Because of this relationship, many pagans aspire toward a sustainable lifestyle and a vegetarian diet. The Pagan Wheel of the Year designates the major holidays, called Sabbats. These holidays follow the cycles of the agricultural calendar, serving as a reminder of the dependence of humankind on the earth. In paying homage to the traditional lifestyle of the European peasantry, these agricultural festivals also serve as a way to commune with and honor the ancestors. There are eight Sabbats focusing on seasons and agricultural periods. While food is central to these holidays, every pagan ritual is also concluded with a feast, both to restore energy and to celebrate the blessings of the Goddess. Pagans also say a prayer of thanks and blessing before beginning a meal, an example being: "Lord and Lady watch over us, / and bless us as we eat. / bless this food, this bounty of earth, / we thank you, so mote it be."

Food also holds an important place in Paganism as offerings to the ancestors, spirits, and the gods. On Samhain, which honors the spirit world and those who have passed into it, food offerings are left for friends and relatives who have passed, as well as for the ancestor. In the worship of ancestral gods, offerings from the gods' locus of worship may be used. For example, a Slavic Pagan may make an offering of honey or grain from that part of the world or one worshipping the Hellenistic pantheon may leave an offering of olives and Mediterranean Sea salt.

Day of the Dead

The holiday Day of the Dead (Día de Muertos) is prominent in Mexico, where the celebration has ancient Aztec and Mesoamerican roots. It is also widely observed in other Latin American countries as well. In Haiti, this holiday combines elements of Christianity with vodou practices and coincides with All Souls' Day, a Catholic occasion to remember the deceased. Day of the

FIGURE 5.5 *Day of The Dead altar with food, Mexico. Credit: Steve Bridger from Bristol, UK, via Wikimedia.*

Dead takes place on November 1 and 2, during which Haitian practitioners are expected to visit the graves of their ancestors, leaving offerings of coffee, fruit, peppered alcohol, bones, flowers, candles, and black crosses. The spirits of Gede, the god of the dead, and Baron Samedi, the gatekeeper of cemeteries, are also invoked, with a special altar set up in the home and offerings of alcohol, peppers, flowers, and candles set aside specifically for the gods.

A feast is also prepared for the celebration, including a spread of beans, sweet potatoes, rice, cabbage, and cornbread. This food is shared with friends, family, and the community as people come together to dance and celebrate.

New yam festivals

Among many residents of Ghana and Nigeria, yams serve as a staple crop whose versatility is celebrated during the harvest season. An offering of yams and goat blood is sacrificed to the gods and ancestors in thanks for the fruitful yield of the harvest. After the ceremony is complete, the remaining members of the community can partake in the feast. In some places, old yams are destroyed and all cooking tools are meticulously cleaned in anticipation of the fresh food. The length of the celebrations and details of the ceremony vary based on region and ethnic group; however, universally this season is met with great anticipation and excitement for the coming of the New Year as well as reverence for this sacred food.

An argument for a vegetable-based diet

In our study, we find that the first references to food in the Bible (Gen. 1–3) are plants and seeds. Some scholars believe that these are the most ideal human foods in accordance with the divine plan. Once the consumption of meat is mentioned (after the flood), it is accompanied with restrictions, including the slaughtering and preparations of animal flesh. Thus, we can infer that such dietary rules regarding the consumption of animal flesh have an underlying ethical principle—minimizing the pain of the animal and acknowledging our engagement with violence toward it.

In addition to ethical concerns, there are other considerations for vegetarianism, such as sustainability and health. For Jains, a vegetarian lifestyle is of highest importance because of the teaching of *ahimsa*, nonviolence, one of the most important tenets of their faith. Buddhists and Hindus also espouse a vegetarian diet due to their religious beliefs of compassion for all creatures. For all three Asian religions, the belief in karma and its effects on reincarnation (the rebirth of our souls) is linked to compassion for all creatures. Reincarnation, depending upon negative karma accumulated in one's life can result in a person's rebirth as an animal.

CONTEMPORARY TRENDS

Ecospirituality, food, and sustainability

The ecological crisis has engendered new theories and activism in an attempt to re-conceptualize and create an organic, non-dualistic relationship between humanity and nature. Gaia theory, named after the Greek earth goddess, Gaia, developed in the 1960s by scientist Dr. James Lovelock, who suggests that the earth and its natural cycles can be thought of like a living organism, an eco-body, which constantly works to balance itself. The metaphor of Gaia, mother earth, common in indigenous religions, can be understood to have coalesced new scientific theories, feminist concerns, and religious movements. Recognizing our ethical responsibility to living sustainably and the importance of honoring the earth and its resources have helped unify the mythic and scientific, the felt experience and the factual.

Ecospirituality is the spiritual component of recent ecological consciousness and activism, elevating the experience of the sacred in our efforts and commitment to live sustainably.

Both the environmental and the feminist movements have recognized the links between the oppression of women and the exploitation of nature and the environment. The term "ecofeminism," coined by French feminist Françoise d'Eaubonne in 1974, applies to the theory and movement which combines both concerns, recognizing their cause under patriarchal societies. As we mentioned in Chapter 2 under recent feminist theologies, ecofeminism is an important aspect of contemporary rethinking of the divine and the earth in feminine terms. Theologian Rosemary Reuther, a leader in the ecofeminist movement, has urged women and environmentalists to work together to end patriarchal systems that privilege hierarchy over collaboration. Some ecofeminists, influenced by nature-based religions, base their positive association of women and nature on spirituality, and see their activism as redeeming the spirituality of both women and of nature.

A unique grassroots movement of organic farming and sustainable practices has been growing in the United States, led by "Green Sisters" or "Eco-Nuns." These nuns believe that they are fulfilling the religious duty to be God's stewards of the land. There are now dozens of farms and retreat centers led by Catholic nuns, focused on cultivating the land, feeding the poor, providing retreat centers for women, and celebrating the beauty of the earth. Retreats commonly include activities like drum circles, labyrinth walking, and bird watching. Sister Barbara O'Donnell, of the Villa Maria convent in Pulaski, Pennsylvania, says, "We see this earth as a gift from God, and we are responsible for it. We want to care for it in a sustainable way, so that we can have a healthy habitat and healthy soil for healthy food for future generations of all species." Villa Maria encompasses a 300-acre organic farm and a 400-acre protected forest. The sisters donate at least half of their produce to local food banks and pantries. The Dominican sisters of Santuario SisterFarm in Texas focus on cultural diversity as well as sustainability. Their motto is, "Dominic's footprint was carbon neutral. Is yours?" The sisters at the Grail in Loveland, Ohio, aim at social and ecological transformation through releasing and empowering the creative potential of women.

Eco-Halal and Eco-Kosher are growing movements among Muslims and Jews, respectively, that have evolved in response to concerns over sustainability. For those who are a part of these movements, it is not enough that their food is labeled "Kosher" or "Halal," but must also have been raised and brought to market in a way that is in line with their larger religious and ethical beliefs. Muslims base these ecological beliefs on the Islamic idea of *tayyib*, meaning "pure." The Eco-Kosher movement takes into account not only the fact that the meat was raised and slaughtered humanely, but also that the workers were treated and paid fairly.

In response to growing concerns about sustainability within the Jewish faith, a group of Conservative leaders met in 2008 to develop a food certification program to convey to consumers that the product they are purchasing was made in line with Jewish ethics and social justice. This certification is called the Magen Tzedek Standard and ensures compliance in the realms of humane treatment of animals, labor concerns and fair pay, environmental sustainability, consumer issues, and corporate transparency. The Magen Tzedek Standard is not meant to replace kosher certification, but rather serves as an additional assurance for the consumer.

Like sports and music, certain Western food practices today resemble what can be called pseudo-religion; this is particularly evident by individuals who have transformed their eating habits in radical ways. The phenomenon of conversion comes to mind when thinking of the process of eliminating the consumption of meat and the act of adopting a vegetarian diet. Whether for health or ethical motives, vegetarians, especially newcomers are passionate about their food choice. This new life style, not only encompasses the rejection of consuming any animal flesh, but also involves the advocacy and activism undertaken for ethical values including working on behalf of animal rights, biodiversity, environmental sustainability, violence, hunger, and overall compassion to all living things.

Questions for review and discussion

1 What food-based practices or rituals do you observe and how do they reflect your beliefs?

2 Which religion-based food practices serve to strengthen community ties and which primarily serve to differentiate one religious group from another?

3 What common themes do you find in cross-cultural comparisons of religion-based food practices?

4 How can dietary laws contribute to religious and political conflict?

5 Is religious fasting the opposite of religious feasting? Why or why not?

6 In what ways can vegetarianism among Westerners today be understood as a pseudo-religion?

7 How do ecofeminists justify the connection between degradation of women and the degradation of the environment?

1, 2, 3, 6, 7

Glossary

Ahimsa-non-harming; Hindu, Jain, and Buddhist principle of nonviolence to all living things.

Ayurveda-traditional health modality of the Vedic culture from India.

Eco-feminism-theory and social movement that recognize connections between oppression of women and the exploitation of the environment.

Gaia Theory-the earth and its natural cycles thought of like a living organism, which constantly works to balance itself.

Halal-permissible food in Islamic law.

Haram-forbidden in Islamic law.

Jhatka-rules for slaughtering animals according to the Sikh religion

Karma-the spiritual principle of cause and effect central to Hinduism, Buddhism, and Jainism.

Kashrut-Jewish religious dietary laws.

Langar-kitchen/canteen at the Sikh gurdwara where food is served for free to all visitors without any distinction of religion.

Pagan Wheel of the Year-annual cycle of seasonal festivals consisting of eight Sabbats, including the winter and summer solstice and the fall and spring equinox.

Prasad-food offerings to deities blessed and shared by devotees in Hinduism and Sikhism.

Transubstantiation-Catholic belief that the bread and wine at the sacrament of the Eucharist transform into the body and blood of Christ.

6

Sustaining the Body: Breath, Harmony, Health, and Healing

In this chapter, we will investigate views and practices of health and healing, establishing that the religious and philosophical perspectives of the body are integral to their cultures and environments. As we review the function and symbolism of breath as the vital force or energy flow which sustains the body, we highlight its conceptualization and use in Asian healing systems, along with notions of balance, harmony, and the interconnectedness of the elements in the body. We consider biblical narratives of healing as well as ongoing tribal practices that are often linked to supernatural beliefs, whether through deities or spirits that exert influence on the body. We complete our study with a discussion of twentieth and twenty-first-century perspectives on health, and the gradual acceptance in the West of religious forms of healing, and Eastern practices that promote a holistic approach that integrates the spiritual and physical bodies in the process of healing.

Traditional healing methods consider the multivalence of human phenomena and its social and environmental, as well as biological factors in addressing health and healing. This grounds traditional healing methods in a series of dynamic interactions of mind, body, spirit, and environment. The traditional Greek, Chinese, Persian, and Indian approaches to health are conceptualized in terms of harmony and balance of the elements within the body. The Greek tradition of medicine, represented by physicians such as Hippocrates and Galen, understands the human being as a composite of four elements: air, earth, water, and fire. These elements are related to four humors or vital "winds": phlegm, blood, yellow bile, and black bile. *Unani*, traditional Persian-Arabic medicine practiced in Muslim cultures of South Asia, follows the Greek tradition by emphasizing the quality and quantity of the four elements in an individual—a person's unique, proper, and proportionate humoral makeup—believed to be the foundation of one's health. The *hakims'* (practitioners) healing practices are based on harmony and balance among the physical, mental, and spiritual aspects of the body.

Breath and soul

Breath, with its function and symbolism, figures prominently in the literature and practices of the world's religions and cultures. In Western traditions, the breath is associated with the soul, and is given metaphysical qualities, associated with one's spiritual life and the afterlife. The interchangeability of concepts of breath and soul has been used to signify the spiritual body of the individual. In Eastern traditions, a broader and holistic connection between the breath and one's mind-body-spirit has been cultivated. In Chinese and Indian cultures, for example, breath has been understood not only as referring to the inner self, but also as the key to one's health. Techniques of breath control in such practices as Tai Chi, yoga, and meditation are fundamental and integral to these traditions, and embody their philosophical concepts of health and healing. Eastern views of health and healing consider the person as a whole, seeing the interconnectedness of every element in the body. Breath then is fundamental to one's body, both physically and spiritually.

Terms such as the Hebrew *neshamah* and *ruah*, Greek *psyche* and *pneuma*, Latin *anima* and *spiritus*, Sanskrit *prana*, and Chinese *ch'i* found in scriptures and other sacred literature shape and inform concepts of human life and death, the soul, and energy. The breath, especially in Asian cultures and religions, has also influenced notions and practices of healing, spiritual discipline, and self-control.

Pre-Socratic philosophers see air, wind, and breath as essential to the description of the soul. For them, the soul has two qualities: movement and knowledge. The Greek philosopher Anaximenes, who lived in the sixth century BCE, describes the soul as having an air-like nature that guides and controls the living being. Diogenes (fifth century BCE) asserts that air was the element most capable of originating movement. Plato refers to the breath in his notion of the soul using the Greek term *psyche*, but instead of emphasizing the breath as the life force as did the pre-Socratic philosophers, for him the soul or psyche was the divine essence, the rational aspect of humanity that is separate from the body.

In the Bible, the Hebrew term for breath as the symbol of life is *neshima*, similarly to the Greek *pneuma*. The Hebrew *nefesh*, which also translates as soul, like the Greek *psyche*, refers specifically to the living person, distinguished from the dead by the breath. Another term, *ruah* means wind or spirit, and as a general principle, is applied to the physical breath, one's moral character, and spirit. A third term, *neshamah,* also translated as soul, derives from the root-word *neshimah* or breath, and shares common meaning as the breath of God breathed into Adam, and as the breath of every living thing.

Breath and harmony in Chinese philosophy and practice

In Chinese philosophy and culture, *Ch'i* (also spelled *chi* or *qi*) is a fundamental concept. Found in Chinese traditional religion but especially Daoism, *ch'i* literally means "air" or "breath," but as a concept it refers to the energy flow or life force that is said to pervade all things. Chinese thinkers debate whether *ch'i* is derived from physical matter or physical matter is derived from *ch'i*.

The balance of *ch'i* is believed to be essential to maintaining health and achieving a long life. In addition to living a healthy life (both physically and psychologically), *ch'i* can be regulated through practices like breath control, Ta'i Chi, massage, and acupuncture. Breath control is essential to balancing the levels of *ch'i* in the body. *Hsing-ch'i* (meditative breathing), allows *ch'i* to pervade the body by visualizing the breath moving through the body. Feng Shui, the traditional Chinese art of placement and arrangement of space is also based on the flow of *ch'i*, the five elements (wood, fire, earth, metal, and water) as well as "yin" and "yang." Each item, its color and shape in a space affects the flow of *ch'i* and with it, impacts the well-being of persons who reside in that space.

While the virtue of harmony is found in numerous cultures and religions, its meaning is particularly essential to Chinese traditions. Harmony is defined as an orderly arrangement of the elements. Harmony in Chinese religions is related to the natural cosmic order of reality. In the social sphere, harmony points to orderliness, rightness, truth, and stability. It is essential in relationships between individuals, and is also imperative in humanity's relationship with nature.

Chinese notions of Yin and Yang

The ancient Chinese belief is that the cosmos and human beings function properly according to the rhythms of yin (female principle) and yang (male principle), which are mutually complementary despite their opposite natures. Yin is described as negative, receptive, passive, and low like the earth to which it is equated, whereas yang is active, positive, aggressive, and high—analogous to heaven. The cosmos represents a cyclical totality constituted by the conjunction of these two alternating and complementary principles. Life, which is in a constant state of flux, is derived from a blending and harmony of these two forces that alternate in cycles.

In addition to the cycle of yin and yang, the basic constituents of the universe are wood, fire, earth, metal, and water, which are called the Five Agents. These five elements form a network of relationships between the human and nonhuman parts of the cosmos. Just as the sun dominates the day and yields its place to the moon at night, the cosmic order is meant to teach humans that heaven and earth operate orderly and with harmony and that human order and harmony should follow the cosmic order.

The spiritual practices, institutions, and beliefs that comprise the Daoist religion were developed by Zhang Daoling, also known as the *Lao Tzu*, author of the philosophical and poetic classic Dao De Jing or Tao Te Ching (The Book of the Way). Daoist teachings integrate elements of Confucianism and village life and include rules by which to live in harmony and protect the environment. Daoism and Confucianism teach that a person must live a harmonious life in accord with the Dao—the eternal principle, the mother of all that is. The Dao is mysterious because it is invisible and nameless. Daoist philosophy is mystical while at the same time, it can be considered a precursor to modern science as it seeks to explain the nature and patterns of life.

Tai Chi Chuan is an ancient Chinese mind-body practice rooted in multiple Asian traditions, including martial arts, traditional Chinese medicine (TCM), and philosophy. Tai Chi Chuan means "perfect boxing," and while referring to the martial art, it is a meditative exercise based upon the philosophical principles of Daoism. It consists of complementary and deeply meditative movements that are graceful and balanced, thus expressing the principles of harmony and yin and yang, derived from the philosophic principles of Dao De Ching. Tai Chi Chuan is much more than a martial art—it is a philosophy founded in traditional Chinese healing, which uses the concept of *ch'i*, the vital force, to explain health and disease. Tai Chi training integrates slow intentional movements with breathing and multiple cognitive skills (e.g., mental focus, heightened body awareness, imagery). The movements of Tai Chi strengthen,

FIGURE 6.1 *Chinese man performing Tai Chi, Credit: SONGMY via Wikimedia.*

relax, and functionally integrate the physical body and mind, and improve health, personal development, and self-defense.

Traditional Chinese Medicine (TCM) is based on the belief that the human body has organic unity. This unity is based on the opposing and complementary relationships of yin and yang. The body's organs and tissues can be classified according to yin yang theory on the basis of their functions and locations. The upper body belongs to yang while the lower body belongs to yin. Other yin/yang pairs in the body include the interior (yin) versus the exterior (yang), the front (yin) versus the back (yang), the inside (yin) versus the outside (yang) of the limbs, and the five yin organs versus the six yang organs. Each organ can also be further divided into yin and yang aspects such as heart yin and heart yang and kidney yin and kidney yang.

According to TCM, health is achieved when yin and yang are in harmony. Yin yang disharmony is the cause of disease and physiological disorders. A primary cause of yin and yang disharmony is the flow of *ch'i* throughout the body. When a person has normal *ch'i* flow, their body functions well and has good immunity allowing them to recover easier from illness. By applying the yin yang theory to treat and diagnose diseases, yin yang harmony can be restored and health maintained.

In practice, the restoration of yin-yang harmony may be accomplished through several means. TCM often combines techniques such as acupuncture; acupressure; massage; cupping; meditation; diet; and the use of herbs, roots, and powders. In acupuncture, tiny needles are inserted at specific acupuncture points to restore harmony within the body by influencing the flow of *ch'i* along the body's channels, or meridians. Western medicine has

FIGURE 6.2 *Acupuncturists at work in the Wangjing clinic in Beijing. Credit: Official Navy Page from United States of America Dominique Pineiro/U.S. Navy, via Wikimedia.*

been gradually embracing traditional healing methods, particularly TCM, which are now categorized as alternative or complementary medicine, providing relief from pain and beneficial for other conditions as well.

Ayurveda, yoga, and meditation in Indian health system

Ayurveda, (Sanskrit: science of life) is an ancient Indian health system whose principles include the inseparability of mind and body, and the mind's central role in healing and transforming the body. Like TCM, it aims to bring balance to mind and body. An individualized approach to healthcare has been a cornerstone of Ayurvedic medicine. Ayurveda, like TCM, understands the body as an integral part of the environment. Diseases are understood largely to be caused by blockages of three humors, wind, bile, and phlegm, energies that course through the body. Ayurvedic diagnosis of the body is based on "body type," referring to *prakruti*, or a person's "essential nature." According to Ayurveda, our body constitution or *dosha* is determined at the moment of conception and consists of physical and emotional characteristics. The three body types or *doshas*, *vata*, *pitta*, and *kapha*, are governed by two of the five elements or *mahabhutas* that make up everything within our bodies and everything outside of our bodies: Earth is solid, grounded, and stable; fire is hot, direct, and transformational; wind has the qualities of movement and change; water is cohesive and protective; and ether carries all the aspects of pure potentiality. A balanced *dosha* brings health, whereas an imbalanced *dosha* fosters discomfort or illness. Ayurvedic healing includes special herbs and oils, massage, a diet of fresh, and organic food which consists of the six tastes (sweet, salty, sour, pungent, bitter, and astringent) in each meal, physical movement, breath control, and meditation.

Ayurvedic and yogic literature recognize breath or *prana* as the vital energy and life force of the body. *Prana* is the combination of the two Sanskrit words, *pra,* meaning constant and *an,* meaning movement. When *prana* is weak, we become physically ill. When the brain does not receive a sufficient supply of *prana,* we experience mental health disorders such as anxiety and depression. We can increase our *prana* through the practice of *pranayama,* the practice of conscious and controlled breathing. It is believed that advanced yogis may become so attuned that they can control the *prana* by sending it to parts of the body that need healing.

Prana is also associated with the belief in a subtle body that is not perceived by the direct action of the senses. The subtle body is structured around three channels (*nadi*) through which vital energies pass: the *pingala, ida,* and the *sushumna.* The *sushumna nadi* is the central axis of the subtle body and is bordered on the right by the *pingala* and on the left by the *ida.* The *ida* and *pingala* intersect the *sushumna* at crucial points called chakras. Each chakra is visualized as a different disc of swirling *prana,* vital life force.

Another manifestation of *prana* is the powerful energy force called *kundalini,* which originates in the base of the spine. The Sanskrit word *kundalini* means "in a coil," represented as the coiled serpent that resides in the lowest chakra. The awakening or raising of the *kundalini* is depicted as the uncoiling of the serpent. When she is awakened, through sustained yogic practices, the *kundalini* courses up through the central channel of the body activating chakras located in various sites in the body.

The first chakra is the *muladhara,* which corresponds with the anus and is associated with the element of earth. It controls the lower limbs and the sense of smell. The second chakra is the *svadhishthana,* which is at the genitals, and associated with the element of water. It controls the arms and hands as well as the sense of taste. The third chakra is the *manipura,* located at the naval and associated with the sense of sight. The fourth chakra is the *anahata,* located at the heart and associated with the element of air. It controls the sexual organs and the sense of touch. The fifth chakra is the *vishuddha,* which corresponds with the throat and is associated with the element of ether. It controls the harmony between the organs and the sense of hearing. The sixth chakra is the *ajna,* which is positioned on the forehead and associated with the transcendent element "*mahant,*" that controls mental activity and the sense of intellectual perception. The final chakra is the *sahasrara,* which is the Absolute and is positioned outside the subtle body. In addition to being

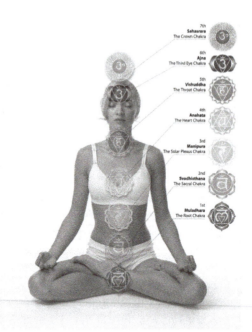

FIGURE 6.3 *Chakra Chart. Credit: Oleksiy Maksymenko, via Getty Images.*

associated with particular sensory powers, the chakras are also symbolized by particular colors, geometric shapes, and sounds, which are also used as meditative aids in the effort to awaken the *kundalini* and energize the chakras.

According to Ayurveda, when these chakras are out of alignment they can negatively impact emotional, physical, and spiritual health. If underactive they become sluggish, but if overactive they can draw energy away from other parts of the body. The chakras can be balanced through meditation and hatha yoga poses. The first stages of yoga regulate and tame the physical body. Through *asana* (yogic posture) and *pranayama* (breath control), one can rebalance the energy centers of the body. For example, the "camel pose" may help to activate the heart chakra. The throat chakra can be activated through poses that stretch the neck, like Matsyasana (the "fish pose").

While hatha yoga and pranayama are beneficial for physical health, the yogic practices of *pratyahara* (the withdrawal of senses from their objects), *dharana* (concentration), and the practices of awakening and raising the *kundalini* are known to bring spiritual health in the forms of illumination, bliss, and wisdom. The ultimate goal of the awakening of *kundalini* is a state of *samadhi*, absorption in the divine, where the *kundalini*, considered to be feminine, reaches the final chakra, the *sahasrara*, which is likened to the abode of Shiva. When *kundalini* joins the *sahasrara* chakra, it constitutes a return to the primal unity of masculine

FIGURE 6.4 *Yoga and Ayurveda camp in India. Credit: Hindustan Times / Contributor, via Getty Images.*

and feminine. This then is the key to liberation. The person who has awakened *kundalini* may finally join the Absolute beyond the cycle of death and rebirth.

Meditation and healing in Buddhism

Buddhism shares many healing techniques with Hinduism, including meditation. Buddhists perform a variety of meditation practices. When done regularly, meditation helps to stabilize the mind from its fluctuations and reactions to external circumstances. Vipassana Bhavana (Mind development through insight) is a technique that originated in the Theravada tradition, and uses mindfulness to note details of our mental and physical experiences. Mindfulness consists of awareness of breathing, thoughts, feelings, and actions in order to gain insight into the true nature of reality. The main focus of this type of meditation is accepting what is occurring without judging.

Folk traditions have influenced Buddhist healing practices that are particularly evident in Tibetan culture. In Nepal, as in rural India, disease is believed to be caused by possession of an evil spirit. Healing is often done as part of the *Cinta* ceremony, a ritualized trance performed by a healer called *dhami*, whose acts include dancing, fighting, and mantra (sacred words) recitations. *Cinta* is intended to remove the evil spirit from the body of the diseased person and restore their health. The system of Tibetan medicine,

Gso-wa Rig-pa, or "The Knowledge of Healing," like Ayurveda, is based upon the appropriate balancing of the body's energies. Healing techniques include herbs, massages, applications of heat, and the use of mantras. In the process of healing, Tibetan Buddhists also invoke the Medicine Buddha or Bhaisajya-guru, who is believed to be an emanation of the Buddha.

Healing in Judaism

Healing in the Hebrew Bible is closely related both to spiritual and physical redemption and to wholeness. The prophets spoke about the healing aspects inherent in turning to God. Ezekiel and Zechariah describe God as the caretaker of the sick. While there is a negative attitude toward sorcery and incantations, incidents of magical healing are mentioned, including Moses's use of an image to heal serpent bites (Num. 21:9). Hebrew priests had no authority as physicians, but rather as the custodians of the health of the community, enforced the laws pertaining to social hygiene. Various diseases are mentioned in the Bible, including many types of skin disease. *Tzar'at* (leprosy) required rigid quarantine as portrayed in great detail in the Book of Leviticus. Persons with leprosy and other skin diseases were considered ritually impure, with the presumption that their skin disorder was associated with transgression or immorality. The priests in charge instructed their separation from the community, and once their skin had cleared, he or she was cleansed through a priestly ritual and welcomed back into the community.

The medical knowledge of the rabbis, like their priestly predecessors, can be seen in the prevention of disease and the care of community health. The rabbis advocated hygienic measures for practical as well as religious reasons. The medical profession was seen as a spiritual vocation in the post-biblical period. Jewish physicians were simultaneously rabbis and scholars in the Middle Ages, as exemplified by Moses Maimonides who was a court physician in Egypt, as well as the author of Judaism's most authoritative legal and philosophical works. On the Sabbath, between readings of the Torah, special prayers are recited on behalf of individual congregants who are ill, and it is customary to recite psalms on behalf of those suffering from an illness.

Healing in Christianity

Stories of Jesus's performance of healing miracles are recounted throughout the New Testament. Within Roman Catholicism, healing has been institutionalized in the sacrament of extreme unction, during which the sick person is

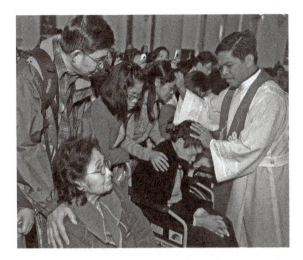

FIGURE 6.5 *Filipino Catholic Priest Father Fernando Suarez lays hand on the sick during a healing mass at Catholic cathedral in Hong Kong, January 20, 2008. Father Suarez is a well-known priest-healer in the Philippines.*

anointed with oil. In Eastern Orthodoxy, this anointing is usually performed at a church with oil from lamps. While Protestantism has denied sacramental status to the anointing of the sick, it too embraces a variety of healing practices, the most well known of which is faith healing associated with Pentecostal denominations. Claiming that they have exceptional gifts experienced by followers of Jesus during the Pentecost, Pentecostal healers often lay hands upon the afflicted and pray in an inspired speech called "glossolalia" that both transmits and symbolizes divine healing power.

The most distinctive healing tradition associated with Christianity is Christian Science, founded by Mary Baker Eddy.

Mary Baker Eddy, known as Mrs. Eddy to Christian Scientists, suffered from several ailments early in her life, and her recovery from a particularly incapacitating illness inspired her to write her seven-hundred-page work entitled *Science and Health with Keys to the Scriptures*, which was first published in 1875. This book, along with the King James Version of the Christian Bible, comprises the whole corpus of writings upon which Christian Scientists' beliefs and practices are based. The Christian Scientists' Mother Church is still located in Boston, Massachusetts, and the organization is active in today's news media with the well-respected, Pulitzer prize-winning publication *The Christian Science Monitor*.

Christian Scientists believe that the physical world is an illusion, and is actually a state of mind. It follows, then, that sin and bodily illness or injury are illusory as well. Medical attention that only treats the body promotes the

FIGURE 6.6 *A Colombian pastor, pressing a crucifix on a believer's head, attempts to evict a supposed demon during the exorcism ritual performed at a house church on March 10, 2016 in Bogota, Colombia. Credit: Jan Sochor/CON / Contributor, via Getty Images.*

illusion of the reality of matter and is thus illusory as well. Prayer is the only way to truly heal, by helping the mind to overcome the illusion of the body, so adherents are expected to pray in the event of injury or illness. The prayers are not for a miracle of healing by God, but instead to release themselves from the illusion of injury or illness. Christian Scientists object to their healing practices being labeled "faith healing" because they believe that faith does not heal their bodies, as their bodies are made up of matter and matter is "nothingness."

Given how it is difficult to discipline one's own mind to regard bodily suffering as an illusion and pray for clarity, there are practitioners of healing prayer within the Christian Science organization who work with illnesses. Christian Scientists also have their own care facilities for the spiritual treatment of their patients. Despite this reliance on prayer for healing, it should be noted that most Christian Scientists go to the dentist and use prescription eyeglasses as needed. It is documented in her biography that Mrs. Eddy herself used pain relievers near the end of her life, and that she believed that people can seek medical intervention if spiritual practice does not provide relief. The decision to seek medical attention or to treat injuries is up to the conscience of the individual, or the parents of a child. Despite this, many former Christian Scientists report pressure from other church members to forgo traditional medicine.

Christian Scientists actively lobby for religious exemptions from public health mandates and requirements, such as laws that require vaccinations and mandatory treatment of illness and injury for children. As a result of their efforts, only a few states have mandatory requirements of this type, making it difficult to prosecute Christian Scientist parents for failing to seek medical attention for their children.

Healing in Islam

In addition to the practice of *unani* medicine mentioned earlier, there are a number of Islamic faith healing traditions. The psychoanalyst Sudhir Kakar writes of a *pir*, or Muslim healer, who was particularly focused on diagnosing cases of possession by *jinn*, or demons. This pir's method of healing would involve the recitation of Qur'anic verses; the chanting of one of the ninety-nine names of Allah as appropriate; and the making of talismans according to a complex combination of mystical squares, Arabic letters, and signs of the zodiac. In recent years, standard Islamic practices such as *salat* or prayer have been touted for their psychological and physiological benefits. Islamic healing techniques rely upon a sense of self brought into equilibrium by submission to God.

Healing practices in indigenous traditions

Native American

Native American healing practices vary depending upon the tribe and their geographic location. Most healing practices tend to approach the person in a holistic way, with treatments that target a person's mind, body, and spirit. In Arizona, for example, some may run at sunrise, which provides a connection between bodily health and spiritual well-being. Generally, Native American healing traditions also incorporate nature and draw upon the natural and spiritual worlds in order to promote individual health and vitality. Categories of traditional Native American healing include, narrative and mythical healing, herbal remedies, shamanistic ceremonies and rituals, and medicine wheels.

One of the most common and well-known forms of spiritual healing is the Sweat Lodge or *inipi*. The practice is often exclusive to native people or members of specific tribes. An individual enters a teepee-like structure that has been sealed to keep the heat, steam, and energy from escaping the structure's confines. The purpose of the ceremony is to cleanse the individual by promoting physical, mental, and spiritual clarity, and encouraging the presence of beneficial human and nonhuman spirits.

Sweat lodge controversies

The cultural appropriation by Westerners of indigenous rituals is an issue of an ongoing debate and concern. The deaths of three people in 2009 while participating in a so-called "sweat lodge" as part of his "Spiritual Warrior" operated by James Arthur Ray, resulted in a prison sentence for this self-help guru. This was not the first time that Ray caused suffering on his innocent followers. In 2005, a number of participants in his retreat were also hospitalized and traumatized as a result of his sweat lodge retreat. The legal issues of Ray's culpability for these people's death and trauma, and his subsequent imprisonment, may have taught his followers and others a lesson, but the emphatic response from the Native American community continues to reverberate, as they actively object to the abuse of their sacred traditions. A Native American leader captures their anger and disapproval: "We call it a 'Purification Lodge', not a sweat lodge, because its purpose is not to sweat as in a sauna, but instead its aim is to purify the body, mind, and soul." This tragedy illuminates not only the issues of cultural appropriation, but also the physical and emotional harm caused by greed and self-aggrandizement of some self-proclaimed spiritual leaders.

Vodou

Vodou (also known as voodoo, hoodoo, *Sévis Gine,* or African service) is a religion derived from African religious traditions (mostly from the Ibo, Kong, and Yoruba people), that were transported to the United States and Caribbean as a result of the slave trade, and combined with Christian practices and beliefs. Today, vodou is most commonly practiced in Haiti; however, it is also observed in parts of the Dominican Republic, Cuba, Brazil, and the United States. The practice and rituals of vodou vary greatly by region. While the religion has been sensationalized by the media as being shrouded in superstition and "black magic," referred to as *Petro* by vodou practitioners, these depictions often overlook the reality of vodou practice, including its emphasis on the importance of health and healing.

Vodou healing practices first begin with an acknowledgment of the "crossroads," namely that the invisible spiritual world and the physical world are intertwined. Male (*houngan*) or female (*mambo*) healers are responsible for conducting and determining the proper ritual and materials needed to resolve an illness or personal dilemma. Some common vodou healing practices include spiritual baths, readings, spells (*wanga*), and protection (*gad*).

FIGURE 6.7 *A traditional healer tends to a patient who bows down in front of fetish objects, Lome 2015. Credit: EMILE KOUTON / Stringer, via Getty Images.*

One of the most common *gads* is called the *gad ko*, which involves cutting an individual's skin and inserting specific herbs into the wound. This is done to protect the individual from harmful *wangas* or accidents. In performing this ritual, the person becomes attached to a *lwa*, or spirit, who becomes responsible for protecting the practitioner from harm.

Contemporary practices and trends

Healing with Ayahuasca

Ayahuasca has recently become a popular drug in the United States. However, those who have used or use Ayahuasca on a regular basis refer to it as medicine, a non-recreational spiritual experience, a gateway into the mind and soul rather than simply a drug. The psychoactive effects of combining the *B. caapi* vine and the *P. viridis* leaf, unleashing the naturally occurring psychoactive compound DMT into the body, were originally discovered and utilized in shamanic practice by the indigenous people of the Amazon rainforest. However, it was not brought into urban consciousness until the

FIGURE 6.8 *Shaman prepares Ayahuasca. Credit: Wade Davis / Contributor, via Getty Images.*

1930s with the founding of the Santo Daime movement in Rio Branco, Brazil by Raimundo Irineu Serra, an Afro-Brazilian rubber tapper, sometimes referred to as Mestre Irineu.

Mestre Irineu claimed that after his move to the Amazon in 1912 he began having visions in which he was led into the forest and taught about the healing and spiritual powers of Ayahuasca. In these visions, he was led by a female figure that he believed was *Nossa Senhora da Conceição Aparecida*, Our Lady of the Appeared Conception, a popular title for the Virgin Mary among the Afro-Brazilian population. This female figure also handed down a religious doctrine, which while relying heavily on Catholicism and indigenous shamanic practice, also integrated African, Hindu, and esoteric elements.

Ayahuasca is taken in a strict ritual environment. Adherents must follow codes of dietary and behavioral conduct for three days leading up to the ritual. The ritual is led by a "Godfather/mother" responsible for maintaining order, obedience, and control of the doses. Central to the ritual space is an altar upon which religious symbols are placed. Participants are separated into groups by sex and age, remaining in their prescribed area for the entirety of the ritual. Music is also highly important in the ritual as the percussions serve to elevate consciousness, while singing connects the participants as they hear their voices in unison.

The First Ayahuasca Church
in the United States

Although Ayahuasca had already been developing a large following in the United States, it was not until December 2015 that an institution was granted the legal right to perform Ayahuasca ceremonies based on the justification of freedom of religion. The church, Ayahuasca Healings Native American Church, is located in Elbe, Washington, and opened in January 2016.

While Santo Daime was the first non-shamanic organized religious movement focused on the spiritual use of Ayahuasca, several other Ayahuasca-centered groups quickly evolved throughout Brazil. Similar movements began to emerge across South America and eventually spread to the United States and around the world. "Ayahuasca tourism" has developed as an industry in Central and South America. Those wishing to participate in the spiritual journey that Ayahuasca promises visit lodges and are led by shamans in multiday ceremonies. This phenomenon of Ayahuasca tourism has spurred controversy as some argue that it appropriates native culture, while others claim that the shamans performing the ritual are not authentic but rather con-artists taking advantage of a new trend, thereby leading to dangerous doses and practices for the visitors.

Brazilian healer: John of God

John of God, or João de Deus, as he is known in his native Brazil, is a world renowned spiritual healer. With no medical training and little formal education, John of God claims that saints and the spirits of famous doctors, which he calls the Entities, use him as a channel in order to perform mystical healings. While others refer to John of God as a healer, he says, "I do not cure anybody. God heals, and in his infinite goodness permits the Entities to heal and console my brothers. I am merely an instrument in God's divine hands." In the 40 plus years that John of God has been a practicing healer, he has treated up to 15 million people, who flock to his institute, Casa de Dom Inacio de Loyola, in Abadiania, Brazil. Most of the surgeries John of God performs are invisible, meaning the Entities may enter the body to heal it without needing to break the skin. While thousands, including such popular self-help authors as Wayne Dyer, have claimed to have experienced miraculous healings from John of God, many are skeptical, claiming that although John of God does not charge for healings, his institution does sell herbs and crystals that could potentially earn him millions each year. However, John of God claims that this money is used to help the poor, and that if he were a fraud, it would not have been possible for him to fool people for over forty years.

Healing in Neo-Paganism

One of the primary concerns of Paganism is health and healing, not just of the body, but also of the mind and soul. Pagans believe that the body, spirit, and mind are intrinsically linked, so physical illness is understood as a symptom of a larger problem. Pagans may look for the cause of illness within the psyche, past lives, or in the psychic field. Illness, then, may be a result of negativity and psychic attack from others, negative spirits, psychological troubles, stress, or actions in a previous life. In order to uncover the root of physical illness an individual may consult a method of divination, undergo a past life regression, or ask for an answer through their dreams. Different healing methods are used in order to find the root cause of disease. For example, one may make a sachet of lavender to induce peaceful sleep, and mugwort to increase psychic abilities, and place it under their pillow in hopes of receiving a healing dream or answer to their questions. This may also be accompanied by a prayer or candle burned to Isis, the goddess of psychic powers and healing, or a similar god or goddess, depending on the favored pantheon of the individual.

The healing process usually begins with a cleansing of the home from negative energy, followed by the burning of sage, also known as smudging, to purify the energy. Once the home is purified, the individual may begin the other healing work that is required, whether it be a form of energy healing like Reiki, aligning the chakras, or a ritual invoking an appropriate deity of healing, like the Hellenistic god Apollo or the Celtic goddess Brigid. Many pagans like to seek outside help when they are in need of healing, like consulting a Native American medicine woman. While outsiders claim that in doing so pagans are guilty of appropriating other cultures, pagans would argue that one of the benefits of their practice is the ability to draw from the wisdom of cultures from around the world.

Modern perspectives on health and healing

Trends such as purely mechanistic views of disease, as well as medicalization beyond biological or natural conditions, have permeated the conceptualization of health and disease in the twentieth century. New perspectives influenced by psychology and the growth of medical technology have shifted to identifying multiple interactive causes of health and disease.

The concept of "medicalization," which was developed in the 1970s, is defined as the way in which medical science is applied to behaviors or conditions which are not necessarily biological. Michel Foucault, the French social philosopher, saw medicalization as a historical process deriving from the redefinition of medicine to include psychological, economic, and social concepts of "health." Feminist sociologists have critiqued this medical model as detrimental to women's bodies and women's lives, according to which natural processes such as pregnancy and childbirth, menstruation, and menopause, are conceptualized as illnesses. Similarly, homosexuality and old age, seen as socially undesirable, have also been medicalized.

The medicalization process has also been applied to disability. As medicalized bodies are pressed against constant normativity of the social body, the disabled body has been stigmatized and excluded. In the context of religion, there is evidence that while religions have contributed to our understanding of health and disease, whether positively or not, at present, religious communities and clergy are challenged to accommodate persons with disabilities with both physical accessibility and spiritual opportunity.

Another consequence of medicalization is the resisting the authority of professionals, and taking responsibility for one's own health, as evident in the growth of the self-help movement. While the medical establishment continues to extend its hegemony over the body, controlling and defining its authority on health and disease, lay knowledge of health, including alternative healing practices has also increased. As our next discussion shows, Eastern practices of yoga and meditation in the West can be understood as taking health into our hands. There is a growing acceptance among medical professionals as well as lay people that spirituality and faith play an important role in health and in the healing process.

Mindfulness and yoga in the west

Yoga first arrived in the United States with Swami Vivekananda in 1893 with his speech at the World Parliament of Religions in Chicago, which opened the door for ideas of Eastern spiritual practices in the West. In 1920, Paramahansa Yogananda, considered the father of yoga in the West, came to the United States and founded the Self-Realization Fellowship in order to bring the benefits of the ancient practice out of India and into the rest of the world. What began as a humble spiritual practice has evolved into a $27 billion industry that includes not just yoga classes and videos but also designer yoga accessories and apparel. Westerners have adapted traditional yoga practices to satisfy fitness trends, with everything from paddle board, to aerial yoga, to equestrian yoga.

Mindfulness experts like Deepak Chopra have become household names, while yoga instructors like Tara Stiles have gained fame through social media. With the documented scientific benefits of various mindfulness practices, major companies and universities across the country are utilizing meditation, yoga, Tai Chi, and other practices to increase productivity and reduce stress. In fact, one-fourth of all major employers offer some kind of stress reduction programming.

This explosion in popularity has led many to question whether yoga and other mindfulness practices, like meditation and Ayurveda, have become too commercialized, and have lost their spiritual roots and significance. On the one side of the debate are those who assert that yoga has simply adapted to Western culture, and that even in its mass, commercialized form is beneficial because it still retains some of the mental, spiritual, and physical benefits, and perhaps serving as a stepping stone into a more spiritual practice. Others hold that the commodification of yoga is a form of cultural appropriation that has led to a cheapening of the practice and other negative consequences.

Some yogis would claim that because of the mass popularity and accessibility of yoga, people enter the practice without the proper knowledge to safely do so. Not only can this lead to physical injury, but it can also cause mental and spiritual strife. In the United States, this has perhaps caused an unfortunate phenomenon sometimes called the "Guru Scandal." These self-proclaimed gurus teach their students that to follow a guru means to mindlessly obey. As Bikram Choudhury, one such leader accused of exploitation and manipulation, says, "I implant my mind into your brain." Choudhury, who has already made millions off his yoga empire, has unsuccessfully attempted to copyright his style of "Bikram" yoga. This has led to a significant amount of pushback from the yoga community in America as well as yogis in India, who were appalled that someone would try to copyright and seek financial gain from the ancient practice.

Kumaré

To explore this phenomenon, filmmaker Vikram Gandhi impersonated a guru, and managed to attract a real following, which he chronicled in his documentary *Kumaré*. Gandhi found that although he had no real experience or insight as a spiritual teacher, people were eager, if not desperate, to follow his teachings and trust him implicitly.

The Westernization of the practices of meditation, yoga, and mindfulness has been adapted as a way to innovate in education, business, and trauma care. In the realm of education, organizations like Mindful Schools and Mindfulness Without Borders, that train teachers and students in mindfulness techniques and meditation have cropped up across the world. These organizations often target schools in areas with high rates of crime and poverty, in hopes that beginning a mindful lifestyle as early as kindergarten can help to break these cycles. Research studies conducted during the years 2011–12 by the Mindful Schools and the University of California at Davis found that meditation in the classroom not only has the academic benefits of reducing stress and increasing concentration and attention, but also helps students develop empathy and positive social skills. Likewise, Google, Aetna, and Target are among the corporations that offer mindfulness training for employees. This shift is not just out of concern for the well-being of employees, but also for the company, as it is estimated that each year stress can cost $200–300 billion in lost productivity. Additionally, meditation has been shown to increase concentration, sleep, and creativity. Aetna estimates that their new mindfulness practices that include free yoga and meditation classes for employees, earn them $3,000 per participating employee each year.

The mindfulness community has also responded to trauma across the globe, trying to bring psychological and physical relief to the suffering. The David Lynch Foundation brings transcendental meditation to schools, veterans, prisons, homeless shelters, individuals living with HIV, and high-risk populations in cities such as Los Angeles and Chicago, and in locations across Africa. Yoga and meditation have also been implemented in prisons with the aim of curtailing recidivism rates. This project has been especially beneficial to incarcerated veterans struggling with chronic pain from injuries sustained while deployed. The director of the Prison Yoga Project says, "Yoga as a mindfulness practice is our tool for re-engaging prisoners with their bodies to restore connection between mind, heart, and body. We use yoga practice to develop the whole person, increase sensitivity towards oneself and empathy for others."

In response to mass shootings and terror attacks, the mindfulness community has been involved in various emergency responses. In Orlando, Florida, after the terror attack at the Pulse nightclub in June 2016, the community came together within a week to offer trauma relief, not just to victims and their families, but to the community at large. An organization called Acupuncturists Without Borders began offering free acupuncture for trauma relief, while the Pranic Healing Center held a two-night benefit featuring meditation, breath-healing, massage, and herbal remedies. The event centered on a concert performed by the meditation choir, The Beautiful Chorus, which offered free downloads of their meditation albums to all attendees.

Regardless of where one stands on the debate of how mindfulness has been adopted in the West, yoga has clearly been adapted to fit Western consumer needs, as new types of yoga evolve from growing fitness and cultural trends. Whether these new styles enhance the spiritual, physical, and mental experience of yoga or distract from it is up for debate. Trends like the popularity of yoga apparel are clearly antithetical to the original goals of yoga, as the high-priced designer clothes distract from the practice by emphasizing body image and materialism. Still, mindfulness techniques taught as a response to poverty, illness, and trauma accomplish the objectives of increasing a greater sense of balance and well-being.

The popularity of alternatives to Western, science-based views of the body in general and medicine in particular shows a desire by lay persons and medical professionals to reintroduce spiritual components to healthcare. Whether prayer practices in post-operative recovery rooms or acceptance of acupuncture as a legitimate pain therapy, or yoga and meditation for stress relief and mind-calming, there is a growing appreciation of the benefits of a spiritual component to health and healing, which is based on the inseparability of mind, body, and spirit.

Questions for review and discussion

1 Is health the absence of disease?

2 Why are Eastern and Western notions of health and healing so different?

3 Why and how should health and healing be integral to religion?

4 Is healing in essence "spiritual?"

5 How is health related to concepts of the self?

6 Elaborate and explain the factors for the enormous popularity of yoga in Western societies. Can we reconcile the tension between viewing it as cultural appropriation, as well as a response to a legitimate desire for spiritual and mental well-being?

7 How are Christian Science and TCM alike in the ways they view the body?

Glossary

Chakras-seven wheels or energy centers in the subtle body that need to be be in balance according to Indian health system of yoga, meditation, and Ayurveda.

Ch'i-Chinese term for breath, vital energy in the body.

Faith healing-prayers and other practices such as "laying on of hands" that are believed to aid in spiritual and physical healing.

Holistic-in medicine, the treatment of the whole person, addressing mental, social, and physical factors.

Incantations-using words as a magic spell.

Mantras-sacred words or sounds used for concentration, meditation, and healing.

Medicalization-defining and treating human issues and conditions as medical conditions.

Pentecostal-Christian movements that focus on baptism in the Holy Spirit, enabling speaking in tongues, prophecy, healing, and exorcism.

Psychoactive-a chemical substance that changes brain functions.

*Samadhi-*a mystical state of bliss understood as being absorbed in the divine as described in Hindu texts.

Talisman-an object believed to have magical power for good luck.

Traditional Chinese Medicine (TCM)-Chinese health system based on the principle of yin-yang harmony and proper flow of chi in the body.

*Vipassana Bhavana-*insight meditation; the oldest method of meditation in Buddhism, believed to have been taught directly by the Buddha. This meditation helps to cultivate acceptance and mindfulness.

1,2,3,4,5,6,7

PART THREE

Disciplining the Body

In Part 3, our focus is on the role that religions play in disciplining our bodies through rules that define behavior, sexuality, modesty, marriage, reproduction, and gender roles. In Chapter 7, "Purity and Pollution," we consider how religions establish the concept of purity and its symbolism. In comparing notions of purity in multiple religions, we note that there is a gender difference in the ways in which religions apply their notions of pollution, often contributing to the denigration of women's bodies. In Chapter 8, "Gender and Sexuality," we note metaphors of gender and body as these have been applied to philosophical and religious writings. We then examine sexual norms, taboos, and practices as they are prescribed in religious texts, and review the shifts in views and changes that have been implemented in recent decades, particularly toward LGBTQ persons. We then consider the impact of sexual abuse scandals on religious leaders and their communities. In Chapter 9, "Marriage and Reproduction," we survey views of marriage in religion, and address the impact of the legalization of same-sex marriage. We tackle the issue of reproductive rights by considering contemporary views and practices related to contraceptives and abortion, and the continued debate within religious communities regarding these issues.

7

Purity and Pollution

In this chapter, we consider how purity functions and what it symbolizes. In comparing notions of purity in multiple religions, we ascertain the sources of pollution and the rituals that restore purity. We clarify how purity is different from the notion of holiness, and whether notions of pollution contribute to a denigration of the body. In many cases, gender figures in concepts and laws of purity, suggesting a qualitative difference between the polluting powers of men and women. We examine biblical notions of purity, followed by Zoroastrian, Islamic, and Hindu beliefs and practices. We apply anthropological theories of the function and symbolism of purity to ancient and indigenous codes and rules that define physical boundaries between purity and pollution, as well as focus on practices that define female impurity and purification rituals. Finally, we reflect on how notions of purity and pollution continue to shape our religious and cultural practices, albeit in subtle and evolving ways.

Purity is related to wholeness, holiness, and normality, and is a symbolic, semantic, and cultural category which is integral to religious traditions and societies. Both purity and its opposite—pollution—bear the potential to create differences and to strengthen cohesion. Pollution, as opposed to purity, disturbs equilibrium, destroys or confuses desirable boundaries, and engenders destructive natural forces or conditions. The term pollution is usually applied to objects and activities that are physically problematic, rather than morally sinful; still, there is a connection between pollution and sin. Furthermore, being in a polluted state requires corrective actions and responses that may stigmatize persons and groups. Found in all known cultures and religions, purification rituals are acts done to reestablish lost purity or to create a higher degree of purity.

Dualistic notions of human purity and pollution shape our attitudes toward the lived body. The biological body is no longer a neutral object or territory.

Rather, it is subject to judgment and control, since it is not independent, but rather conceived as part of the social body—the body as a symbol of social cohesion. When intact, the lived body is integral to the social group of which it is a part. When it is not congruent with established norms, it is deemed unfit to be integrated into the social body, and is subject to isolation and removal from the group. Thus, the body either reinforces or detracts from group cohesion.

While the category of purity intersects with topics such as religious rituals in general, and specific practices including marriage, reproduction, sexuality, dietary rules, and death rituals (addressed in other chapters in this book), it is vital to distinguish between impurities associated with biological conditions and processes, and those resulting from moral choices. We identify and clarify bodily states and biological processes that render a person physically impure in order to highlight the symbolic nature, yet practical consequences, of the dualistic view of purity and impurity.

Anthropologists William Robertson and James Frazer (nineteenth and early twentieth centuries) deployed the Polynesian word "taboo" to designate avoidance behavior which they claimed originated in the primitive mind's fear of blood and demons. Sigmund Freud in *Totem and Taboo* dismissed religious prohibitions as irrational and useless. British anthropologist Mary Douglas's scholarship (particularly *Purity and Danger*, 1966) brought new perspectives to our understanding of the role of purity laws. She examined the underlying structures and meanings that guide diverse cultural beliefs, rules, and practices of purity and pollution, and explained rules and practices found in "primitive worlds" as well as complex civilizations. Her theory shows how purity stands for (and stresses a recognition of) clear boundaries and orders, while pollution invites unwanted ambiguity, confusion, and disorder. According to her, societies at times relate pollution to their moral values and devise ways of clearly demarcating, ordering, and controlling sources of pollution, with the overall goal to protect their social and cosmological orders.

Douglas theorizes that the grand sense of social order (macrocosm) is mirrored in the very physical body. In other words, the physical body manifests the purity concerns of the social body. Just as the social body is concerned with maintaining safe boundaries (city walls, gates, front door of a house), so too the physical body is the object of concern as to its surface (skin, hair, clothing) and orifices (eyes, mouth, genitals, anus). Just as strangers crossing through our social boundaries is of concern, what flakes off the body surface and what pours from or into its orifices are comparably of concern. Substances, especially blood and semen, are matter which is "out of place" and therefore dangerous or "unclean."

Douglas suggests that minority groups such as the ancient Israelites expressed anxiety about the body's states of pollution when the boundaries of their social and political identity were threatened. Accordingly, this anxiety was mirrored in their scrupulous care for the purity and integrity of the physical body.

In general, the more universalistic religions—Christianity, Buddhism, and Islam—seem to de-emphasize pollution concerns, and to subsume them within their frameworks of moral and religious beliefs. The New Testament and Christianity manifest a sharp decrease in rules of specific pollution avoidances compared to the Hebrew Bible and later rabbinic thought. Similarly, Buddhism, in contrast to the multiple and detailed purity regulations of Hinduism, stresses the necessity for cultivating one's spiritual and moral development instead of concerns for rituals and rules of avoidance.

Purity and pollution in Judaism

In the Bible, there are commands to distinguish persons, places, and certain things as either "*kadosh*" (holy) or "*chol*" (common), "*tahor*" (pure or clean) or "*tameh*" (impure or unclean). But terms such as "holy" and "pure" are not identical. What is pure is not necessarily holy. Furthermore, there are multiple meanings to purity, including moral and ritual purity and impurity. "Moral impurity" has to do with grave sins, such as murder, incest, and idolatry. "Ritual impurity" concerns contact with substances related to birth, death, and genital discharges. The ritual purity system revolved around the Temple in Jerusalem and the sacrifices performed by the *kohanim* (priests). These had to be guarded from impurities. As in Zoroastrianism, corpse impurity was considered to be the most severe form of pollution; in biblical law, it required purifications over a seven-day period. Contamination related to death could have been linked to other sources of impurities, such as menstrual blood, stillbirth, childbirth, and other genital discharges.

According to biblical law, a person or object can become *tameh* (impure) in several ways, including direct contact with a dead body; being present in a building or roofed structure containing a dead body; coming in contact with certain dead animals (Lev. 11:29-32); contact with certain bodily fluids, such as *niddah* (menstruation) or *zav/zavah* (seminal discharge) (Lev. 15); giving birth to a child (the time of *tumah* is seven days for a boy, followed by thirty-three days of *taharah* and fourteen days for a girl followed by sixty-six days of *taharah*); and contracting certain diseases, such as leprosy (Lev. 13).

While it is tempting to view ritual impurity as a concern for health, there is no direct association between health and purity in the Bible. The sources of ritual impurity which include birth, death, sex, disease, and discharge are natural and unavoidable. They are not considered sinful, and convey temporary contagion, generally of a short duration such as one day or seven days during which the person is unfit to encounter the sacred at the Jerusalem Temple. In these cases, sacrifices purify and transform the impure to pure. Paradoxically, while priests are in charge of safeguarding the boundaries of purity and impurity, certain procedures that are associated with their role in removing impurity, result in their own state becoming one of impurity, which then requires that they themselves undergo purification rituals before resuming their role.

Like many other ancient cultures and religions, Judaism views menstruation with a complex combination of awe and fear, as a potential source of both life and death. Biblical and rabbinic attitudes toward the menstruant woman (*niddah*) reflect ancient blood taboos. In the Torah, a menstruating woman is declared to be impure, and a man is prohibited from engaging in any physical contact with her. The Book of Leviticus declares that a woman is ritually impure for seven days during her menstrual flow, at which time sexual contact is forbidden: "When a woman has a discharge, if her discharge in her body is blood, she shall continue in her menstrual impurity for seven days; and whoever touches her shall be unclean until evening. Everything on which she lies during her menstrual impurity shall be unclean, and everything on which she sits shall be unclean" (Lev. 15:19-20). In biblical times, menstruant women were physically removed from the community for the duration of their menstruation, as commonly practiced in indigenous cultures. As discussed in Chapter 4, the Red Tent Movement is a contemporary adaptation of this ancient ritual practice, understanding the bonding and social cohesion engendered among women during this time.

Although there are certain symbolic affinities between the biblical laws and tribal religions, the rules of segregating women in their state of *niddah* as practiced in Judaism have been modified. The woman may cook but not serve her husband; any physical touch and sexual relations are strictly forbidden during this time in Orthodox Judaism. At the same time, since notions of impurity stem in part from the proximity to the sacred space of the Temple in Jerusalem, the prohibition against participating in public worship does not apply in post-biblical Judaism. In contrast, both Islam and Hinduism have continued to forbid women from public worship during menstruation.

On the other hand, rabbinic law made *niddah* more severe by extending the biblical law from seven to twelve days, prescribing a five-day minimum for the menstrual flow and seven "clean" days afterward. Following this twelve-day period, the *niddah* immerses herself in the *mikveh* (ritual bath) and is then permitted to resume sexual activity with her husband. The *mikveh* is a special bath that contains rainwater or water of a natural river/stream/spring. The *mikveh*, while also used by orthodox men before holy days, is nevertheless primarily a women's ritual. Laws of *niddah*, according to the rabbis, regulate a married couple's sexual life, and rabbinic statements acknowledge the mutual benefits of periodic sexual abstinence.

FIGURE 7.1 Mikveh *in Speyer, Germany. Credit: Chris 73 via Wikimedia.*

Purity and pollution in Christianity

In the New Testament, there is little emphasis on ritual purity. Ritual purity laws, including dietary laws, were challenged by Jesus and his disciples as evidenced in stories where Jesus is engaged in healing of persons considered to have been in a state of impurity, such as healing a leper. While ritual purity practices before entering the Temple in Jerusalem continued, there is a general critique of the Pharisees who took ritual purity laws to excess (Mk 7:1-5). Nonetheless, two rituals are associated with the notion of purity: Washing of the Feet and Baptism. The ritual of the Washing of the Feet is recounted in Jesus's performance of this act and in his instruction to his disciples:

> If I then, your Lord and Teacher, have washed your feet, you also ought to wash one another's feet. For I have given you an example, that you should do as I have done to you. Most assuredly, I say to you, a servant is not greater than his master; nor is he who is sent greater than he who sent him. If you know these things, blessed are you if you do them (Jn 13:14-17).

Washing of the Feet, a ritual which signifies both purity and humility, and honoring a person through service, is observed by various Christian denominations, following the example of Jesus. Historically, this ritual was often performed by popes to their deacons during Holy Week. In 2013, Pope

Francis radically changed this papal ritual when he washed the feet of two women and several Muslims at a juvenile detention center in Rome. Whereas historically this ritual permitted only males, the Washing of the Feet had been revised to permit women to participate during Holy Week. In 2016, Catholic priests around the world washed both women's and men's feet on Holy Thursday.

Baptism, the Christian practice of purification, is a ritual common to all Christian denominations, and for most denominations the application of water onto a believer's head or full bodily immersion in water is an outward symbol of the spiritual conversion that has taken place in the believer's soul. For Roman Catholics, however, the ritual is distinct in practice and meaning. The pouring of the water on the infant's head three times while saying the requisite prayers is not only an initiation into the Catholic community, but also the washing away of original sin, which Catholics believe all humans are tainted with at birth, and no human can be saved without this cleansing. Christians understand sin as moral transgression and therefore a form of pollution. In order to remove it, a person must repent and atone. For Catholics, the practice of confession is an atonement which restores one's purity.

The neglect of ritual purity and justification against it in the New Testament is a subject of debate among scholars. It is also important to note the shift from the dualism of ritual purity and impurity as prevailing in biblical books such as Leviticus, to one where the spirit is pitted against the flesh in the

FIGURE 7.2 *Parents having baby baptized in church. Credit: Sollina Images, via Getty Images.*

Christian Bible. The example of Paul's statement in Phil. 3:3 is indicative of such a shift: "We, who perform cultic service by the Spirit of God and boast in Christ Jesus, and are not persuaded by the flesh, are the circumcision." The emphasis on spirit is suggestive of the elevation of moral purity or uprightness over physical purity. Purity is thus now associated with understanding, patience and kindness. The importance of the distinction between spirit and flesh is relevant to the issue of the holiness of the community, and the holiness and authority of the apostle. While rejecting the Israelite cultic practice of circumcision, Paul still invokes a principle from the purity system, namely that "the spirit and not the flesh" imparts holiness, in this case defined as being the new people with faith in God through Christ.

Purity and pollution in Zoroastrianism

Zoroastrianism is a religion known for its dualistic views of the cosmos which was created wholly good and pure by the God, Ahura Mazda, but contaminated by the evil polluting force named Ahriman, as expressed in the Avesta (Zoroastrian sacred text). Accordingly, Ahriman, an independent cosmic force, is responsible for destroying all the good that Ahura Mazda has created in the world, by his association with decay, disease, and death. The creation story and theology of this cosmic struggle are fundamental to understanding purity and pollution, which are identified with their notions of good and evil. Zoroastrian teachings attribute a major role to their priests as well as lay persons in restoring cosmic purity.

Zoroastrianism advances a system of purity rules whereby its teachings and Pauline identify and explain sources of pollution, describe the consequences of contamination, and finally the process of removing pollution and restoring purity to objects and spaces. Two major sources of pollution for Zoroastrians are dead bodies and menstrual blood, which are seen as manifestations of the demons. Fire is the great purifier in Zoroastrianism, and purification rituals including ablutions, ritualized conscious washing of body parts, reciting prayers and performing ritually prescribed actions, such as pouring and drinking of ash from the fire at the Temple, mixed with water, sand, and bull's urine.

Purity and pollution in Zoroastrianism are not only signifiers of cosmic good and evil, but also serve as a disciplinary method for maintaining social order. All materials that leave the body are polluted and polluting: breath, blood, and all other bodily fluids, as well as solids such as dead skin, nails, and hair. These must be carefully disposed of. It is interesting to note nonetheless that even though the body is the source of these polluting substances, the living

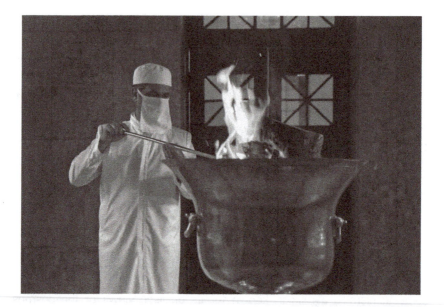

FIGURE 7.3 *A cleric stokes the coals of the "sacred eternal flame" at the Zoroastrian fire temple in Yazd, Iran. Credit: John Moore / Staff, via Getty Images.*

body itself is not considered impure. In fact, the living body is celebrated and embraced; pleasure and enjoyment of the body are valued, and asceticism and punishment of the body are discouraged or prohibited. As will be pointed in our chapter on death rituals, Zoroastrians consider the corpse to be the greatest source of contamination, and care must be taken against any contact except for purification purposes. The corpse of a virtuous person is more polluting because the victory of the evil Ahriman is greater when the dead person was virtuous. In addition to menstruation, childbirth and stillbirth are seen as major causes of defilement and require both social segregation and ritual cleansing.

Zoroastrian dualistic views of reality are not the same as the Greek dualism of spirit and matter. Rather, theirs is cosmic dualism—an eternal battleground between the divine powers of good and their evil opposition. Identifying the forces of evil with Ahriman—an external and independent cosmic power—suggests that the body is not considered guilty of impurity. Rather, the body is seen as a victim of Ahriman and therefore, as long as humans choose to follow God, Ahura Mazda, the creator of all that is good, they participate in the cosmic drama to defeat Ahriman. Humans who follow the teachings and rules of God are seen as God's helpers in destroying evil, by embracing all that God created, while leading a moral life. Purification rules maintain order in the physical body, the social body, and the cosmic body. Eventually, Ahura Mazda and his followers will be victorious against evil, defeat death, and gain immortality.

Purity and pollution in Islam

Purity and pollution in Islam parallel earlier Zoroastrian and Jewish views. Like Zoroastrians, Muslims pray five times each day at specified times. For them, it is not enough to simply perform the prayers at the right time and in the proper manner; practitioners must perform ablutions, meaning that they must cleanse areas of the body before praying in order to properly approach God. These ablutions are so important that it is believed that the prayer will not be effective if the body has not been properly cleansed.

For Muslims, the basic ritual ablution involves washing with water that has been specified for ablutions. The body parts in this purification ritual include the hands up to the elbow, the face, neck and head, flushing the nostrils, rinsing the mouth, and cleaning the feet up to the ankle. Most of these areas must be washed three times successively and the right side should be washed first, then the left, then alternate two more times. One ablution may suffice for more than one prayer, if the ablution has not been nullified by a polluting activity, in which case ablutions must be performed again. Muslim ablutions must be performed carefully, because washing in preparation for prayer cleanses the body of not only dirt, but one's sins as well. Washing the face, mouth, and nose cleanses sins of those parts; washing the hands cleanses the sins done with the hands; and washing the feet cleanses sins toward which one has walked.

FIGURE 7.4 *A Muslim man in Afghanistan performing ablutions.* Credit: *NOORULLAH SHIRZADA / Stringer, via Getty Images.*

There are many variations concerning ablutions, depending on activities and state of health of the person. Cleansing of additional body parts and more thorough washing is required under certain circumstances. *Ghusl* is the Arabic term referring to the full body washing ablution mandatory before the performance of various rituals and prayers. *Ghusl* is mandatory for any adult Muslim after having sexual intercourse or semen discharge. Women are also required to perform Ghusl after the end of their menstrual period in order to be ready to resume daily prayers. All of this care and concern for ritual purity is to ensure that worshippers approach prayers with awe, reverence, and respect, and to ensure that the prayers are acceptable to Allah.

Purity and pollution in Hinduism

In Hinduism, correct practice is the primary vehicle for maintaining religious values. The religious elite—the Brahmin priests—preserve the sacrificial traditions, purity codes, and dietary regulation of this tradition. In the Dharma Sastras, the Brahmanical legal codes, the body is considered the locus of polluting substances associated with occasions such as birth and death, as well as with bodily processes and secretions such as urine, feces, semen, menses, and saliva. A hierarchy of purity is established and attributed, in addition to humans, also to animals and plants, which is based on past and present lives. Reincarnation, a fundamental belief in Hinduism, means that after each life, a soul is reborn into a new physical body. A soul's new form depends upon the virtuousness of its previous behavior. The principle of purity is essential to the justification of the four *varnas* (castes). The four *varnas* emerge from the divine body in creation based on their level of purity, and since the Brahmins are born from the mouth of God (with the mouth being rendered the purest part of the body), their caste is the purest.

Ritual purity is linked to the system of caste interactions. The strictest purification rules are generally prescribed for Brahmins, especially those engaged in the temple worship. Brahmins must avoid any association with blood or death as these are considered sources of pollution. They can only accept food from and eat together with people from their own caste. Their purity is maintained by their occupation as scholars, teachers, and priests, as well as by adhering to a strict vegetarian diet. Occupations that require sweeping or contact with leather, dead humans and animals, toilets and sewers are deemed to incur pollution, and are usually relegated to the lowest caste.

According to the Bhagavad Gita, *varna* is conferred on the basis of the intrinsic character of the person, which is a combination of three *gunas* (qualities): *sattva* (purity), *rajas* (passion), and *tamas* (dullness). The degrees of purity are also expressed in the Bhagavad Gita by Krishna, who compares the community to a human body, where the Brahmin caste represents the head, and the others the arms, legs, and bowels. The caste determines possible occupations, permissible food, the social circle, and selection of a marriage partner.

In addition to one's birth in a particular caste, one's bodily state is constantly subject to accumulation of impurities depending upon the choices the person makes, both temporary ones such as sexual conduct and food choices, and permanent ones such as marriage (to someone of the same or, of a different caste). Factors that impact women's bodies and render them impure are birth and menstruation; due to these biologically polluting processes, women were not permitted to study the Vedas and perform the sacrifices.

Hindu sources associate hair and pollution, especially hair that belongs to women. To come into contact with water that has been used to wash hair is forbidden and seen as potentially dangerous. It is believed that hair is made from the impure waste produced in the process of digesting food. Another interpretation for the polluting quality of hair is that, like nails, hair does not absorb water, which is the ultimate means of purification; the third explanation for the impurity of hair is because, like nails, hair is dead skin.

Water is an essential agent of purification in Hinduism. Ritual bathing in holy rivers is an auspicious way to cleanse oneself of spiritual pollution. In general, holy places are located on the banks of rivers, coasts, seashores, and mountains. Sites of convergence between land and two, or even better three rivers carry special significance and are especially sacred. The rivers are generally associated with female divinities, food and life-bestowing mothers. There are seven sacred rivers: Ganges, Yamuna, Godavari, Saraswati, Narmada, Sindhu, and Kaveri. The holiest river in which to perform ritual purification is the Ganges River, where the pure are thought to be made even purer and the impure have their pollution removed, even if only temporarily. In these sacred waters, it is believed that the distinctions imposed by castes are assuaged, as sins fall away. Some Hindus also believe that life is incomplete without bathing in the Ganges at least once in one's lifetime.

Purity and pollution in indigenous religions and cultures

The notion of physical segregation of menstruant women and exclusion from normal relations and activities seems to be universal among indigenous groups and religions including Aborigine Australian, African, Native American, Indian, and Nepalese. Some indigenous tribal religions have tended to regard

FIGURE 7.5 *Thirteen-year-old Nepalese village girl sits inside a traditional* chhaupadi *house isolating menstruant girls and women. Credit: PRAKASH MATHEMA / Stringer, via Getty Images.*

menstruation positively. In these, the first menstruation of a girl is often accompanied by female-only ritual practices. A period of seclusion is followed by a ceremony, at which the girl's new status as a woman is celebrated.

The ritual segregation at menarche stems from the belief that natural secretions from the female body—such as milk, placenta, and blood—have inherent danger and power. Many tribal traditions dictate strict rules including physical separation of the menstruant woman in a designated dwelling and restrictions from normal daily activities such as cooking, cleaning, and sexual relations.

Australian Aboriginal women's religious ceremonies—especially those surrounding menstruation and childbirth rituals convey not simply a state of pollution, but also the sacredness of female blood and fertility. Pregnant and menstruating women are often secluded, because menstrual blood is thought to be dangerous for men. Fathers are not allowed to be present during their child's birth and do not see the baby until the child is four or five days old. The placenta is buried in a secret place in order to prevent men and children from coming into contact with it.

This process of seclusion is often misunderstood as indicating that menstrual blood is seen as "unclean." In fact, Aboriginal Australians avoid menstrual blood because of its profound sacredness and spiritual power. Some groups of native Australians carry out rituals that allow men to mimic menstrual bleeding by forms of sub-incision or piercings. Through this process, men are able to release the "bad blood" that women rid themselves of naturally. It is only after these processes—after men adopt the menstrual-like qualities of women—that they may learn about secret female rituals.

Bamana women in rural parts of northern Mali undergoing the circumcision ceremony will wear *bogolanfini*, a traditional form of mud cloth created by them in order to prevent spirits—*nyama*—from harming them. Part of the cloth's value comes from both its ability to heal and protect the woman during this dangerous, polluting time, and its ability to absorb blood released during and after the ritual. This demonstrates just one of the ways that *bogolanfini* has become inherently tied to female sexuality, including its potential dangers as a source of pollution.

Despite the changes in attitudes toward purity and pollution in modern Western society, and the trend of sanitizing our bodies and our physical spaces, certain conditions of the lived body remain de facto taboo. While boundaries of purity and pollution are more fluid than those in ancient traditions or tribal cultures, the ideal of purity is still sought after. This is represented in symbols such as the white wedding dress, or the products of the multimillion-dollar industry of feminine hygiene products through which women are able to function productively during their menstrual cycle. The healthy body is the accepted norm and the diseased body is stigmatized, marginalized, or removed from view and contact. Even death is hidden from our view and is handled by our professional funeral home industry. Notions of purity and pollution continue to shape our religious and cultural practices, albeit in subtle and evolving ways.

Questions for review and discussion

1   What are the primary concerns that underlie the purity system in the Bible?

2   How is purity related to holiness?

3   Why is sexual activity considered polluting in some traditions? How do we reconcile that with God's first commandment to humans in the Bible to "be fruitful and multiply"?

4   In what ways do purity rules in the Bible serve to enforce social control by the priests over laypersons and women?

5 Why are the functions of women's bodies considered "unclean," even though they are the very processes by which humanity procreates, thus obeying God's commandment to "be fruitful and multiply?"

6 Why was Jesus critical of the purity laws and practices in his time?

7 In what ways do purity laws function to discipline the body?

8 Why and how are female sexuality and reproduction often tied to pollution?

9 How do the ablutions performed by Muslims and Zoroastrians prepare them for prayer?

10 What roles do purity rules play in the twenty-first century?

1, 2, 3, 7, 8, 9, 10

Glossary

Ablutions-religious ritual of purification involving washing one's body.

Ahura Mazda-the God of Zoroastrianism.

Ahriman-a spirit of darkness and evil in Zoroastrianism.

Avesta-Zoroastrian sacred text.

Baptism-the Christian purification ritual of sprinkling water on a person's forehead or of immersion in water.

Brahmin-a member of the priestly Hindu caste.

Ghusl-mandatory washing of the body as a purification ritual prior to religious worship in Islam.

Menarche-the first occurrence of menstruation.

Niddah-the state of a menstruating woman in Jewish law.

Nyama-harmful spirits in African traditions.

Original Sin-Christian doctrine of humanity's inherited state of corruption and sin after the disobedience in the Garden of Eden.

Reincarnation-a belief in the rebirth of the soul in a new body central to Hinduism, Buddhism, Jainism, and Sikhism.

Ritual Purity-rituals to remove pollution prior to religious worship.

Taboo-something avoided or forbidden.

Varna-caste; traditional class system of Hindu society.

Washing of the Feet-a ritual practiced by Jesus; practiced especially during Holy Week in various Christian denominations.

8

Gender and Sexuality

In this chapter, we will begin with a brief consideration of the metaphors of gender as applied to philosophical and religious writings. We will review sexual norms, taboos, and practices in a selection of classical literature from Judaism, Christianity, Islam, and Hinduism. We will also compare traditional and changing views toward gender and sexuality, as these have been and continue to be fervently debated issues. This contemporary debate is accentuated by thinkers such as Judith Butler and Michel Foucault whose study of the discourse of the body informs us about issues of political and religious power and social manipulations of the body in terms of gender and sexuality. We will highlight two important contemporary issues: sexual scandals in religion and views of transgender persons in a variety of traditions including Buddhism, Sikhism, and Native American religions. Finally, we will consider evolving trends in religion such as the ordination of women, and reflect on gender and sexuality as some of the most dynamic areas in the academic study of religion.

The contemporary debate regarding gender and sexuality has been influenced by philosophers such as Michel Foucault and Judith Butler, whose study of the discourse about the body elucidates political and religious power and social manipulations of the body. Two ideas in particular have contributed to the evolving ways we view gender and sexuality: the body as culturally constructed category and the body as the central locus of power. These have informed the critique of essentialist, fixed, and binary views of gender and sexual orientation. Furthermore, these fundamental notions have influenced feminist critiques of various forms of social control over women's bodies and the oppression of women based on biological difference.

Sex, gender, and sexuality are terms we employ to think about our body and our identity. Gender can refer to an individual's concept of themselves (gender identity) in terms of one's innermost concept of self as male, female, a blend of both or neither. When a person does not identify with a single fixed gender, it is referred to as a fluid or unfixed gender identity. Gender figures prominently in the cultural expectations or the social roles of a male or female (gender roles).

Sex refers to the biological differences such as the genitalia and genetic differences between males, females, and intersex individuals (persons who have genetic, hormonal and physical features typical of both male and female at the same time, so their biological sex is not clearly male or female). Sex also refers to sexual intimacy and intercourse. In the history of religion, sexuality has often been highly regulated. Views against lust and rules against premarital sex, homosexuality, rape, and incest are prevalent in most religions.

While sex and sexuality have been disciplined and constrained in religious legal texts, the positive aspects of sexuality, particularly the pleasure of sex as elaborated by religious adepts, is also integral to some traditions. An interesting phenomenon in the history of religion (as was highlighted in Chapter 3) is the mystics' proclivity to express their love of and desire for God in highly erotic terms. Spiritual adepts, often monastics and renouncers of marriage and sex, have expressed erotic desire for the divine in their autobiographies, poetry, and in their commentaries to sacred texts.

Sexuality can be understood as an interplay between body image, gender identity, gender role, sexual orientation, eroticism, intimacy, relationships, love and affection, and religious orientation. A person's sexuality includes their attitudes, values, and behaviors. The manner by which people express their sexuality is influenced by their families, culture, society, faith, and beliefs. Our scientific understanding continues to evolve as contemporary research delves into the varied nature of sexuality and gender.

In most societies, gender roles have been constructed to favor men and disadvantage women. Social, economic, and religious hierarchies often led to rigid gender roles where women were relegated to second-class status. Moreover, gender symbolism employed in myth and other discourse have reinforced essentialist (fixed) views of gender.

Gender has also been employed symbolically to describe notions such as heaven and earth, passivity and activity, form and matter, spirit and flesh. From the beginnings of philosophical thought, gender has been applied to the categories of nature and culture. Aspects of femaleness were metaphorically associated with the earth, with nature, and with the mysterious power of fertility, whereas maleness was identified with culture and reason. In one of the earliest descriptions of gender binaries found in the Pythagoras scheme, female is associated with formlessness, and male with form. Aristotle believed that men and women naturally differ both physically and mentally as his writings on politics and biology explicitly state. For example, Aristotle states "as regards the sexes, the male is by nature superior and the female inferior, the male ruler and the female subject" (Politics, Book 1.1254b).

Aristotle also attributed gender to his basic concepts of matter and form, which according to his philosophy constitute every physical object. In this way, he associates matter with female qualities, and form, which is superior to matter, he identifies with male characteristics. The philosophy of the modern thinker, Rene Descartes, follows Greek philosophical trends of gendering reason and objectivity as male, the body and emotions as female.

In the history of religious literature, we find, in addition to views of gender roles in their respective societies, the symbolic function of gender in beliefs about the sex or gender of deities and religious figures. As we discussed in Chapter 2, monotheistic religions generally attribute masculine language to their deities, albeit interpreting these as generic. In religions with multiple male and female deities, female deities often take the typically gendered role of women, recognized as dependent upon their male partners, and representing sex, fertility, beauty, and loyalty. It should be noted however, that although powerful female deities have existed for millennia, social roles for women in their respective societies have not been positively impacted by them.

The correlation, or the lack thereof, between the gender of the divine and social gender roles is indeed worthy of further exploration. Daoism, an ancient, nature-based Chinese religion without a belief in a deity, conceptualizes the spiritual path in feminine terms. In several verses in their classic text, the Dao De Ching, the composer/philosopher Laozi employs traditional and essentialist gender characteristics, whereby the male is identified with the sun, heat, light, and activity, and the female with the moon, cold, dark, and passivity. Despite these so-called "negative" qualities, he advises his followers to follow the *dao* (the way) which he conceptualizes as female, thus reversing the traditional gender hierarchy of the superiority of the male over the female. The Daoists may have been the exception to traditional discourse which designated spirit, mind, God in masculine terms. The ubiquitous role of the body in religion then, can be seen in the gendering of the ideal, whether as a deity or as a spiritual path in religious and philosophical discourse. In recent decades there has been an increasing acceptance among theologians that God is also synonymous with Mother Nature, and also feminine, rather than exclusively masculine.

Sexuality in Judaism

While modesty is an important value in Judaism, sex is not considered evil or a taboo subject; in fact, the rabbis were keen on understanding sexuality as the following first-century Talmudic story suggests. Rabbi Kahana hid under the bed of his master, Rabbi Abba (also known as Rav), as the latter was having sex with his wife. Kahana, shocked at the type of frivolous language used by his mentor, commented that Rav was behaving ravenously. Rav exclaimed, "Kahana, you're here? Get out! It's not proper!" Kahana replied, "It is Torah—and study it I must."

Jewish attitudes toward sexuality span from negative and reserved, to positive and liberal. Overall, the Jewish approach is focused upon restraint and moderation. The prevalent rabbinic view is based on the two urges within us, *yetzer ha-tov* (the good inclination) and *yetzer ha-rah* (the bad inclination), with which the sexual urge is usually identified. The rabbis considered sex to be one of the most difficult instincts to control as revealed in the following question and response: "Who is mighty? He who subdues his lust" (Avot 4:1).

According to the rabbis, sexual desire is essential to the existence of the world. The first commandment in Genesis 1 is *pru urvu* (procreate and multiply) indicating the pivotal and positive role of reproduction. Conversely, celibacy is frowned upon. There are references in the narratives of the Torah to sexual activity, yet instead of a specific verb, these stories employ euphemisms such as "Adam *yada* (knew) his wife and she conceived (Genesis 4:1)", "Jacob . . . went in unto her" (Gen. 29:23), and "He took her, and lay with her" (Gen. 34:2).

The notion that man and woman are to become "one flesh" (Gen. 2:24) suggests that sex is good—and because of the rabbis' positive view of the body, the attitude to sexual relations in the Talmud and Midrash is on the whole positive.

The Torah advocates proper sexual relations between husband and wife, and condemns homosexuality, adultery, and incest as capital crimes. There is also a rabbinic prohibition against masturbation, referring to the act as "spilling seed in vain." Sexual relations between husband and wife include the obligation for the husband to fulfill his conjugal duty (*onah*) to his wife on a regular basis, and the obligation to be fruitful and multiply. In the Talmud, there are extensive rules of proper sexual conduct within marriage (such as the laws prohibiting sex with a menstruant woman). In the Shulchan Aruch (the most widely accepted code of Jewish law), we find additional rabbinic rules that aim to prevent lewd thought and sexual transgression, even among spouses. Non-consensual sex is prohibited. One rule which is meant to guard against illicit intimacies among men and women outside of marriage is the prohibition against private meetings (behind closed doors) between individuals of the opposite sex.

In certain philosophical and Kabbalistic writings, there are divergent positions that range from positive views that legitimize sexual pleasure, to negative opinions that advocate self-restraint or even some forms of abstinence. Some Kabbalists regard the sexual experience as one of impurity and as a barrier on the path to the holy. Others see sexual desire as a source of inspiration for one's devotion to God. As Elijah de Vidas in the sixteenth century claims, "Whoever does not desire a woman is comparable to a donkey, and even inferior to it. The reason is that the one who becomes excited (from the sexual act) must have a sense of divine worship" (Reshit Hokhmah, Sha'ar ha-Ahavah, ch. 4).

Not only are sexual desire and proper sexual conduct necessary for the continuation of the world, but they also have cosmological importance. The best-known Kabbalistic construct, the ten *sefirot* (or attributes) of the divine, consists of the eternal and dynamic union of the masculine and feminine emanations. According to the thirteenth-century Kabbalistic text Iggeret ha-Qodesh, the unification of the male and the female in the sexual act reflects the divine order of the universe. As such, the sexual act is for more than the purpose of procreation—it is a mystical experience in which man and woman are believed to promote the analogous union between God and His female consort—the Shekhinah, one of the ten *sefirot*. Thus, marital sex is religiously significant for its sacramental value. It is also interesting to note that in the Talmud, devotion to God in the context of Talmud Torah (ongoing learning of Torah) is sometimes represented in erotically charged language. Nonetheless, the obligation to fulfill the *mitzvah* (commandment) of *pru urvu* and *onah* presumes a balance of family life along with devotion to God.

There are various views, positions, and explanations of the biblical law in Leviticus 18 that strongly prohibits male homosexual intercourse. Nonetheless, the Orthodox community has officially maintained its stance against homosexuality. On the other hand, the Jewish Reform Movement was the first to accept gays as equal members of the community, and in 1977 called to decriminalize homosexual sex and to end all discrimination based on sexual orientation. Both the Reform and the Reconstructionist movements have ordained LGBTQ rabbis, and have conducted same-sex marriage ceremonies. The Conservative Movement's philosophy of pluralism has accepted as valid both the orthodox position and the liberal position of homosexual ordination and same-sex marriages, leaving it to individual rabbis and synagogues to determine whether they will hire an LGBTQ rabbi or perform same-sex marriages.

Sexuality in Christianity

In the early Christian Church, the unmarried, sexually abstinent, or virginal person was considered the paragon of Christian virtue for several reasons. A celibate person is not distracted by the pleasures of the flesh and can better focus on spiritual matters. Additionally, through the transgression of Adam and Eve, considered original sin, lustful sexual activity simultaneously introduced death into the world. Some leaders of the early Church, such as Tertullian, even questioned whether the commandment given to the first couple in Genesis "be fruitful and multiply" remained in force after Jesus Christ, or if it had accomplished the purpose of leading to the birth of the messiah, essentially rendering sexual activity and procreation obsolete.

The exaltation of celibacy and virginity became evident with the promotion of the idea that sexual activity causes irreversible spiritual pollution that binds one's spirit more closely with the material world, and creates a barrier to the spiritual world.

In the New Testament, we find this warning: "Flee from sexual immorality. Every other sin a person commits is outside the body, but the sexually immoral person sins against his own body" (1 Cor. 6:18). Viewing sexuality with disdain and suspicion is typified by St. Augustine's claim that prior to the Fall, Adam and Eve performed the sex act without lust or desire, but merely in fulfillment of God's order to "be fruitful and multiply" (Gen. 1:28). He further argues that lustful sexual congress only occurred as the result of Eve's disobedience, which rendered it a sinful act. And as a result, all people are born bearing the taint of original sin. For strict Roman Catholics, although children are considered a blessing, the act that creates them is considered a necessary evil. Moreover, since it is an essentially sinful act, it should be performed only when the conception of children is possible. Thus, any kind of contraception is unacceptable because sex for the sake of pleasure alone is forbidden.

Protestantism, on the other hand, has more varied and generally more positive views on sexuality, depending on biblical interpretation. While there are conservative Protestant denominations that view sex with suspicion, most Protestants view sex within the bond of marriage as the way, not only to fulfill God's commandment to procreate, but also to fulfill the apostle Paul's direction: "The husband should give to his wife her conjugal rights, and likewise the wife to her husband" (1 Cor. 7:3). Pleasurable sexual activity, the becoming of "one flesh," strengthens the marital bond in the view of many Protestants.

This generally positive view of sex by Protestants applies only to married couples. Sex outside of marriage is sinful, and people, particularly women, should be virgins prior to marriage. Adultery—that is, any sexual activity by a married person with someone other than his or her spouse—is strictly forbidden. There are varied interpretations among Protestants concerning which sex acts are permissible, but all agree that sex only belongs within marriage. There is also a variety of views concerning contraception among Protestant denominations. While few denominations outright forbid contraception, most encourage openness to the possibility of creating a new life with each sex act.

Since Christians view sexual activity as acceptable only within the bond of marriage, and the purpose of sexual activity is procreation, homosexual activity is forbidden by many Christian denominations. At earlier points in history, all Christian denominations forbade same-sex relations, but within the past half-century, a few Protestant denominations, such as the United Church of Christ and the Evangelical Lutheran Church of America, have accepted it and even perform same-sex marriage.

Sexuality in Islam

Islamic teachings hold that sex between a man and a woman is not shameful but rather, is a part of human nature as created by God. Since marriage and the family are seen as the foundational element of an ideal religious life, celibacy and monasticism are forbidden. Premarital sex and masturbation are also forbidden based on an interpretation of the Quranic verse, "The believers are those who protect their sexual organs except from their spouses. . . . Therefore, whosoever seeks more beyond that, they are the transgressors" (23:5-6). While sexuality between husband and wife is celebrated, sex is not permitted during menstruation, based on the verse from the Qur'an:

> Menstruation is a discomfort (for women). Do not establish sexual relations with them during the menses and do not approach them sexually until the blood stops. Then when they have cleansed themselves, you go into them as Allah has commanded you (2:222).

Sex is also forbidden during daytime in the month of Ramadan, when on pilgrimage to Mecca, and during the postnatal bleeding period (ten days). According to Islamic law and in parallel with Judaism, sexual intercourse on a regular basis is one of the basic rights of the wife. The husband is therefore required to have sex with his wife regularly. It is also important that both parties receive pleasure from the encounter. In one hadith, the prophet Muhammad says the man who has sex with his wife without foreplay is one of the three kinds of cruel men in the world. Thus, sexuality in Islam is viewed not only for procreation but also as an important source of pleasure.

Although the Qur'an condemns homosexual behavior, scholars of Islam differ in their views of LGBTQ persons. While homosexual attraction has been expressed in Arabic literature, and has been a recognized aspect of Muslim societies for many centuries, this has not been translated into an endorsement of homosexuality as an acceptable identity in Islam. To the contrary, homosexuality in numerous Muslim countries continues to be prosecuted, and in several countries, is still considered a capital crime. At the same time, there has been significant media coverage of the plight of LGBTQ Muslims and an increase in the number of support groups for them, particularly in the West.

Sexuality in Hinduism

Hindu texts on sexuality encompass spiritual wisdom, science, and laws. This literature addresses a rich diversity of topics including marital sex aimed at reproduction, heterosexual, same-sex, and transgender sexual relationships, the psychology of eroticism, sexual pleasure, as well as ritualized sex aimed toward union with the divine. The wisdom and science of *kama* (pleasure) is elaborated in a number of Hindu texts, including the fourth-century text Kamasutra, authored by Vatsyayana, to whom sex for human beings is a matter of culture, not simply nature. The subject of the Kamasutra, broadly understood, is the science of love and of living the good life. This involves care of the body with the use of oils and massages, learning to play music and to enjoy concerts and dance performances, the reading of poetry and participations in literary salons, the pleasures of intoxication, and the enjoyment of a cultivated level of sexual pleasure. According to scholar of Hinduism, Wendy Doniger, the Kamasutra has attained its classic status because it is essentially about the psychology of eroticism, which is timeless and universal, and addresses the human proclivity toward such desires as lust, seduction, and manipulation.

The Laws of Manu, an ancient authoritative moral and legal text, provides an orthodox view of sexuality within marriage. The text specifies that sexual relations are highly recommended during the wife's fertile period, and avoided during her menstruation (Laws of Manu, Ch. 3). It is particularly important for the married couple to aim for the birth of a son since sons perform the rituals

FIGURE 8.1 *Erotic sculptures at Vishvanatha Temple, Khajuraho, Madhya Pradesh, India. Credit: Aotearoa, via Wikimedia.*

upon the death of their parents. Contraception is permitted and *kama* (sexual pleasure) is considered to be good within the context of marriage.

Other textual sources that address sexuality are classified under the term *tantras*, an esoteric tradition in Hinduism and Buddhism which recognizes that sexual energy can be harnessed to achieve union with the divine. The Sanskrit term *tantra* ("loom, weave") refers to traditions that combine yogic and meditative practices in order to achieve *moksha* (liberation). Sexuality is only one facet of the tantric texts. Spirituality is embodied in the philosophy and practices of *tantra*, employing yoga, meditation, mantras, and *mandalas*, as well as ritualized sexual acts to unify and worship the male and female aspects of the divine. For example, it is believed that energy stored in the lowest chakra, at the base of the spine, may be directed up to the crown chakra, which is in the head, through disciplined and ritualized sexual intercourse. By redirecting sexual energy in this way, it is believed that the female divine aspect, *Shakti*, joins with the male divine aspect, *Shiva*. The goal of this unification is spiritual enlightenment. As a whole, the sexual techniques of *tantra* are intended to be practiced in an appropriate ritual context, and only by spiritually advanced practitioners. At the same time, not every practitioner of *tantra* employs sexual intercourse to seek their spiritual goal, since union with the divine may be achieved through meditative practice.

Hair, sexuality, and religion

Scholars have theorized hair as symbolic of an individual's sexuality, as well as being linked to social control and exclusion. Women's hair is rigorously regulated in some traditions because of the imputed sexual attractiveness associated with it. Hair can also be an important symbol of masculinity. For example, images of Shiva's matted hair represent masculinity and sexuality, further solidifying the association of hair with sexual virility.

Hair is a major symbol in culture and religion, as it is one of the most visible signs of one's identity. Hair is a physical marker that shapes and constructs an individual's religious, gender, and sexual identity. Religious mandates surrounding the cutting, cleaning, covering, and configuration of hair—particularly when the hair belongs to women—can be found in a variety of religious texts and practices. Men's hair, especially facial hair, has also been subject to strict religious rulings. In Sikhism, hair is perceived as a divine gift which must remain uncut. In Orthodox Judaism and Islam, facial hair can be trimmed but cannot be shaved.

Women's hair is associated with feminine beauty, sexuality, and modesty. The covering of women's hair in Orthodox Judaism and Islam, and its control in

Hinduism, exemplify how religions have influenced views on female modesty. Furthermore, such views and practices link feminine sexuality and masculine temptation, and place the responsibility of maintaining sexual ethical conduct upon women. Hair is not only an internal personal reminder of faith to the believer, but also functions as a public affirmation of individual identity, religion, and society.

Hinduism requires that both male and female practitioners neatly maintain their hair. For men, this requires keeping facial and head hair trimmed, while women are expected to keep their hair tied back or even covered. The unknotting of the hair is a signaling of "sexual receptiveness," as it symbolizes the unknotting of a woman's sari. To allow a woman's hair to be loose outside of the home could indicate promiscuity, rejection of traditional values, or a state of impurity, such as menstruation or mourning. Loose hair often connotes a level of sexual intimacy because traditionally, women would only allow their hair to fall loose when in the presence of their husbands.

While Hinduism primarily focuses on women's hair, Sikhism instead uses this religious symbol to connect long hair to masculinity and the tenants of the Sikh faith. Preserving hair is extremely important in the Sikh tradition, because hair is viewed as "a gift from the Divine," and thus symbolizes adherence to tradition and devotion to the faith. While both men and women are prohibited from cutting their hair, only men wear the turban. Interview-based studies with young Sikh men have shown that, even today, Sikh youths see kesh (including the turban or pagh, that men wear to hold and protect their uncut hair) as the most prominent and important visual symbol of Sikhism, especially to outsiders.

FIGURE 8.2 *An Indian woman's hair tied back. Credit: Veronique DURRUTY / Contributor, via Getty Images.*

Transgender issues

With the rise of the LGBTQ rights movement and the legalization of same-sex marriage in the United States in 2015, questions about transgender rights have increasingly come to the forefront. Though a variety of traditions have recognized transgender people or transgender deities for millennia, contemporary discussions on trans rights have only recently begun to take center stage.

Religious leaders are facing decisions on whether gender reassignment surgery should be permissible, and how modern trans people challenge or uphold religious doctrine.

In contemporary parlance, "cisgender" is defined as a person who feels that their gender identity aligns with their biological sex. In contrast, transgender is an umbrella term for people whose gender identity and/or expression is not aligned with their biological sex or cultural expectations. Being transgender, however, does not imply any specific sexual orientation. Therefore, transgender people may identify as straight, gay, lesbian, bisexual, etc. Furthermore, some people strive to more closely align their outward appearance or sex organs with their gender identity. They undergo a process of transition, where they might begin dressing, using names and pronouns, or be socially recognized as another gender. Others undergo physical transitions in which they modify their bodies through medical interventions such as hormone therapy and surgery.

Transgender and androgynous figures can be found in many religions. Aboriginal Australians recognize a rainbow serpent god called Ungud, who is able to transition between being male and female, and is associated with rainbows and the fertility of shamans. In Hinduism, Ardhanarishvara became part man and part woman when Shiva and Parvati chose to be conjoined into one person. The story of Ardhanarishvara is meant to teach that each person has half masculine/half feminine qualities. Avalokiteshvara (also known as Guanyin or Kuan Yin) is a Buddhist *bodhisattva* of compassion who has the ability to transform into any form, and frequently changes gender in order to best support those in need of help. As we indicated in Chapter 1, both the Greek creation myth in the Symposium and the rabbinic interpretation of the creation story in the Book of Genesis envision the original human as an androgynous being.

These stories acknowledge the phenomenon of androgyny as a sexual body type and in some cases as gender identity of both the divine and the human. While some faiths may see androgyny as a reflection of the divine nature, other religions have developed rigid definitions of sex and gender, thus complicating the presence of transgender or androgynous persons within that religious community.

Transgender in Hinduism

Some religions have also celebrated transgender people, believing that they have heightened spiritual abilities and intimate proximity to the divine. In south Asia, especially in India and Pakistan, the term *tritiya-prakriti* (third gender), is applied to those who identify as transgender, intersex, or homosexual men who prefer to dress in women's clothing. A well-recognized group of the third gender is the *hijras*. Most *hijras* leave their original families and communities and move into or create a *hijra* family with a senior person serving as a mother or a guru figure.

Same-sex relations and third gender people have been acknowledged, debated, and celebrated in a variety of ancient Hindu texts, including the Vedas, but despite their recognition in religious texts, *hijras* have often been socially stigmatized and marginalized. They generally have a very difficult time accessing healthcare, education, and employment opportunities. Many *hijras* use their acclaimed mysterious spiritual power by offering to bestow blessings on families, invited or uninvited, at events such as weddings or births. Even though the *hijras* are estimated to account for approximately two to three million members of the Indian population, they were not legally recognized as a third gender until 2014; Pakistan recognized *hijras* as a third gender in 2012.

FIGURE 8.3 *Transgender people in India. Credit: R D'Lucca, via Wikimedia.*

Nonetheless, many *hijras* experience severe discrimination, harassment, and abuse, and many have been forced to turn to sex work in order to survive or pay for their reassignment surgeries. This has led to a staggering prevalence of HIV/AIDs among members of the *hijra* population, especially in large Indian cities, such as Mumbai.

Muxe (Third Gender in Indigenous Mexico)

Believed to have originated from the Spanish term for "woman" (*mujer*), *muxes* represent an ancient phenomenon predominantly found in communities in Oaxaca, where tolerance toward people identifying with this third gender is generally higher than in many other parts of Mexico. Like the *hijras* of India, *muxes* are (broadly speaking) biologically male but dress and act in ways typically associated with females. Their sexuality is fluid: some consider themselves gay, others consider themselves women, but most *muxes* choose to be *vestidas* (wearing female clothes). *Muxes* have a variety of lifestyles: many live with or take care of their parents; some of the *muxes* have families; others live in partnership with men, while still others live with women. They tend to live in rural areas, where they are more accepted than in major Mexican cities.

Transgender people in the Native American traditions

In the United States, ancient Native American traditions have also held those who are androgynous or transgender (referred to as "two-spirit") in high regard, since they reflect the unity of the spirit world. Seen as holding both the spirit of a man and a woman, some tribes have regarded two-spirits as possessing spiritual gifts, being talented artisans, or providing an economic advantage to their family due to their ability to fulfill both male and female roles. It is important to note that the role of two-spirits cannot be generalized across all native tribes, as each tribe views and reveres two-spirits in different ways and for different reasons. It was not until the influx of foreign explorers that two-spirit people began to be seen as homosexual or viewed as a deviant identity. Spanish and English colonists began to refer to two-spirit people as "berdaches," a term meaning "intimate male friend" or "homosexual." Many people now view the term "berdache" as a misunderstanding and misrepresentation of the two-spirit identity.

Transgender people in Islam

In many Muslim-majority countries, such as Iran, transgender people have become more welcomed than those that identify as gay or lesbian. Ayatollah Khomeini declared gender reassignment surgeries to be permissible in Iran in 1987, since he believed that persons are born transgender, whereas individuals choose to be gay or lesbian. Egyptian scholars at Al-Azhar University echoed this sentiment in 1988. Today, those who are able to receive the surgery in Iran obtain a variety of support, including an expedited name-change process and assistance in finding housing after the surgery is complete. Some institutions also view gender reassignment surgeries as a way to "correct" homosexuality by changing the individual's gender to "correctly" align with heterosexual norms.

Transgender people in Judaism

While some branches of Judaism are welcoming to trans people, Jewish law has been interpreted as condemning gender reassignment surgery and promoting a binary interpretation of sexuality and gender. Leviticus outlines that no animal should be offered to God if it has had its testicles "bruised or crushed or torn out" (Lev. 22:24). This verse has served as a basis for has the prohibition against gender reassignment surgery, and by association, trans individuals. However, some synagogues and religiously affiliated spaces are accommodating of transgender people. Joy Ladin for example, is a Jewish professor, author, and transgender woman at Yeshiva University in New York City, an Orthodox institution.

Transgender people in Christianity

In 2014, Tia Pesando became the first transgender woman to become a Catholic nun. After undergoing hormone treatments, she felt her calling to join a convent of Carmelite nuns living in Canada. While the Catholic leadership has not addressed issues specifically related to transgender people, Pesando's acceptance into the order may be a step toward trans acceptance and visibility in the Catholic Church.

Views of transgender people in Christianity vary depending upon denomination, with many churches not having yet adopted a formal or public stance on transgender identity. As opposed to its views of the lesbian, gay, and bisexual identities, the Bible neither supports nor prohibits transgenderism or gender reassignment. Thus, the experience of Christian trans people varies widely depending upon their culture, community, and local denomination. Below is a list of the stances that various Christian denominations have taken on transgender people and transgender issues:

Supportive/Welcoming of Transgender People	Non-Supportive of Transgender People and/or Gender Reassignment Surgeries	Have Not Publicly Taken a Stance or Stance is Unclear
Disciples of Christ	Eastern Orthodox	African Methodist Episcopal Churches
Episcopal	Presbyterian Church, United States	Alliance of Baptists
Metropolitan Community Churches	Southern Baptist Convention	American Baptist Church United States
Presbyterian Church		Church of God in Christ
Religious Society of Friends (Quaker)		Church of Jesus Christ of Latter-Day Saints (Mormon)
Unitarian Universalist		Church of the Nazarene
United Church of Christ		Evangelical Lutheran Church in America
United Methodist Church		National Baptist Convention USA Inc.
Unity		Old/Independent Catholics
		Oriental Orthodox Church
		Pentecostals
		Roman Catholic Church
		Seventh-day Adventist

Transgender people in Buddhism and Sikhism

Both Buddhists and Sikhs believe that transgender people are allowed to practice and worship within their respective faiths. For Buddhists, it is of prime importance that the individual does not harm others, but as long as she does not do so, they are allowed to be a part of the Buddhist faith. In Thailand, a largely Buddhist society, transgender persons are called the *kathoeys* (ladyboys). Thailand remains one of the world's most tolerant societies toward transgender people. Males undergoing sex-change operations are common occurrences, but they are still regarded as men on their identification documents. Similarly, in Sikhism, all individuals are welcomed in Sikh temples and are permitted to attend *langar*—a free meal that is open to Sikhs and non-Sikhs alike. It is important to note that while these religions may be open and welcoming to transgender people, the cultures in which these religions are practiced may not always reflect these values.

Sexual scandals in religious communities

Sexual abuse and scandals occur across religions and cultures and in various circumstances. The intense emotional connection that can develop between a spiritual leader and a follower seeking personal counsel and guidance can evolve into inappropriate intimate relations. Sexual abuse in religious communities includes those that are and are not officially designated as celibate.

The practice of clerical celibacy within the Catholic Church for example, has recently caused many, both within and outside of the Church, to question whether the practice is practical or even possible, given that celibacy demands suppression of a natural and potent human urge. There are those who have claimed that the strict rules on celibacy for priests have contributed to pedophilia and the sexual abuse of minors. In 2014, Pope Francis spoke about allegations of sexual abuse within the Church, claiming that the Vatican believes about two percent of the clergy are pedophiles, which equates to roughly 8,000 priests worldwide. Pope Francis has called this "intolerable," and vowed to address this problem head on. When pressed about the question of celibacy in the Church, Pope Francis pointed out that celibacy for priests was adopted 900 years after the death of Christ, but did not clearly assert his personal beliefs beyond that.

The sexual abuse of children at the hands of religious officials is not restricted to the widely reported instances within the Catholic Church. Sadly, the abuse of children occurs in the communities of many religious traditions, including Judaism, Islam, Hinduism, and Buddhism. Both boys and girls are vulnerable to sexual abuse, and children are particularly vulnerable to sexual abuse when contact with adult religious authorities occurs in religious communities in which the child is apart from their parents—in a Buddhist monastery or an Islamic madrassa, for instance. Three conditions within a religious community make children especially vulnerable to sexual abuse. The first condition is the existence of a rigid hierarchy within the community, in which religious authorities are unquestioned, and to whom obedience is required. The second condition is the existence of fear in the community. The fear may be of many distinct matters, including fear of people high up in the hierarchy, fear of exile from the community, and even fear of offending their deity for defying religious authority. A third factor which makes sexual abuse of children more likely to occur is the isolation of a religious community from mainstream society, reducing the likelihood that abuse will be reported to secular authorities. The all-encompassing nature of the separated religious community strongly reinforces the authority of the religious leader in all matters in life, including control over the bodies of children.

Complicating matters for the victims of sexual abuse by religious leaders is a near-universal denial of the pervasiveness of its occurrence. Given that many religions forbid homosexuality and sexual contact outside of marriage, the religious authorities to whom the abuse is first reported often find the mention of it in connection with their community abhorrent, leading to denial of the occurrence. Reports of sexual abuse are often treated with great skepticism by religious officials, and frequently the motivations of the victim are brought into question for reporting the abuse. Exacerbating the trauma of abuse is that victims and their parents are often discouraged from reporting these criminal acts to secular authorities. Instead, many communities prefer to handle the crime within their own groups, and thus the perpetrators are rarely brought to justice. Nonetheless, in our era of social media and constant news coverage, there is reason to hope that more perpetrators will be caught and prosecuted.

Toward a new openness and evolving perspectives on sexuality and gender in religion

Sexuality and gender continue to be one of the most dynamic fields in the academic study of religion. Textual, historical, and ethnographic scholarship of diverse attitudes and behaviors in the area of sexuality illuminate the complexity and diversity which exist within a single religion. While some texts espouse negative views toward sex and the need to control it, others see sex as a source of pleasure or a vehicle toward spiritual wholeness. Likewise, views toward same-sex and transgender sexuality vary in the history of religions, and continue to evolve. Our increased openness to speaking about a subject that was once seen as taboo can result in greater understanding of the power of sexuality.

Changes that are occurring in our knowledge and appreciation of gender and the evolving state of gender roles in religion are also deep and pervasive. We have been addressing issues in this category in several chapters, including our discussions of creation myths, representations of the divine, erotic desire and divine love, new women-centered rituals, and purity and pollution. We provided an account of feminist interpretations of creation myths, theological conceptualizations in which the divine is imagined in feminine terms, rituals celebrating women's bodies and life cycles, and the rise in women's religious leadership roles. Although the ordination of women has been accepted in a variety of liberal denominations and religions, it remains a controversial subject in conservative and orthodox traditions such as Orthodox Judaism and Roman Catholicism. In our next chapter, our examination of marriage and reproduction will cover both traditional religious norms and the evolving meaning of marriage in terms of gender and sexuality.

Questions for review and discussion

1   Given heterosexuality as the dominant social paradigm, what are the motives for some societies such as Native American and Hindu cultures to perceive and value transgender persons as possessing sources of spiritual power?

2   How do liberal Jewish denominations such as the Reform movement reconcile its endorsement of gay marriage with the biblical taboo against homosexuality?

3   How could conforming to modern standards and beliefs regarding gender and sexuality compromise a religious group?

4   Are religious teachings of compassion and loving the neighbor as oneself in contradiction with rejections of same-sex marriage?

5   What are the benefits and detriments for religions that do not have one organized governing board?

Glossary

Adultery-sexual intercourse between a married person and a person who is not his or her spouse.

Celibate-abstaining from marriage and sexual relations, typically for religious reasons.

Hadith-the collective body of traditions relating to Muhammad and his companions.

*Hijras-*transgender persons in India and Pakistan who live in separate communities.

Incest-sexual intercourse with a parent, child, sibling, or grandchild.

Kamasutra-4th century Hindu text about the science of love and living the good life.

*Laws of Manu-*an authoritative Hindu text consisting of moral and legal teachings.

*Muxe-*Third gender persons in Mexico.

Pedophilia-romantic and sexual attraction and activities of adults toward children.

Tantra-esoteric tradition in Hinduism and Buddhism that includes practices such as yoga, meditation, and ritualized sex in order to achieve liberation.

Third Gender-individuals categorized and or identify themselves as neither male nor female.

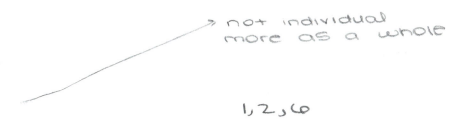

respect
agreeing towards
their actions

> not individual
more as a whole

1, 2, 6

9

Marriage and Reproduction

In this chapter, we will explore views, rules, and practices of marriage in several religions as these are represented in their history and sacred texts. In this context, we will underscore regulations and procedures pertaining to divorce, and emphasize how views and practices of modesty impact gender roles and control women's social and religious status in particular. We will highlight the shift that has taken place with the increased acceptance of same-sex relations and the legalization of same-sex marriages in several European countries and the United States. We will consider the growing phenomenon of interfaith marriage in the West, a contemporary trend which influences religious identity. We will then turn our attention to reproduction and reproductive rights, and consider contemporary views and practices related to contraceptives and abortion, and their continued debate within religious communities.

Prior to the modern era, most marriages were arranged by the parents, and represented a strategic alliance between families, satisfying social and economic objectives. Attraction and sexual desire were not important factors in marriage until about a century ago. While religious attitudes and practices relating to marriage vary, religions typically incorporate prescriptions for marriage comprising rituals and rules of conduct. Moral and social codes of marriage commonly regulate sexuality, reproduction, and modesty, and stipulate restrictions in marital and family sexual relations.

Marriage in Judaism

Marriage is a fundamental imperative in Judaism, and its purpose extends beyond procreation. Refraining from marriage is considered unnatural and untenable; the Talmud says that an unmarried man is constantly thinking of sin. The primary aims of a Jewish marriage are companionship, love, and intimacy. According to the rabbis, the woman was created because "it is not good for man to be alone," and not because she was necessary for procreation. The Talmud specifies that a woman can be acquired by marriage only with her consent, and not without it. The *ketubah* (marriage contract), which the husband gives his wife at the wedding, delineates his obligations to the wife during marriage, conditions of inheritance upon his death, and obligations regarding the support of children. It also specifies providing for the wife's support in the event of divorce. A husband is responsible for providing his wife with food, clothing, and sexual relations. Marital sexual relations, and specifically sexual pleasure, are the woman's right (*onah*). A man cannot force his wife to engage in sexual relations with him, nor is he permitted to abuse his wife in any way. As for property rights, a married woman retains ownership of any property she brought to the marriage, while the husband has the right to manage the property and to enjoy profits from the property. While marriage is highly valued in Judaism, divorce is permitted. Despite the responsibilities of the husband and the rights of the wife in marriage, the procedure of obtaining a woman is likened to the acquisition of "property." Therefore, divorce is a unilateral procedure whereby only the husband can grant a divorce (*get*), and must do it of his free will.

According to the Torah and the Talmud, it is permissible for a man to marry more than one wife. Although polygyny (marriage to more than one wife) was

FIGURE 9.1 *An Orthodox Jewish wedding ceremony under a chuppa (canopy). Jerusalem, Israel. Credit: Dan Porges, via Getty Images.*

permitted, it was not common. The Talmud never mentions any rabbi with more than one wife. Around 1,000 CE, European Jewry banned polygyny, yet it continued to be permitted for Jews in Islamic lands until the middle of the twentieth century following Islamic practice.

Marriage in Christianity

The early Christians' views of marriage were shaped to a large extent by the anticipation of the "end of days" and the return of Jesus. Following the Essenes (a first-century ascetic Jewish group, also known as the Dead Sea community), they believed that in order to prepare themselves for these cataclysmic events, they should live a life of purity, emphasizing frequent ritual bathing, and renunciation of sex and marriage. After Christ's ascension into heaven, the early Christians believed that his return to earth would occur in a relatively short time. As the years passed, however, it became clear that in order to ensure the continuity of the faith, procreation within marriage needed to endure. Although celibacy and virginity were regarded as exalted states in the early Church, the apostle Paul (in an opinion similar to the Jewish rabbinic position) recognized the need for some men to marry in order to avoid excessive lust and fornication, as indicated in his directive in 1 Cor. 7:9 "But if they cannot contain, let them marry; for it is better to marry than to burn."

Marriage, then, while grudgingly accepted in the early Church, was subject to particular strictures. The first stricture is that a marriage involves one man and one woman. Polygamy was practiced by other cultures and religions at the time of the early Church, but New Testament authors drew justification from Genesis for their embrace of monogamy. God created only one wife for Adam, and Adam declared that they would be "one flesh" (Gen. 2:24). Paul supported Adam and Eve's monogamous model by stating in 1 Cor. 7:2 "let every man have his own wife, and let every woman have her own husband."

While in the beginning of the Church, priests were married, a preference for sexual abstinence was later developed. This was declared by the Church Fathers as early as the fourth century, but was not formally required until the first Lateran Council of 1123, when celibacy became a requirement for entering the priesthood. As sexually abstinent, unmarried man's loyalties would not be divided between his duties to the Church and to a wife, which would eventually bring familial responsibilities. Nuns also take a vow of celibacy. They are considered "Brides of Christ," echoing the ancient social order that dictated that women needed to be defined by their relationship to a man, in this case, Jesus Christ.

The Protestant Reformation rescinded the prohibition on marriage for clergy, and embraced marriage as the earthly foundation of the Christian community. From the beginning of the Reformation, marriage was viewed in a positive light. Protestants referred to the Old Testament writings about marriage and family for their argument that marriage was the state God intended for human beings. They also pointed out that Jesus himself supported marriage, as demonstrated by the miracle reported in the Gospel of Jn 2:1-10, in which he transformed water into wine at a wedding feast in Cana.

Marriage became one of Roman Catholicism's seven sacraments only in the twelfth or thirteenth century. For Protestants, in contrast, marriage was not a sacrament, and therefore, it could be dissolved. But even so, for both Protestants and Catholics, divorce is vigorously discouraged, and for Catholics, it is an anathema for any reason except adultery. The verse found in the Gospel of Mk 10:9 states in no uncertain terms that when a marriage has occurred, it cannot be reversed: "What therefore God hath joined together, let not man put asunder." The view that a man and a woman who joined in marriage have become "one flesh" is taken very seriously. Remarriage and sexual activity after divorce is considered fornication in some Christian traditions, particularly in Roman Catholicism. The Roman Catholic Church will in some cases grant an annulment of a marriage, which essentially means that the marriage was invalid from the beginning.

Marriage in Islam

Within Islamic cultures, marriage is seen as the cornerstone of society, and family law (marriage, divorce, and inheritance) is central to the *shariah* (Islamic law and path). An ideal marriage is a microcosm for a stable Muslim community. The prophet Muhammad is believed to have said "whoever marries, has completed half of his faith," placing marriage at the center of religious life. Marriage is not just an earthly social construct; husbands are promised to be reunited with their spouses in heaven. According to the Qur'an, in order to be married, a man must secure permission from the bride's family and then pay the bride a marital gift, or *mahr*. Before the wedding, the bride's family may throw a *mendhi* party in which they decorate the bride's hands with henna. The wedding ceremony itself must be witnessed by two people. During the ceremony, called the *nikah*, which is usually very intimate and private, the couple signs their marriage contract. While this is the bare minimum that must occur in order to have a valid Islamic marriage, other customs have evolved over time. The *nikah* is often followed by a feast and celebration known as the *walimah*.

Polygyny, the practice of being married to more than one spouse at a time, is a permissible practice under Islamic law. One man is allowed a maximum of four wives, with the condition that he treats them all equally; at the same time, the Qur'an points out that such treatment is impossible (Qur'an 4:3, 129). Muslims who oppose polygyny note that the Qur'anic directive was not an incipient law, but a restriction on the limitless number of wives a man was hitherto permitted and a temporary solution aimed at gradually abolishing the practice.

Muslim men are also allowed to marry Jewish or Christian women, while Muslim women can only marry within their own faith. While this practice is abused in some parts of the world, notably through the practice of taking child brides, Muslims claim that polygany was meant to be a compassionate practice, established in response to the social welfare issues of the time. Because of the wars and conflicts that plagued the early Muslim community, men had a much higher mortality rate, leaving behind widows and fatherless children. Polygany began as a way to ensure that these women and children would be cared for. The prophet Muhammad himself had eleven wives. Islamic scholars believe that these marriages were performed to cement important alliances for the early Muslim community, or in other cases to protect widowed women. Polygyny is declining today, and many Muslim countries have severely restricted or banned it completely. Many argue that polygyny is no longer a practical option, claiming that the same social welfare problems that existed 1,400 years ago, and inspired the early Muslim community to maintain the practice, no longer exist or at least can be addressed in other ways. Divorce in Islamic law is permitted and follows different procedures for husband and wife. If the husband wishes to divorce his wife, he can pronounce it or submit it in writing. Similarly to Jewish law, the husband may be obligated to his wife in financial terms, and is required to consent in cases where the wife initiates it.

Marriage in Hinduism

Marriage in Hinduism is not only considered as a union between a man and a woman, but also understood as a sacrament of two souls. In the Rig Veda, the husband pledges to the wife a partnership that is not confined to one life, but transcends several lives. The two souls are intertwined for the purpose of spiritual progress and *moksha* (liberation). Arranged marriages have been the norm and entail consent from the parents on the basis of caste, family background, and occupation.

The three prescribed functions of marriage in Hindu teachings are: *praja*, *dharma*, and *kama*. *Praja* is the continuance of a family line over the generations. *Dharma* relates to virtuous conduct and the right way of living. *Kama* denotes not merely sexual pleasure, but more broadly sensual pleasure—music, good food, perfume, and so forth. Ancient Indian texts regard *kama* as one of the three goals of human life, the other two being *dharma*—duty, religion, religious merit, morality, social obligations, the law, justice, and so forth—and *artha*—power, politics, success, and money. Where *dharma* regulates the socio-religious world and *artha,* the political world, *kama* legitimizes the world of the individual, or the cultivation of the self.

Sexual union between married couples for the purpose of procreation is the ideal, and sex within the parameter of marriage is the prescribed behavior in Hinduism. The balanced life of an individual is possible by channeling sexual energy within the system of marriage. So it is the life of a *grihastha* (person settled in marriage) that sets the norm of sex and sexuality in Hinduism. While "love marriages," or marriages that result from the couple's interaction with each other, have become trendy in modern Hindu society, arranged marriages are still highly prevalent. Today, many couples seek to play a more central role in arranging their marriages and as a result, "semi-arranged marriages" have become more popular, with both the parents and the children having a say in the selection of a mate.

Given that in ancient Hindu society marriage was understood as a sacrament, similarly to Catholicism, rather than as a contract as it is in religions such as Judaism and Islam, a formal divorce was not an option. At

FIGURE 9.2 *A wedding ceremony in Rajasthan, India. Credit: Xavier Zimbardo / Contributor, via Wikimedia.*

the same time, Hindu texts such as the Laws of Manu discuss circumstances in which a husband may abandon his wife, while for women, abandoning their husband was impossible, since once married, women were obligated to remain with their husbands during his life and even after his death. Like other patriarchal religions, the subject of marriage and divorce brings to light the subordinate status of women in the Hindu tradition. Divorce was finally legalized and enforceable after the Parliament of India in 1955 introduced the Hindu Marriage Act, which stipulats procedures for divorce for both men and women.

Modesty in religious texts and practices

Modesty is one of the highest virtues and often one of the most rigidly enforced practices in religion. Modesty is maintained by disciplining behaviors and dress. Guarding against the temptations that are believed to result from improper dress, particularly the improper dress of women, exemplifies the control of the body in religion.

In contemporary cultural and feminist studies, it has been argued that the power of those in religious authority is exerted upon the bodies of members of a religious group by means of disciplinary practices (Foucault). Religious narratives such as the story of the Garden of Eden present women as temptresses against whom one must be guarded. Women's bodies— their hair in particular—are seen as a source of sexual temptation to men in patriarchal traditions. Therefore, women's bodies, dress, and daily practices must be regulated and controlled, especially when they are in public spaces. Though the *burqa* (outer garment worn by women in some Islamic traditions and countries to cover their entire bodies when in public) is often seen as an extreme example, other traditions, including Orthodox Jews, Mormons, and Amish, also promote modest dress to various degrees for both men and women.

Veiling

The practice of veiling is not an invention of Islam, but was actually quite prevalent in the ancient Near East during the second millennia BCE. The earliest mention of veiling occurs in a thirteenth century BCE Assyrian legal text, which ironically forbade prostitutes from the practice. In Greco-Roman pre-Islamic Byzantium and Iran, the veil was worn by elite women as a status symbol. Female veiling is also seen in the stories of the Hebrew Bible. For example, in the Book of Genesis, Tamar dons the veil in order to disguise herself as a prostitute and trick her father-in-law, Judah, into sleeping with her: "When Judah saw her, he took her for a harlot; for she had covered her face" (Gen. 38:14-15). In Christian art, even in modern times, Mary, the mother of Jesus, is almost always depicted as wearing a veil or some other kind of head covering.

Modesty in Islam

There is a close association between women's virtue and man's honor in ancient religions such as Islam. Modesty (*haya* in Arabic) and one's honor and dignity are of primary importance in preserving the moral fiber of society. While modesty is the concern of both men and women, it is often focused on women.

> [Prophet], tell believing men to lower their glances and guard their private parts: that is purer for them. God is well aware of everything they do. And tell believing women that they should lower their glances, guard their private parts, and not display their charms beyond what [it is acceptable] to reveal; they should let their headscarves fall to cover their necklines and not reveal their charms except to their husbands, their fathers, their husbands' fathers, their sons, their husbands' sons, their brothers, their brothers' sons, their sisters' sons, their womenfolk, their slaves, such men as attend them who have no sexual desire, or children who are not yet aware of women's nakedness; they should not stamp their feet so as to draw attention to any hidden charms. Believers, all of you, turn to God so that you may prosper (Qur'an 32:32-33).

In the canonical Hadith collections, only one can be said to address explicitly the requirement of women's covering. This Hadith is recorded by the ninth-century Hadith compiler Abu Dawud, and reports an incident involving an encounter between Muhammad and Asma, who is the daughter of Abu Bakr, the prophet's closest friend and first Caliph after the death of the prophet:

> Asma, daughter of Abu Bakr, entered upon the Apostle of Allah wearing thin clothes. The Apostle of Allah turned his attention from her. He said: O Asma', when a woman reaches the age of menstruation, it does not suit

FIGURE 9.3 *African Muslim girlfriends wearing traditional colorful dresses and chadors. Credit: Anthony Asael/Art in All of Us / Contributor, via Getty Images.*

her that she displays her parts of body except this and this, and he pointed to her face and hands (Book 32, Number 4092).

The Hanbali and Shafi'i schools of *shariah* (law), the more conservative of the four schools, require Muslim women to cover their entire body, including their face and hands. The other two, the Maliki and Hanafi believe that the entire woman's body, except for the face and hands, has to be covered. With the growth of the Muslim population in Europe, opposition has developed to the display of conservative Islamic dress. France was the first country in Europe to ban Islamic full-face veils, such as the *burka* (which covers the entire body) and the *niqab* (which covers head and face) in public places. This controversial ban took effect in April 2011, and made it illegal for Muslim women to appear in public with their faces covered. Since 2016, Germany, the UK and the Netherlands have called for the ban, while other European countries have officially banned face veils in public areas including Belgium and Switzerland. In the summer of 2016, the *burqini*, a swimsuit that covers the whole body except for the face, hands and feet, was banned in beach towns such as Cannes, Villeneuve-Loubet, and in Sisco on the island of Corsica. Some view these bans as political measures driven by Islamophobia in reaction to the rise in Islamist extremist attacks. In an attempt to defend these measures as not being targeted only at the Muslim community, in some cases, the ban has been extended to apply to all forms of identifiable religious dress, including the Jewish yarmulke or skullcap worn by religious Jewish men.

FIGURE 9.4 *A woman wearing a* niqab, *Marrakech, Morocco. http://www.flickr. com/photos/babasteve/5687993/, via Wikimedia.*

Modesty in Judaism

Modesty (*tzeniut*) connotes a moral quality that can be applied in multiple contexts, including speech, dress, and sex. In the Bible, modesty is most often related to humility. Many rabbinic rules seek to curb lewd thought and immodest conduct, even among spouses. In later rabbinic and Kabbalistic literature, the concept of modesty acquires particularly gendered and sexual connotations.

Views of modesty for men are expressed in general terms. A man is to be modest in all ways: in food and drink, in speech, and with his wife. In contrast, female modesty is almost exclusively located in the sexual realm. The prevalent assumption underlying the strictures incumbent upon men is that the male sexual urge is greater than that of women. The traditional architectural guidelines for the construction of synagogues, in which the women are seated separately from the men (traditionally on a second-floor balcony), are founded on this assumption, mainly to prevent men from looking at women, and not the opposite.

The apprehensions concerning women and their sexuality intensified in the medieval period. Statements were made by rabbis regarding women's seductiveness. When Eve was seduced by the serpent in the Garden of Eden, women acquired the quality of seduction. Consequently, women naturally seduce men, and may themselves be easily seduced, so their modesty must be scrupulously maintained. According to the medieval Kabbalistic book, the Zohar, women's eyes should be cast down; a woman's hair must be completely covered and her voice should not be heard since it is a source of temptation. To this day, Ultra-Orthodox men will not attend any performance in which a woman sings, and Orthodox women can only sing in front of other women. At Ultra-Orthodox weddings and other celebrations, mixed dancing is prohibited, and the men and women dance separately on opposite sides of a *mechitza* (a physical separation barrier).

The veiling of women's hair is also part of the Jewish laws of modesty, which requires that women wear a scarf or a wig in order to cover up their real hair. Women's hair is considered *ervah*, or erotic stimulus, which must therefore be covered, just as other parts of a woman's body that provide erotic stimulus must also be covered. The law also requires that the neck (below and including the collarbone), the upper arms (including the elbow) and knees of a married woman be covered both in public and within the confines of her own house. These dress rules continue to be followed in the Ultra-Orthodox community, as well as in significant parts of mainstream Orthodox Judaism.

Modesty in Christianity

In Christianity, modesty is understood as the virtue of moderation and humility in all behavior, and is a common theme in Christian literature. Here too we find the explicit link between modesty and women's dress. Paul's injunction in 1 Cor. 11:3-16 that women should cover their heads during worship is usually understood in this vein, as is his advice in 1 Tim. 2:9 that "women should dress modestly, with decency and propriety." These instructions were strictly followed by Christians until recently, although members of Orthodox Churches, Baptists and the Amish continue to adhere to traditional head-coverings, especially during religious services. Since Christianity is in general less law or rule-based religion than Judaism or Islam, restrictions on women's behavior and dress related to the virtue of modesty tend to be a function of denominational and geographic customs and traditions.

Contemporary issues

Birth control

While an overpopulated world is an ethical issue, most religions continue to view having children in a positive light. Religious views on birth control vary widely. The Reconstructionist, Reform, and Conservative branches of Judaism as well as Buddhists support and often advocate on behalf of reproductive rights for women, which includes the use of contraceptives. Most schools of thought in Islam also approve of the use of birth control, so long as it is a birth control method that prevents conception, rather than a method, such as the Intrauterine device (IUD), that prevents the already fertilized egg from attaching.

The Catholic Church does not support the use of contraception of any kind, but encourages married couples to practice Natural Family Planning, a method of monitoring a woman's fertility in order to conceive or avoid conception. The Church does acknowledge, however, that there may be legitimate medical reasons for a woman to use the birth control pill, for example to regulate hormones or to prevent migraines. In these cases, it is acceptable for the woman to use oral contraception, so long as the intention is to alleviate suffering, not to avoid conception.

In general, most liberal Protestants accept the use of birth control, while conservative Evangelicals continue to debate what types are acceptable.

Abortion

Abortion was declared a legal right under the US Constitution in 1973 with the Supreme Court case Roe v. Wade. Nonetheless, certain religious groups have continued to contest this decision, making abortion one of the most politicized issues of religion and the body.

Buddhism

Although there is no official Buddhist position on abortion, one of the primary tenets of the faith is compassion for all beings and to do harm to none. Buddhists hold that life begins at conception because of the belief in karma and rebirth; the fetus already bears the karma and identity of previous incarnations. However, whether the termination of a pregnancy results in the accumulation of negative karma is dependent on the specifics of each individual situation. The Dalai Lama asserts that although abortion is an act of killing, each circumstance must be examined and judged on an individual basis. He has also said that if a child were to be born with disabilities, or if the pregnancy would cause serious harm to the mother, these cases may be an exception.

Mizuko Kuyo

In Japanese Buddhism, abortion is not a stigmatized practice. In fact, a ceremony called Mizuko Kuyo, "water child memorial service," was developed to mourn and honor aborted fetuses and stillborn babies. The ceremony consists of paying homage to the god Jizo, who is responsible for leading the unborn to the other world. Traditionally, the fetus or child, called the mizuko, "water child," is buried beneath the parent's home or in a special park outside of the temple that contains statues of the god Jizo, toys, and playground equipment, where the parents may return to pay their respects. This ceremony is meant to ensure the child or the fetus's rebirth as well as to allow the parents to mourn.

Christianity

The Catholic Church has historically been one of the loudest voices in opposition to abortion, basing their argument on the Fifth Commandment, "Thou shalt not commit murder." To the Catholic Church, life begins at conception, and therefore terminating a fetus constitutes an act of murder. The Catholic Church does not support abortion in instances of rape and incest, but does in the case of an ectopic pregnancy that threatens the life of the mother.

In September 2015, Pope Francis, in conjunction with the jubilee Year of Mercy, issued a statement urging priests across the world to offer forgiveness to women who have had an abortion and have "sincerely repented." Under ordinary circumstances, a woman who has terminated a pregnancy could be excommunicated, and an individual priest does not have the authority to revoke that penalty; rather, this particular situation falls under the authority of the local bishop. During the Year of Mercy, priests had the authority to forgive the sin as well as the penalty of excommunication. The Southern Baptist Convention, Church of Latter-day Saints, and Evangelical Christians all reject abortion except in cases when the mother's life is at risk, while the Episcopal Church is a strong advocate for reproductive rights.

FIGURE 9.5 *Pro-life march against abortion in Rome. Credit: NurPhoto / Contributor, via Getty Images.*

Planned Parenthood shooting

In 2015, Robert Lewis Dear attacked a Planned Parenthood clinic in Colorado Springs, wounding nine and killing three. Dear declared himself to be a "warrior for the babies," and openly admitted his guilt in court, leading many to label his attack as an act of Christian terrorism. This attack is the worst among many incidents of anti-abortion violence. The Naral Pro-Choice America Foundation reports 6,900 reported acts of violence against abortion clinics, doctors, and staff. There is an irony in committing murder to demonstrate support for pro-life values, and this is indicative of the extreme divisiveness of this issue in contemporary society.

Hinduism

Hinduism rejects abortion based on the principle of *ahimsa*, nonviolence. For Hindus, conception is the moment when the soul is reborn, and thereby enters the fetus. To terminate a fetus is not only an act of murder, but also an affront to one's duty to society to produce offspring. Abortion is, however, permitted if the life of the mother is seriously at risk. In practice, there has been a growing problem in India of the abortion of female children, based on the idea that it is more beneficial for parents to have a son. This practice has been widely condemned by religious authorities, and laws have been enacted to forbid clinics from revealing the gender of the fetus. The government of India, in a 2011 report, has begun better educating all stakeholders about its MTP (Medical Termination of Pregnancy) and PCPNDT (Pre-conception and Pre-natal Diagnostic Techniques) laws. In its communication campaigns, it is clearing up public misconceptions by emphasizing that sex determination is illegal, but abortion is legal for certain medical conditions in India. The government is also supporting implementation of programs and initiatives that seek to reduce gender discrimination, including media campaign to address the underlying social causes of sex selection.

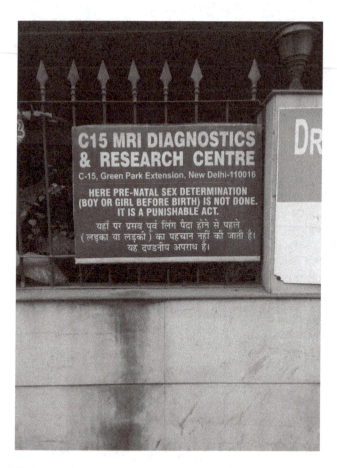

FIGURE 9.6 *Prenatal Determination Act sign in Delhi, 2015. Courtesy of David Greenberg.*

Intercultural abortion controversy

In 2013, a Hindu woman named Savita Halappanavar was admitted to an Irish hospital due to prenatal complications. She was told that the baby would not survive. However, due to the fact that she was in a Catholic hospital, in a Catholic country with strict abortion laws, she was not able to obtain the abortion that she needed, and passed away in great pain. Savita's death sparked international outrage and protests in Ireland over the right to abortion and religious freedom.

Judaism

The Reform, Reconstructionist, and Conservative branches of Judaism all respect a woman's freedom to choose. However, Orthodoxy is more divided on this issue, with some believing abortion should be allowed only in the instance of a threat to the mother's life and health (including mental health), and others asserting that each abortion should be decided on a case by case basis.

Islam

Because there is no one governing body in Islam, there are many different views on abortion. Like Judaism, abortion is always permitted if the woman's life is in danger. However, outside of this case, the Islamic perspective is more complicated, with some views holding that abortion should always be permissible during the four months, based on the argument that the fetus only develops a soul after four months. Others believe abortion, if not a threat to the mother's life, should only be allowed in the case of rape and incest.

Interfaith (interreligious) marriage

Promoting marriage within one's faith community has been a common view and practice in most religions. Interfaith marriage, or the marriage between members of different faiths, has traditionally been prohibited, rejected, shunned, and stigmatized. Many cultures and religions reject marriage with outsiders in their desire to protect the cohesion of their social body. In some cases, the marriage contract can only be binding upon persons of the same faith, such as the Jewish *Ketubah*. Attitudes toward interfaith marriage are becoming more liberal in the Western world, as multiculturalism and secularism have challenged rigid religious views and the place of religion in society. While the Hindu and Baha'í religions have traditionally been tolerant toward interfaith marriages, it is only recently that liberal and progressive denominations within Judaism and Christianity have become more inclusive in their attitudes toward interfaith marriage. At the same time, Orthodox Jews, Muslims, and Catholics have remained firm in their stance against interfaith couples unless the outsider undergoes proper religious conversion.

Marriage equality (Same-Sex Marriage)

The U.S. Supreme Court decision in 2015 to unequivocally legalize same-sex marriage across the United States has forced religious groups within the United States to explore and perhaps re-envision their stance on marriage equality. While some societies such as the ancient Greeks accepted same-sex relations, many religious groups, such as Catholics, insist upon remaining rooted in their tradition, while others have not come to a consensus at all. Making matters more complicated for Christians and Jews is the condemnation of homosexuality in the Book of Leviticus. The debate over same-sex marriage presents the larger problem that all religions are now facing: Do they conform

FIGURE 9.7 *First gay couple marriage ceremony in Los Angeles County, 2008. Credit: Ted Soqui / Contributor, via Getty Images.*

to changing times and risk losing their identity, as some would advocate, or do they turn toward tradition, but risk alienating some of their members?

Same-sex marriage precedents

Historic records indicate a tolerant attitude toward homosexuality in Japanese Buddhism, at time even praising it for its mystery. Today, there are no religious or political limitations on homosexual behavior in Japan, but there is not yet legal recognition of homosexual unions. Same-sex marriage has been practiced in societies such as Native American tribes and China. In Native American tribal groups, same-sex marriages were accepted; men who adopt female gender roles, called two-spirit men, enter into formal marriages with other men. Same-sex marriages were often temporary in places such as China and Africa. In the Chinese province of Fujian, homosexual love was accepted, and older men would marry youths for several years, at the end of which the elder partner would help the younger find a wife to raise a family. Similarly, in the Azande African tribe, older men would temporarily marry male youths.

Christianity

Catholicism has rejected the idea of same-sex marriage based on the biblical story of the creation of Adam and Eve, based on the belief that this story indicates that marriage is between a man and a woman only. Homosexual desires, however, are not in themselves sinful; it is acting on these desires, whether through masturbation or sexual activity, that is a sin. Conversely, the Eastern Orthodox Church does condemn homosexuality as being inherently sinful based on scripture and Church tradition. While many within the Catholic Church and LGBTQ community were initially optimistic about Pope Francis's stance on homosexuality, these hopes were diminished as Pope Francis rejected the possibility of same-sex marriage, calling it a threat to the family in January 2015.

The American Baptist Church, Seventh-day Adventist Church, Southern Baptist Convention, and the United Methodist Church all reject same-sex marriage based on their interpretation of the biblical creation story. The Church of Latter-day Saints also rejects same-sex marriage, and has actively advocated against marriage equality.

In 2015, the Episcopal Church officially accepted same-sex marriage into canon law. However, individual clergy can opt out of performing same-sex unions if they do not feel comfortable doing so. As of 2014, the Presbyterian Church allows same-sex marriage ceremonies, also at the discretion of local church government and ministers. The Religious Society of Friends, or the Quakers, unequivocally accepts LGBTQ individuals as welcomed members of the Church. Whether to recognize and perform same-sex marriages has been left up to local Meetings.

Islam

In the Qur'an, homosexuality is condemned in the story of Lot's people (26:165). *Shariah* (Islamic law) is concerned primarily with actions as opposed to emotions, and therefore does not condemn same-sex attraction if it is not displayed in public. Islamic law requires a certain number of male and female witnesses to the homosexual act to testify in court, and calls for severe punishment if gay sexuality is proven, but is less harsh regarding lesbianism. Same-sex intercourse carries the death penalty in five Muslim nations: Saudi Arabia, Iran, Mauritania, Sudan, and Yemen, while in the United Arab Emirates the law is unclear. In some Muslim-majority nations, such as Turkey, Jordan, Egypt, or Mali, same-sex intercourse is not forbidden by law. While mainstream Islam rejects the idea of same-sex marriage, there is no overarching governing body in the West to enforce it. While there had been occasional reports of same-sex unions in Islamic communities, most have been met with significant protests.

Judaism

Same-sex marriage within Orthodox Judaism has been sharply condemned, and the legalization of same-sex marriage in the United States has been strongly resisted by Orthodox individuals and rabbis. However, Rabbi Steven Greenberg, who is an openly gay Orthodox rabbi, has officiated at same-sex commitment ceremonies.

The Conservative Movement accepts marriage equality, pointing to the importance of family and marriage as a sacred act between couples. However, individual synagogues and rabbis are not required to perform same-sex marriages. As early as 1990, the Rabbinical Assembly's Committee on Jewish Law and Standards stated that they would work for equal civil rights for LGBTQ individuals.

In 1996, the Reform movement affirmed their support of marriage equality, and in 2000 recognized the right of Reform rabbis to perform same-sex marriage ceremonies, asserting that same-sex couples and their commitment to each other should be affirmed through a Jewish ritual. The Reform movement does, however, accept the decision of rabbis who would prefer not to perform same-sex marriage ceremonies.

The Reconstructionist Movement is considered by some to be the most welcoming among Jewish denominations toward LGBTQ individuals. In 2004 the Reconstructionist Rabbinical Association called for civil rights for LGBTQ couples, including child custody and inheritance rights.

Buddhism

The focus in Buddhism is on the individual experience, and therefore it is not possible to make an overarching claim about a Buddhist stance on marriage equality—the decision is largely left up to the individual. Siddhartha Gautama did not specifically speak about homosexuality, and no majority Buddhist country has legalized same-sex marriage. The Dalai Lama's stance on same-sex marriage has not been definitive or canonized, implying it should ultimately be left up to the individual to decide.

Same-sex marriage activism

Dignity New York is a nonprofit founded in 1972 that seeks social justice, acceptance, and legal reforms for LGBTQ individuals, while encouraging these individuals to maintain their Catholic faith and become more active in the Church. The American Friends Service Committee, an independent group of Quaker activists, has been advocating on behalf of the LGBTQ community since the 1960s. Activist movements within Islam include Muslims for Progressive Values and the Muslim Alliance for Sexual and Gender Diversity, which holds annual retreats for LGBTQ Muslims. In fall of 2015, MECCA, an online school for Muslim research on inclusive interpretations of Islamic texts was established. Keshet, meaning rainbow, is a national organization that works toward inclusion for LGBTQ individuals in Jewish life. Likewise, the organization Nehirim functions as a community for Jewish LGBTQ individuals and their families.

Questions for review and discussion

1   Traditions such as Judaism and Hinduism affirm pleasure as an important aspect of life, and sexual pleasure as a valid purpose of sexual activity in marriage. What are the implications of such views for understanding God and holiness?

2   What do modesty rules say about self-control and the issue of personal responsibility when facing potential temptations?

[handwritten margin note, top-left: ς/2/6]

3   What kinds of problems, if any, do veiling practices present in a largely secular world?

4   Discuss similarities and differences in marriage rituals and practices cross-culturally.

5   Discuss the tensions between religious views on abortion and women's rights.

6   How do traditions whose scriptures prohibit homosexuality reinterpret the institution of marriage to include same-sex couples?

[handwritten: Origin Stories stand as templetes — Story of adam and Eve, same sex marriage is seen as a paradim ⟶ myth]

Glossary

Adultery-sexual intercourse between a married person and a person who is not his or her spouse.

Celibate-abstaining from marriage and sexual relations, typically for religious reasons.

Hadith-the collective body of traditions relating to Muhammad and his companions.

Interfaith marriage-marriage between individuals who belong to, or identify with different religious traditions.

Laws of Manu-moral and religious law of Hinduism, delineating code of conduct in inter-caste relationships and all areas of life.

Marriage contract-a contract between prospective spouses which states their respective rights and obligations in the marriage.

Polygamy-the practice of having more than one wife or one husband.

Polygyny-the practice of having more than one wife.

Sacrament-(Roman Catholic)the rites of baptism, confirmation, the Eucharist, penance, anointing of the sick, ordination, and matrimony.

Veiling-the act of covering a woman's face with a veil.   *[handwritten: ⟶ through exclusion Church bringing order]*

[handwritten margin note, left side, vertical: To have something ordered, you must have something disordered]

[handwritten at bottom:]

2021
Vatican opposing same sex marriage —

- Homosexual relationships are seen as disordered
- Control over the normative
- Not judging yet creating a rule
  ⟶ God's words are above all the Pope may think one thing while God (above all) believes another

Relationship of self and Body:
Catholic normative views
Body is to act one way when
soul can act another way
↳ soul, mind, heart contradicted
by what your body does
Subverting to bodily urges

PART FOUR

Asserting
heteronormativity
↳ desires vs. what
the body does

Social control
of body,
Religion is a way
to keep people in order

Roots always
to Creation story
↳ women
created for
men

Modifying, Liberating, and Honoring the Body

Bodily
union of
2 people
is the issue

In the last part of the book, we will examine rituals and practices that manifest religious beliefs that are marked on the body, that liberate the body from attachments and desires, and that honor the temporality of the body and the eternity of the soul. In Chapter 10, "Marking and Modifying the Body: From Rituals to Biotechnology," we explore body modifications as practiced cross-culturally from ancient times until the present. Our focus is on circumcision and tattoos and their significance in several traditions and cultures, while considering issues of cultural relativism. We also account for current body modification practices that employ biotechnology for procedures such as organ transplantation and gender reassignment, and ponder the impact of science and technology on traditional religious views of the body. In Chapter 11, "Asceticism: Spiritual Technologies of Detachment," we examine the role that ascetic practices play in religion and their intended objectives. Here, we also consider the benefits gained by women adepts as they embrace a life of renunciation. We also explore the reasons why some traditions reject the ascetic path and maintain the primacy of family life, and see no contradiction between physical pleasure and spirituality. In Chapter 12, "Death and the Afterlife," we review and address notions of purity as these pertain to treatment of the body after death. We also analyze how practices of burial and cremation reflect their respective religious world views on the afterlife. In the case of burial, there is often the belief in heaven and hell as well as Judgment Day and the resurrection of the body. Cremation is often associated with the belief in the continuous rebirth of the soul and its final liberation from the body.

10

Marking and Modifying the Body: From Rituals to Biotechnology

In this chapter, we will explore body modifications as practiced cross-culturally from ancient times until today. We will address evolving perspectives and practices of ancient rituals such as tattoos and circumcision in the West. Circumcision, originally a religious obligation for Jews and Muslims and shunned by Christians, became a routine hospital procedure performed on newborns since the early twentieth century. Tattoos were employed in ancient Egypt and Polynesian culture as marks of one's social and religious rank, as well as protective amulets. In Chinese culture, they served to mark criminals, and later identified sailors. The recent renaissance of tattoos in the West opens new ways of looking at tattoos and what they mean. The tattooed body can be understood as challenging the control of religion and culture. The decision to tattoo can be understood as affirming one's personal agency to shape one's body and produce change and transformation. We will raise issues of cultural relativism in the context of controversies such as female circumcision. Finally, we will also review the influence of biotechnology on such procedures as organ transplantation, gender reassignment, and the transhumanist movement as we assess the impact of science and technology on the body.

Body modification is any form of permanent or semi-permanent alteration of one's physical body. Body modifications in a religious context have been physically, socially, and spiritually ritualized. Regardless of the degree, method, and goal of body alteration, modifying the body is as ancient as human history and integral to religious and social identity. From tattoos to circumcision, religious traditions have celebrated the modified body and its rich symbolism. While the motives for and process of body modifications differ cross-culturally, they reflect the belief in the mutability and potentialities of the body to signify gender, age, class, ethnicity, and religion.

As science and biotechnology are penetrating and shaping our bodies for aesthetic, medical, and gender reassignment purposes, there is a significant debate about the moral and religious implications of such practices. Cosmetic surgery often caters to the need to conform to popular trends. In an attempt to attain an idealized standard of beauty, some women and men resort to surgery; in some cases, this desire becomes compulsive; and plastic surgery addiction is now recognized as a behavioral addiction. Although some have developed an unhealthy relationship with cosmetic surgery, others claim that it can be empowering. Plastic surgery to combat the effects of aging and achieve current beauty standards is a billion-dollar industry. As a solution to biological impairment, prosthetics give the disabled possibilities for movement and active participation in society; and gender reassignment procedures enable transgender people to attain their desired gender identity.

As most religions adhere to different notions and rules of purity and impurity as was discussed in Chapter 7, they also view marking the body through practices such as tattoos and scarifications quite differently. There is a wide disparity across cultures regarding permissible and prohibited body modification. While traditions instruct their adherents to perform one type of body modification, they abhor other forms of modification. Judaism and Islam, for example, prescribe body modification of circumcision, yet forbid other types of modification such as tattoos for disturbing the integrity of the body, which to them is created in the image of God. Some cultures employ the body as a canvas for decoration on which to mark social identity and rites of passage.

Historical note on tattooing

The oldest documented tattoo belongs to Otzi the Iceman who died in 3,300 BCE. After Otzi, the next evidence of tattoos is found on Egyptian mummies, particularly females. During the Roman Empire tattoos were prohibited by Emperor Constantine, who decreed this form of body modification to be unholy. Romans also were known for tattooing numbers on their slaves. Tattoos were also associated with criminals during this period. These reasons contributed to the negative reputation tattoos once held. It was in the eighteenth century that tattoos began to gain popularity once again, particularly with British sailors. From there, the trend caught on and led to the birth of our modern-day tattoo industry. Throughout history, tattoos have been associated with personal and group expression and identity.

Tattooing, scarification, and piercing

In countries throughout the world, ceremonies and rituals are employed to mark major transitions in a person's life or religious practice. Some examples of popularized rites of passage include "Sweet Sixteen" parties in the United States, Quinceañeras in Latin America (especially Mexico), and Bat/Bar Mitzvahs in Judaism. While not all of these examples are directly connected to a religious tradition, all three embody the participant's transition into or toward adulthood and social maturity within their respective culture and/or religious tradition. These "coming of age" traditions mark only one form of rites of passage in which religious practitioners across the world participate. In other traditions, these rites of passage take the form of permanent body modifications.

Tattoos were employed in ancient Egypt and Polynesian culture as marks of one's social and religious rank, as well as protective amulets. In Chinese culture, they served to mark criminals, and later identified sailors. The recent renaissance of tattoos in the West opens up new ways of looking at tattoos and what they signify. The tattooed body can be understood as challenging the control of religion and culture. The decision to tattoo can be understood as affirming one's personal agency to shape one's body and produce change and transformation.

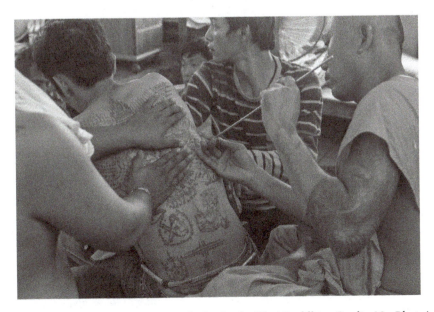

FIGURE 10.1 *A monk tattooing the back of a Thai Buddhist. Credit: NurPhoto/ Contributor, via Getty Images*

Scarification, also known as cicatrization, has been utilized by a variety of African ethnic groups for thousands of years as a way to mark an individual's social belonging and social maturation. The scarification process, design, and meaning vary, depending upon each group that practices this tradition. Generally, scarification is performed using a sharp object, such as glass, razors, metal, stone, or thorns, to cut designs into an individual's (usually a young person's) skin. This is usually not completed in one sitting and may be prolonged in order to demonstrate the individual's maturation and social status over time.

The designs of scarification are unique to every ethnic group that practices it, and can often be used to identify the wearer's belonging to a specific ethnic group, or may even indicate the bearer's family line. For example, the Bessoribe people, a tribal group in Benin, a country located in western Africa, uses scarification to mark rites of passage for both men and women, from a child's birth and initiation into the group's social structure, to marriage.

FIGURE 10.2 *A young Mursi tribal woman is seen displaying her body modification, including scarification of the shoulder and the extension of lower lip and earlobes. Credit: Rod Waddington, via Wikimedia.*

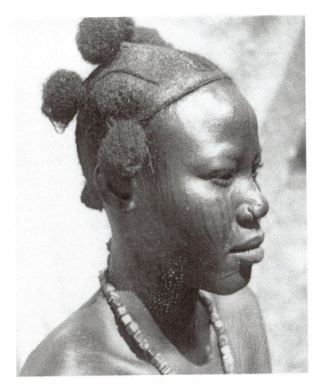

FIGURE 10.3 *A Woman with scarification. Credit: John Atherton, via Wikimedia.*

Body modification practices such as scarification and piercing are often puberty rituals found in Africa. Suri and Mursi tribal groups from Ethiopia choose to engage in scarification ceremonies, as the scars are viewed as marks of strength and beauty. Another modification practice among the Mursi women is lip piercing in preparation for wearing a lip-plate, although today, some women choose to pierce their lower lips without wearing a lip-plate. This is a puberty ritual signifying the woman's transitioning to adulthood, marriage, and childbearing.

The Nuba women of Sudan participate in their scarification ritual as they begin puberty. As the woman ages, she will receive scars that span the length of her body. Besides marking sexual maturity and social status, the Nuba believe that specific marks prevent diseases, such as hepatitis. Based upon archaeological evidence and cave paintings, it is thought that scarification is not unique to Africa, and that it may have been practiced among Aboriginal Australians and ancient Mexican peoples. For example, in the Sepik Region of Papua New Guinea, this process is also used as an initiation process for young men. They believe that the crocodile created human beings, and the scars are used to resemble marks left on the young man being swallowed by a crocodile.

Today, the process of scarification has become less common, particularly in cities in Africa where Western colonial influences have discouraged the practice. The abandonment of this traditional practice has been attributed to a variety of factors, including the influx of Christianity, education surrounding the transmission of diseases and infection as a result of cutting the skin, and encouragement to detach from "tribal" roots. However, many people throughout the continent of Africa continue to adhere to this ingrained cultural practice by participating in scarification rituals.

Tattoos in Judaism

Prohibitions or endorsements of body modifications are found in sacred religious texts such as the Torah. Here we find examples of individuals with body markings that are not only endorsed but also have positive connotations as divine protection. In Gen. 4:15 we read: "And the Lord put a mark/sign (*ot*) on Cain so that anyone who finds him will not kill him." This brand mark is intended to protect Cain from avengers. In Isa. 44:5, the prophet Isaiah stresses God's covenantal allegiance to Jacob/Israel and, in turn, the people's loyalty to Yahweh (God) in the aftermath of Jerusalem's destruction and the ongoing Babylonian exile. The prophet explains that one way for the faithful to exhibit their allegiance to God is to write on their hand "*lyhwh*," meaning "belonging to Yahweh."

On the other hand, there is an explicit prohibition against marking the body in Lev. 19.28: "Incisions/gashes for the dead you will not make in your flesh, nor incised marks (tattoos) on yourselves." It is possible that the ban in Leviticus may have applied only to certain types of markings that were reminiscent of pagan, non-Israelite cults, whose tattoos represented devotion to another deity besides the Hebrew God; whereas the "positive" examples of body marks refer to individuals or a group as devotees of God, or under God's protection. Today, the popularity of tattoos, particularly in Israel, where tattoos stand out among a population that traditionally prohibited them, has opened rabbinic discussions on the practice. Tattoos have been historically prohibited and discouraged on the basis of their original association with pagan worship, and the belief that our bodies are created in the image of God, and therefore should not be subject to modification according to personal decision. While prohibited in the Torah, contemporary rabbinic views are mixed, with various degrees of tolerance, and there are no legal consequences such as denial of burial for those with tattoos in a Jewish cemetery. The issue remains extremely sensitive for Jews, given the association of tattoos with the

Holocaust, with the dehumanizing Nazi practice of tattooing numbers on their Jewish victims' arms.

Tattoos in Christianity

While some Christians are opposed to tattooing on the basis of the Leviticus prohibition, there is no explicit rule against the practice under the authority of the Catholic Church. Others might disapprove or approve of tattoos as a social phenomenon with no implications for their religious identity. 1 Cor. 6:19-20 exhorts that our bodies are not our own but rather are temples of God. This verse is sometimes employed by conservative Christians to support a prohibition on violation of the body with a tattoo.

Tattoos in Islam

While there is no prohibition against tattoos in the Qur'an, the majority of Muslims consider permanent tattoos against the tradition of the prophet Muhammad. Legal scholars base this view against the practice of tattoos on the Hadith. According to one source in the Hadith, the prophet cursed the lady who tattoos (herself or others) and the one who gets herself tattooed.

Tattoos in Hinduism

There is no prohibition on tattooing in Hinduism. Hindus have had traditions of permanent as well as temporary tattooing that have been practiced for several thousand years. In the Vedas, we find a prescription for the use of a plant called *mendikha* (commonly referred to as henna in the West) and *Haldi* (turmeric) for the purposes of marking the body. The *bindi*, or the red dot on the forehead, serves as an important social marker in Hindu culture and society as a common symbol of the married woman. *Tilak*, on the other hand, also called *kumkum*, is made from turmeric powder and placed on the same spot on the forehead, but serves as a spiritual symbol. Representing the third eye, it is applied by a Hindu priest during religious ceremonies at the temple, and is a mark of auspiciousness and a reminder of spirituality as the supreme reality of life.

Various other symbols have been used in tattoos to depict peace and divine consciousness, such as AUM. Temporary tattooing using *mendikha* has evolved into a popular art-form in India, and is applied during Hindu weddings and festivals such as Diwali. Permanent tattooing has been widely practiced by tribal communities in northwest India and is called *godna*. *Godna* is considered to be a permanent ornament using the human body as the canvas.

FIGURE 10.4 *A female hand with henna design, Zainubrazvi, via Wikimedia.*

Tattoos in Buddhism

In Buddhist teachings, everything is in a state of flux and therefore nothing is permanent. To avoid suffering, we must develop an attitude of detachment toward all things, including the body. Buddhist teachings generally do not forbid tattoos. In fact, there is an annual Buddhist tattoo festival in Thailand, where Thai monks pray while performing the ritual of tattooing using their tools to mark the images into the flesh. This ritual renders tattoos as amulets, protecting the wearer from demons and providing spiritual strength in the face of crisis. A few of the most popular Buddhist tattoo designs are *mandalas*—intricate designs meant to represent the layers of the universe, *dharma* wheels or *dharmachakras*, representing the wheel of truth and law or the eightfold noble path, and lotus blossoms which are considered to be a Buddhist symbol of purity. Other Buddhist tattoos often used to represent the Buddha include the lion and the Bodhi Tree, where Buddha is believed to have achieved enlightenment.

Tattoos in Neo-Paganism

Tattooing is a popular ritual in Neo-paganism, as a way of connecting to the ancestors, or as a way of expressing their devotion to a specific god. Tattooing is also used in ritual spell work as a sort of blood sacrifice. Although tattooing is an accepted and celebrated practice within paganism, it is not without controversy. While many pagans choose to adorn their bodies with the symbols of what they believe to be their ancestral religion, others appropriate images from Jewish, Hindu, and Native cultures.

Tattoos in Contemporary Culture

Tattooing has been accepted more broadly as a way of reclaiming and empowering the body. Many women have claimed that tattoos and body piercings have been a means to reject gender norms and idealized standards of beauty, while survivors of abuse have utilized tattoos to declare freedom from their trauma. Tattoos are also commonly used to memorialize the passing of a loved one. In Flint, Michigan, The Bridge Church, a contemporary church dedicated to nontraditional methods of worship, actually houses a tattoo parlor within its doors, offering tattoos as a kind of "permanent prayer." In opening the tattoo parlor, The Bridge Church acknowledges tattooing as a valid form of worship and spiritual expression. Others find a mystical experience in the physical pain of certain modifications like tattooing. While many people casually enjoy tattoos and other body modifications, these experiences have actually been categorized and developed into a religion. The Church of

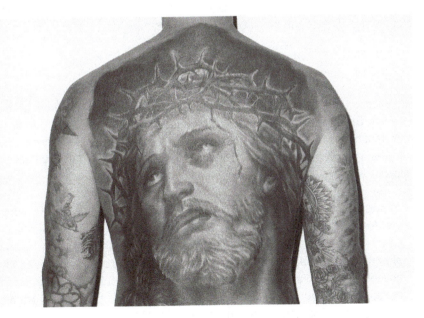

FIGURE 10.5 *A man poses with a full back tattoo of Jesus Christ, Australia, 2016.*

Body Modification, a nontheistic organization, was established (without a geographic location) to encourage and support the use of ancient and modern practices of body modification as a way to strengthen the bond of mind, body, and soul. With this goal, members of the church are committed to a variety of body modifications such as tattooing, piercing, suspension, and corsetry, believing that these result in transforming the spirit and the psyche. Although adherents of this church claim their modifications are mentally and spiritually beneficial, some psychologists argue that this behavior may qualify as a form of self-harm.

Circumcision

Circumcision, originally a religious obligation for Jews, adopted by Muslims, and shunned by Christians, became a routine prophylactic procedure for newborn boys in the West in the early and mid-twentieth century. More recently, a campaign against routine newborn circumcision emerged in Europe and the United States. On the one end of the spectrum are those who object to it on the grounds of needless pain for the newborn, calling it barbaric, and equating it with genital mutilation. On the other hand, many choose the procedure of circumcision to be done in hospitals given ample medical evidence in support of it reducing the prevalence of a range of diseases, including urinary tract infections, syphilis, herpes, penile cancer, and HIV. Still, those who are against circumcision dispute the medical evidence for its benefits.

Circumcision in Judaism

Circumcision (*brit milah* in Hebrew) is literally and figuratively the mark of the covenant God made with Abraham and his descendants. It is one of the most important rituals that are part of the life cycle in Jewish family life. Followed by the great majority of Jews for millennia, this ritual is commanded by God as follows: Then God said to Abraham,

> As for you, you must keep my covenant, you and your descendants after you for the generations to come. This is my covenant with you and your descendants after you, the covenant you are to keep: Every male among you shall be circumcised. . . who is eight days old must be circumcised. . . . My covenant in your flesh is to be an everlasting covenant. Any uncircumcised male, who has not been circumcised in the flesh, will be cut off from his people; he has broken my covenant (Gen. 17:9-14).

The ritual act of male circumcision on the eighth day after birth has since been the marker of Jewish identity, as the sign of the covenant between Abraham, his tribe, and God. The ritual is a joyous occasion for the family, a celebration welcoming the boy into the community. Although any Jew may perform the procedure, it is often a trained person called a *mohel*, who conducts it. The procedure is performed as family and the gathered community witness, and is followed by a festive meal. The circumcision ceremony welcomes the male child, and since there is no equivalent event to celebrate the female newborn, Jewish feminists, as we discussed in Chapter 4, have created a new ceremony for welcoming daughters. Conversion to Judaism requires circumcision, and even a gentile who underwent medical circumcision as an infant, must undergo a procedure called *tipat dam*, literally a drop of blood where a small but symbolic incision is made.

Circumcision in Christianity

The Christian Church abandoned the Jewish practice of circumcision because of St. Paul's teachings that the practice was no longer relevant, since Christ had abolished circumcision and other Jewish rituals. In Paul's view, Christian circumcision should be spiritualized into a "circumcision of the heart." "But a Jew is one inwardly, and circumcision is a matter of the heart, by the Spirit, not by the letter" (Rom. 2:29). This change had major consequences as it permitted free admission of gentiles into the Christian Church. Circumcision became a mark of difference between Christians and Jews. Despite the abolishment of the ritual of circumcision among Christians, Catholics have continued to celebrate the Feast of the Circumcision of Christ on the New Year.

Circumcision in Islam

Circumcision (*khitan* in Arabic), is a religious custom practiced since the beginnings of Islam, and an established practice by all Islamic schools of jurisprudence. Mentioned in the Hadith but not in the Qur'an, it is strongly encouraged and considered an important ritual whose main purpose is to ensure cleanliness or *tahara* (purification). An additional motive offered by Muslim scholars for this practice is to emulate Abraham's example, from whom Muslims consider their lineage to come. It is debated as to whether circumcision should be required upon converts to Islam. In comparison to the ritual in Judaism, the rules for performing circumcision are flexible regarding the age at which it is performed. Depending on regional traditions, some circumcisions are performed as early as seven days after birth, while others as late as puberty. The procedure is usually carried out in a hospital where the medically trained circumciser is not required to be a Muslim. In some Islamic countries, such as Malaysia, circumcision is performed as a puberty ritual to mark the boys' introduction into adulthood.

Female circumcision

According to the World Health Organization (WHO), female circumcision (also known as female genital mutilation (FGM) or cutting is a procedure that is meant to "intentionally alter or cause injury to the female genital organs for non-medical reasons." The most common form of FGM is clitoridectomy, the partial or total removal of the clitoris and/or the prepuce. The amount of tissue that is removed varies widely from community to community. While it is a subject of debate as to whether it is required or recommended in Islamic Hadith, scholars address the fact of decreasing women's sexual desire as a primary reason for the practice. The procedure is practiced throughout various African and Middle Eastern ethnic groups, and is often carried out in unhygienic conditions and without anesthesia. Women who have undergone the procedure report severe problems, including chronic pain, genital sores, bleeding, as well as fear of intimacy.

Some groups claim that this ritual is a way to maintain modesty and prevent the young woman from engaging in premarital sex. Generally speaking, cultures that preserve the ritual of FGM hope to properly prepare young women for the responsibilities of adulthood and marriage. Others, such as the Rendille, do not undergo "cutting" until a woman is ready to be married; in this case, the practice is used to induct the woman into life with her husband's family, and to remove a part of the body that is viewed as "masculine."

Global organizations, including the United Nations and WHO, have labeled the practice as a human rights violation against girls and women, and have condemned the practice for the unnecessary harms it causes to those who undergo it, such as infections and complications during childbirth. Many African countries have also taken steps to outlaw the practice, including Egypt, Ghana, and Burkina Faso. Despite prohibitions against the practice, cutting remains ingrained in many countries throughout the world. Many that participate in the ritual view it as an extremely important part of maturation and a part of being a "proper," "clean," and/or "responsible" woman. Some women who receive the cutting may also view it as a source of pride; however, even those who do not agree with the practice may continue to perpetuate it because of the significant value and importance that it carries within their ethnic, religious, or social group. Opponents of FGM view it as an extreme example of patriarchal oppression of women, yet ironically, the defenders and performers of the practice are mostly women. While some opponents to male circumcision in the West have called male circumcision a form of genital mutilation, some feminists and human rights advocates reject attempts to equate male circumcision in the United States with FGM in Africa and the Middle East.

As increasing numbers of African and Middle Eastern refugees and immigrants move West, the question of how to address traditional cutting or female circumcision practices has become a point of contentious debate. While many countries, such as the United States and United Kingdom, have outlawed the practice, some doctors continue to assist those seeking to engage in the cultural ritual in the hopes that they will be able to make the procedure safer. According to the Population Reference Bureau, more than 500,000 girls and women are at risk of experiencing FGM in the United States alone, signaling a significant rise over the past ten years. This issue has left policymakers and medical professionals at a standstill between condemning the practice and ensuring that those who continue cutting practices are able to engage in the practice in the safest way possible.

Castration and Eunuchs

Castration, or removal of the testicles, has appeared as a religious and social practice throughout history. Castrated men—eunuchs—often served as servants of monarchs in imperial palaces, and guardians of harems in South and East Asia, the Middle East, Europe, and Africa. Castration was also an aspect of religious devotion and was common among the Galli priests and devotees of Cybele in Roman society. Some members of the _hijras_ (transgendered individuals in India and Pakistan) are eunuchs and constitute a social and religious group deemed to have spiritual gifts. Judaism strongly opposes and prohibits the practice of castration, and biblical law excludes eunuchs or any males with defective genitals from the priesthood. If a man is castrated, he is forbidden to marry, or if married, he must divorce his wife.

In the New Testament, there are references to eunuchs who are either born as such or choose to become one: "For there are eunuchs who have been born that way from their mother's womb, and there are eunuchs who have been made eunuchs by men; and there are eunuchs who have made themselves so for the sake of the kingdom of heaven. He who is able to accept this, let him accept it" (Mt. 19:12). Ritual self-castration was observed among some devout Christians since the second century as an act of chastity. The theologian and celibate Origen is known to have castrated himself. Although celibacy was an ideal, in response to this phenomenon, the First Council of Nicaea prohibited clergy members from voluntarily castrating themselves.

In modern times, castration was a central tenet of the Russian sect *Skoptsy*, whose name is derived from the term *oskopit*, meaning "to castrate." This secret sect, which existed until the mid-twentieth century, believed that the best way to combat sexual lust and fulfill Jesus's proclamation of human purity and perfection was the removal of the sexual organs of both men and women.

Despite the Leviticus laws against castration, we find in the Book of Isaiah a sympathetic nod toward eunuchs:

> Let no eunuch say: "And I, I am a dried-up tree." For Yahweh says this: To the eunuchs who observe my Sabbaths, and resolve to do what pleases me and cling to my covenant, I will give, in my house and within my walls, a monument and a name better than sons and daughters; I will give them an everlasting name that shall never be effaced.

While the exact intent of Isaiah's statement is open to interpretation, and may represent a statement of inclusion and compassion for victims of forced castration, it clearly indicates the presence of eunuchs at that time.

Biotechnology: From gender reassignment to transhumanism

Gender reassignment is a medical procedure wherein an individual decides to have their internal and/or external sex organs changed to align with their appropriate gender identity. While some transgender people choose this surgery, many may choose to only undergo nonsurgical procedures such as hormone therapy, or may choose to transition without significant body modification. As we discussed in Chapter 8, acceptance of transgender persons varies greatly across different religions and societies.

With the rise of the LGBTQ rights movement, including the legalization of same-sex marriage in the United States in 2015, questions about transgender rights have increasingly come to the forefront. Though a variety of traditions have recognized transgender people or transgender deities for millennia, contemporary discussions on trans rights have only recently begun to take center stage. Religions throughout the world are only beginning to make decisions on whether gender reassignment surgery should be permissible, and how modern trans people challenge or uphold religious beliefs. For example, the Union for Reform Judaism in fall of 2016 passed a transgender rights policy that called for "spreading awareness and increasing knowledge of issues related to gender identity," including the use of preferred pronouns and, when needed, gender-neutral language in religious and social settings. At the same time, the Jewish Orthodox movement, while addressing the importance of compassion toward the transgendered, and also considering questions of prayer and social interaction inside and outside religious settings related to transgender persons, has vacillated on the issue of body modification in order to transition genders. Rabbi Tzvi Hersh Weinreb, executive vice president emeritus of the Orthodox Union, in his talk on February 2017, was ambivalent; on the one hand, he denied the permissibility of modifying the body to transition genders, while at the same time citing possible exceptions under Jewish law.

Christian responses to current issues of gender reassignment have also been divided. Progressive Christians have expressed compassion and acceptance, and have compared transgender people who suffer with "Body Identity Integrity Disorder" to cancer patients who must undergo chemotherapy to remove cancerous cells from their body. On the other end of the Christian spectrum are the Catholics and the Southern Baptists who emphatically reject the surgery and other forms of transitioning that modify the body. In an address in 2012, Pope Francis strongly denounced gender theory in general and transgender choices:

> The manipulation of nature, which we deplore today where our environment is concerned, now becomes man's fundamental choice where he himself is concerned. From now on there is only the abstract human being, who chooses for himself what his nature is to be. . . . When the freedom to be creative becomes the freedom to create oneself, then necessarily the Maker himself is denied, and ultimately man too is stripped of his dignity as a creature of God, as the image of God at the core of his being.

In 2014, the Southern Baptist Convention issued a resolution in which they oppose altering one's bodily identity (e.g., cross-sex hormone therapy, gender reassignment surgery) to refashion it to conform with one's perceived gender identity, while extending love and compassion to those experiencing conflict between their biological sex and their gender identity.

The prevalence and acceptance of transgender individuals in Hindu cultures in India and Pakistan was discussed in some detail in Chapter 8 under gender and sexuality. With advances in biotechnology, social media, and global expansion of liberal values, the acceptance of diversity in general and gender choice in particular will likely increase.

Organ Transplantation

Organ transplantation has largely been seen in the Christian faith as following the biblical injunction to love your neighbor as yourself, as well as expressing

Christ's love and compassion on earth. The Anglican, Episcopal, Catholic, Baptist, Eastern Orthodox, Presbyterian Churches, and the Society of Friends all encourage and accept organ donation. Seventh-day Adventists, Lutherans, and Christian Scientists leave this moral decision up to the individuals involved. Interestingly, even the Amish consent to organ donation, while Jehovah's Witnesses will consent under the stipulation that all blood be drained from the organ prior to transplantation. All four branches of Judaism encourage organ donation. In Islam, it is generally accepted that organ transplantation and donation are permissible as these fulfill the requirement of the preservation of human life.

Embryonic stem cell research

Stem cell research shows potential for treating a wide variety of diseases, including alzheimer's, parkinson's, and diabetes. However, the stem cells most useful to this kind of research come from embryos, usually performed on the excess fertilized egg cells made in Petri dishes for couples and individuals undergoing in vitro fertilization. These embryonic stem cells are particularly useful and effective because they multiply quickly and can develop into any cell of the human body, and if not used would be otherwise discarded. For religious people, embryonic stem cell research raises the question of whether or not the frozen fertilized eggs constitute human life, and thus should be used in research and treatments.

All four branches of Judaism accept embryonic stem cell research for medical and therapeutic purposes, rejecting the idea that the frozen fertilized egg should be considered human life. Additionally, rabbis point to the fact that these cells would have been discarded and therefore would not have become a human life anyway. For Jews, the potential for saving lives and relieving suffering is the more important issue. Likewise, the Episcopal, Presbyterian, and Methodist Churches also stand in favor of embryonic stem cell research based on the argument that the embryos would have been discarded, but are instead being used to benefit the suffering. On the opposite side of the spectrum stand the Catholic Church and the Southern Baptist Convention. Both parties voice strong opposition to embryonic stem cell research, claiming that life unequivocally begins at conception. Buddhism, Islam, and Hinduism do not have an official stance on embryonic stem cell research.

Transhumanism

Transhumanism is a multifaceted movement that promotes the use of technology to improve the bodies and minds of human beings. The term transhumanism was coined by Julian Huxley in 1957, and in the late 1980s and 1990s, as biotechnology, neuroscience, and nanotechnology were making great strides, a group of scientists and futurists, including Max More, Marvin Minsky, and Ray Kurzweil began to formulate the major themes of what will become known as transhumanism. Those who adhere to the movement, most of whom are atheists or agnostics, believe that human evolution may be guided and sped up through the embrace of technological interventions. Despite the overwhelming claim of atheism, they envision what in religious parlance is an eschatological event or an end to human life as we know it. This event, which they imagine will occur after "the Singularity," is predicted by futurist Kurzweil to occur around the year 2030.

The Singularity is the point at which computers become more intelligent than humans, and thus are able to accelerate their own evolutionary development, outpacing the human brain. The belief is that since the human mind created the technology that will lead to the Singularity, this event will cause sentient supercomputers to extend their existence.

Transhumanists believe that the lives of currently living humans can be improved through technological interventions, including body modifications, such as the implantation of identification and payment devices or magnets beneath the skin. These examples are simple, but they can go as far as applying devices or chemicals to the brain to enhance cognition, and modifying eyes and ears to enhance the senses. While critics urge caution, transhumanists point out that radical medical interventions that use advanced technology to modify the body are already in use, such as the replacement of a knee or shoulder joint with an artificial device, or the use of a cochlear implant to enable a deaf person to hear. Transhumanists believe that technology should be used not only to help people with injured limbs or senses, but also to improve the physical capabilities of any human.

The ultimate goal of transhumanists is to modify the human body and mind to the point that it becomes disembodied, or "post-human." The name of the movement itself, transhumanism, indicates their belief that humanity is in transition from our current state to a post-human state. They believe that they can ultimately conquer death through technological means, and many transhumanists adhere to strict diet and exercise programs so that they can live long enough to enjoy these inevitable advances that will be available when we reach the Singularity.

Transhumanists advocate genetic engineering of human beings to enhance intelligence and physical capabilities, enabling people to become superhuman through the postponement of death and the achievement of immortality. They believe that the soul, the intellect, and the personality all reside in the brain. The mind arises from the brain and is essentially information from which the individual personality arises. The goal is to upload the minds of people into robots, and thus ensure immortality of those minds. These advances brought on by the sentient supercomputers will free humans and allow them to transcend space and time.

It is not surprising that several religious groups find transhumanist ideas threatening. Some feel that they are treading on God's prerogatives as the Creator and that these changes will render humans no longer in God's image as unique and embodied individuals. It is difficult to escape the irony that a movement that is derived from a materialist perspective of the body seeks as its ultimate goal what has traditionally been the telos (purpose) of religion, eternal life.   *buddhist monk robot*

Questions for review and discussion

1   How have perspectives of body modification changed over time?

2   Why have body modifications been adopted and appropriated by persons of different classes and social roles?

3   Could religious and cultural rituals that inflict pain (either initially or over time) be considered under the category of violations of global human rights and therefore subject to prosecution?

4   Is it a contradiction to oppose the practice of tattoos while commanding circumcision?

5   Why has the practice of tattoos become so popular in the West, while other body modifications such as scarification have not?

6   Can the widespread use and acceptance of tattoos today be understood as an expression of people's spirituality or of personal empowerment?

7   How would you compare male and female circumcision?

8   Why would a tradition such as Buddhism, that emphasizes impermanence and detachment from embodiment, encourage marking the body as a way of gaining spiritual insight or protection?

9   How does our reaction to certain body modification practices and our reaction to critiques of these practices help us think through what religion means, how it functions, and how it relates to the body?

10 How is the quest for the immortality of the brain in transhumanism different from traditional religious views of the immortality of the soul?

Glossary

Circumcision-the ritual cutting off the foreskin of a male.

Female circumcision-the ritual removal of some or all the external female genitalia.

Embryonic stem cells-derived from embryos that develop from eggs that have been fertilized in an in vitro fertilization clinic.

Initiation-the ritual of passage marking entrance or acceptance into a group or society. It could also be a formal admission to adulthood in a community or one of its formal components.

Organ transplantation-an operation in which a damaged organ in the human body is removed and replaced with a functioning one.

Scarification/cicatrization-forms of body modification, where a design is cut, etched or scratched into human skin to make a permanent scar.

Tattoos-a permanent mark on the body by insertion of pigment under the skin or by production of scars.

Transgender-people whose gender identity is the opposite of their assigned sex; may also include people who are not exclusively masculine or feminine.

Transhumanism-a movement developed over the last three decades with the belief in the future evolution of humanity by promoting the development of technologies to enhance human intellectual, physical, and psychological capabilities.

3, 4, 5, 6, 7, 8, 9, 10

11

Asceticism: Spiritual Technologies of Detachment

Asceticism from the Greek *áskēsis*, (exercise or training) is the doctrine that one can reach a high spiritual state through the practice of self-denial or self-mortification. In this chapter, we will examine the role that ascetic practices have played in Christianity, Jainism, and Buddhism. In our investigation, we will address specific rules, vows, and exercises followed by monks and nuns, with a focus on celibacy, fasting, and poverty as the most common forms of renunciation, as well as various extreme forms of corporal mortification methods. In our study, we will assess the differences between moderate and extreme forms of asceticism, and their link to fundamental views toward the body. We will also highlight social factors, spiritual motives, and religious goals for the ascetic lifestyle, and consider the spiritual and material benefits gained by women renunciants. Contrasting religious views of the ideal of asceticism, we will discuss the negative stance toward extreme forms of asceticism long held by traditions such as Zoroastrianism, Islam, and Judaism.

Generally speaking, religions can be understood as spiritual paths with a set of beliefs and practices aimed at worldly and otherworldly goals for advancing the soul's journey beyond death, alternately expressed as redemption, salvation, enlightenment, or liberation. For Buddhists, rigorous meditation practices are aimed at the realization of the impermanence of life. For Christian monks and nuns who practiced an arduous regimen of fasting, particularly in the medieval period, the goal was to reenact the physical pain of Christ on the Cross in order to unite with him. For Jains, ascetic practices are meant to eliminate attachment to the body and to material existence in order to gain *moksha*, liberation from the cycle of birth, death, and rebirth.

All religions demand spiritual and physical discipline as part of one's commitment and adherence to their respective traditions. Mastery over one's mind and body can be applied toward material goals such as athletics, as well as to spiritual ends such as enlightenment.

Some religions require and even idealize ascetic behavior such as celibacy, fasting, silence, and various extreme forms of corporal mortification, while others shun such practices. Ascetic practices at times represent a negative view of the body, particularly when they embody extreme forms of renunciation, self-denial, and pain. Yet, periodic and moderate ascetic practices can also be viewed as positive if they are performed with the objectives of cultivating virtue, discipline, and proximity to the divine. Furthermore, in some traditions, in earlier historical periods and even today, embracing asceticism as part of the monastic life has been beneficial to women, as it has provided them with greater personal freedom and access to education and spiritual authority. Asceticism continues to be practiced in some traditions, albeit to a lesser degree in contemporary religious observance and identity.

Asceticism in Christianity

The idea of self-discipline and ascetic practice is particularly prominent in the New Testament and in Christian teachings. Christianity expresses the need to fight against the desires of the flesh for the sake of the life of the spirit. There are at least three forms of asceticism in Christianity: fasting, renunciation of worldly possessions, and chastity.

Fasting as a form of asceticism was a common practice during the time of Jesus, when messianic expectations were particularly high. It was especially common among the Essenes, a group also known as the Dead Sea community, who withdrew from conventional life, became celibate, and adhered to a strict regimen of purity practices and fasting. In speaking about the practice of fasting, Jesus taught that fasting should be done with quiet resolution: "When you fast, anoint your head and wash your face, that your fasting may not be seen by others but by your Father who is in secret. And your Father who sees in secret will reward you" (Matthew 6:16–18). In addition to fasting, the renunciation of all earthly possessions is demanded: "Jesus said to him, 'If you would be perfect, go, sell what you possess and give to the poor, and you will have treasure in heaven; and come, follow me'" (Mt. 19:21).

Furthermore, the ideal of chastity is alluded to in this way: "For there are eunuchs who have been so from birth, and there are eunuchs who have been made eunuchs by men, and there are eunuchs who have made themselves eunuchs for the sake of the kingdom of heaven. Let the one who is able to receive this receive it" (Mt. 19:12). St. Paul sums up the same ideal thus: "For if you live according to the flesh you will die, but if by the Spirit you put to death the deeds of the body, you will live" (Rom. 8:13). Despite the belief in love of God and divine grace, the consequences of original sin in Christian theology are inevitable. For that reason, it was understood as a requirement, especially for those committed to the spiritual path, to fight against the world and the flesh as these were seen as sources of temptation and sin.

Celibacy in Christianity

Celibacy became regarded in Christianity in a way that is absent from Jewish and Muslim traditions. Veneration of celibacy often correlates with the celibacy (or lack thereof) of a religion's key figures. The absence of central celibate figures eliminates the need for, and inherent value of, celibacy in Islam and Judaism. This difference is significant; even for Muslim and Jewish mystics, devotional life does not preclude familial bonds with wives, husbands, and children. In fact, both Judaism and Islam strongly oppose celibacy and monasticism; whereas in Christianity, celibacy is an integral practice of its purest and most pious devotees.

Christianity has revered celibate figures from the beginning. Early Christians relied upon the lives of both Jesus and John the Baptist as examples of a pure celibate existence. Although Jesus did not call attention to his own celibacy, Christians used his example as a basis for their high regard of the practice. Furthermore, the virginity of Jesus's mother Mary heightened the significance of celibacy for early Christians. The apostle Paul's missionary works and writings after Jesus further stressed the importance of celibacy for the devout. From these examples early Christians found reason to equate celibacy with religious purity, even though the rule requiring celibacy for priests, nuns, and monks was not issued by the Roman Catholic Church until the Second Lateran Council held in 1139, and has been maintained since.

Celibacy was further bolstered by the belief that marriage and sexual relations resulted from the original sin of Adam and Eve, and is therefore tainted. Paul preached: "Now the body is not for fornication, but for the Lord; and the Lord for the body" (I Cor. 6:13). Not only is celibacy pure, but sex itself is wicked. Although all individuals could strive to live a good Christian life, only those who refrain from sexual intercourse are unblemished. As a result, celibate monks and nuns practiced the purest form of Christianity.

The body, then, was seen as a dangerous site of potential human sin, even if it is controlled through celibacy and other ascetic practices. Greek dualistic ideas of the split between soul and body were introduced into the Christian tradition in the second and third centuries, and further influenced the early Church Fathers' denigration of the body. By the fourth century, ascetic views and practices became a major trend in Christianity, and not just a short-term response of first-century Christians who awaited the imminent return of Jesus as Messiah.

In the five hundred years following the birth of Jesus, Christian philosophers and leaders such as St. Ignatius, Cyprian, Origen, Ambrose, Augustine, and John Chrysostom continued to extol celibacy and virginity, thereby solidifying its stature as a major tenet of the religion. Church Fathers Clement of Alexandria and Origen were influenced by the Stoics and their belief that asceticism purifies the soul. They explained that ascetic practices were necessary for demonstrating love of God. In Origen's writings, we find the value of asceticism as preparation for martyrdom. With regard to his personal life, it is told that Origen, followed Mt. 19:12 literally and castrated himself.

The monastic way of life was the consequence and embodiment of the ideals and practices of asceticism. These include separation from the world, solitude, silence, celibacy, poverty, fasts and vigils, bodily penitential practices, manual labor, life in community, and obedience to a superior. Although the Protestant Reformation of the sixteenth century altered the course of Christianity and ultimately removed the celibacy requirement for many Christian denominations, celibacy continues to be extolled in Catholicism.

The Desert Mothers

The Desert Mothers are an example of a group of Christian ascetics who, along with the Desert Fathers, dwelled in the deserts of Egypt during the early fourth through fifth centuries CE. The Desert Mothers practiced an extreme form of asceticism, working to "perfect" themselves and become like the angels, who do not have sexual relations, eat, sleep, bathe, or concern themselves with bodily comforts.

Some of the Desert Mothers were widows who embraced chastity and the contemplative life after the death of their spouses, but others were penitent prostitutes. These women wished to perfect themselves by going into the wilderness to pray, contemplate, and wrestle demons as Jesus had done, as reported in the Gospel of Mk. 11:12-13. Many of these women wished to fulfill the promise in the New Testament that in Jesus there is "no woman nor man" (Gal. 3:28).

The fasting practiced by the Desert Mothers caused profound changes in their bodies. Their breasts shrank, their faces and bodies became gaunt, and their menstrual cycles ceased. As a result, the appearance of many of these women was indistinguishable from men. Among the motivations for the Desert Mothers to shed their overtly feminine appearance was to escape societal penalties for femininity, as well as to reconfigure their physical forms to more closely resemble the presumed androgyny of the first human Adam, before the fall.

The title of Desert Mother, or "amma," (or abba, in the case of a Desert Father) was an honorific given to spiritual authorities. Christians, both male and female, sought the spiritual guidance of these ascetics in the desert wilderness, and by embracing this rigorous lifestyle, a woman might achieve a position of honor and authority that would not otherwise be available to her in the world of the late Roman Empire.

There was no formal organization among the Desert Mothers and Fathers; these were not ordained priests or nuns, but lay individuals seeking spiritual fulfillment. As the fourth century continued, however, groups of ascetic women and men formed spiritual communities, separated by gender, and these eventually became monasteries. By the middle of the fifth century CE, the period of the Desert Mothers and Fathers was over, and monasteries became the dominant venue of dedicated Christian spiritual life.

Asceticism in the Medieval period

In the Middle Ages, there was a growing devotion to the humanity of Christ, especially to his suffering, also known as The Passion (from the Latin, *patior*— "to suffer"). As St. Paul says in his letter to the Colossians: "Now I rejoice in my sufferings for your sake" (Col. 1:24). The spiritual path of Christian adepts was embodied in a penitential attitude and a pessimistic view of life. Extreme forms of asceticism were implemented, manifesting the desire to reenact the sufferings of Christ. Penitential and devotional asceticism became popularized, and included mortification of the flesh in the forms of flagellations and the wearing of chains. Mortification of the flesh is an act by which an individual seeks to mortify, or put to death their sins, as part of the process of sanctification. Considered an element of the mortification of the flesh, flagellation was a common practice in Christian religious orders in the past, done to reenact the suffering of Jesus prior to his crucifixion. Christian monks and nuns who chose such extreme forms of asceticism interpreted Christ's pain in a literal way, whipping themselves in order to personally experience a degree of his suffering.

In contrast with practices of self-inflicted pain, the miracle of the stigmata— the miraculous appearance of body marks, blood, sores, or sensations of pain in the hands, wrists, and feet—was and continues to be a uniquely Christian example of rendering sacred pain and suffering. The stigmata wounds,

FIGURE 11.1 *Ecstasy of St. Francis, the seventeenth century. Credit: RwGSW85y8rlqsg at Google Cultural Institute, via Wikimedia.*

corresponding to the crucifixion wounds of Jesus Christ, were popular in the medieval period, with St. Francis of Assisi being the first recorded stigmatic in Christian history. It is believed that the stigmata are bestowed on the bodies of pious Catholic saints, the great majority of whom are women. It enables the saint to suffer in union with Jesus, thus participating in Christ's act of redemption.

In addition to the phenomenon of monastic life, the Medieval period also saw an explosion of ordinary laywomen who chose to embrace a strict religious life characterized by tireless service and a penitential asceticism. In Northern France and the Lowlands, women known as *beguines* formed sisterhoods, wherein they lived austere, chaste lives set apart from the world, devoting themselves to prayer and the care of the sick and the poor. Most supported themselves with occupations such as weaving and dyeing, although some had family money. Interestingly, they had no formal ties to a monastic order, took no vows, and were often viewed with suspicion by the Church. Certain women in southern Europe, known as *tertiaries*, also embraced a life of penitential asceticism along with prayer and charitable works. But unlike their *beguine* sisters, allied themselves with a religious order such as the Franciscans or the Dominicans. In Northern England and the Lowlands, women called *anchorites* elected to leave their families and all their worldly possessions, and upon celebrating a rite of consecration, which in effect was a funeral rite declaring them dead to the world and reborn to a life in spirit, dwelled enclosed in a tiny cell attached to the village church. There they lived the remainder of their lives in solitude and contemplative prayer, and were often sought out for spiritual advice.

In the very early Church, but especially in the Medieval Church, it was believed that a life of penitential asceticism could purify one's soul and thereby realize redemption, transformation, protection, transcendence, and a sacred union with the divine. Thus, despite the fact that practices such as fasting sometimes led to illness and starvation, prayerful vigils to extreme sleep deprivation, and isolation to seeming madness, a significant number of women in the Middle Ages embraced the ascetic path.

The Sacrament of Penance

Penance is an act of self-abasement, mortification, or devotion either voluntarily performed to show sorrow or repentance for sin, or imposed as a punishment for sin by a church official. It is also a sacrament in the Roman Catholic and Eastern Churches, consisting of repentance and contrition for sin, confession to a priest, satisfaction as imposed by the confessor, and, ultimately, absolution.

In 1215, the Fourth Lateran Council led by Pope Innocent III formally declared penance a sacrament of the Catholic Church, and made private confession mandatory once a year, generally during the season of Lent. One either complied with this rule or risked excommunication, which was a grave punishment. Penance, along with the Church's renewed emphasis on original sin and emulation of Christ's suffering, all of which emphasized human weakness and fallen state, created a climate rife with self-doubt and uncertainty, out of which emerged a deep yearning for the divine and for a place in God's kingdom.

With the newly mandated Sacrament of Penance now joined with the Sacrament of the Eucharist, membership in Christ's Church became the purview of church officials. What used to be a ritual of public confession in the Church, by the sixth century evolved into a private confession. Over the next five centuries, the practice of confessing into the ear of a confessor spread throughout Christendom, and along with it, punitive measures that included sleep deprivation, fasts, and isolation.

The implications of the penitential rite for women were profound, since they were deemed responsible for the fall of man through original sin, and thus remained at the base of the medieval world's social hierarchy. While early

Christians embraced fasting as a purification ritual intended to prepare the body and soul to receive Christ, late medieval Christians, especially women, strove to imitate Christ's suffering through their own self-inflicted pain. To share in Christ's suffering was to be one with him. Consequently, an alarming number of women embraced fasting practices so extreme that historian Rudolph Bell's referred to their condition as "Holy Anorexia," which may be interpreted as a response to social structural factors and the patriarchalism of medieval Catholicism. Feminist scholars argue that these women were using one of the few tools they had—food—to affect control of an otherwise powerless existence.

Confession, the Sacrament of Penance, is largely ignored by young Catholics today. According to a recent study, only about 2 percent of Catholics in the United States go to confession regularly while three quarters of them never go, or go less than once a year. In Europe, the numbers have declined so much that groups who study Catholic practice have stopped even asking about it on their questionnaires. Fifty years ago, the majority of Catholics privately confessed their sins to a priest as they awaited spiritual direction and sought absolution. Protestant views of confession are quite different insofar as they believe that no intermediary is necessary between the individual and God in order to be absolved from sins. Accordingly, many mainstream

FIGURE 11.2 *Pope Francis confesses during the penitential celebration in St. Peter's Basilica at the Vatican City, on March 4, 2016. Credit: MAX ROSSI / Stringer, via Getty Images.*

Protestant Churches include a public and corporate confessional prayer in regular worship.

Asceticism in Jainism

Jainism has a tradition of ascetic practices that is central to the religion. The ultimate goal of Jain ascetic practices is to eliminate attachment to the flesh in order to achieve *moksha,* liberating the soul from bodily existence by escaping from the cycle of birth, death, and rebirth known as *samsara.* The concept of *ahimsa* (nonviolence) guides all of the actions and thoughts carried out by Jains, especially by monks and nuns. Jains recognize the souls of all living beings—plants as well as animals and humans. Thus, nuns and monks walk mindfully and avoid causing harm to any living being by, for instance, accidentally stepping on a blade of grass or an insect. Their teachings and practices of nonviolence have influenced numerous Indian spiritual and political leaders, including Mahatma Gandhi, whose leadership of India's independence movement incorporated Jain ideals.

The Digambara (naked or "skyclad"), whose male ascetics shun all property, do not admit women into their order and are always naked. The Shvetambara (White-robed" or "White-clad") ascetic is allowed to have fourteen possessions including loin-cloth and shoulder-cloth, but the Digambara ascetic

FIGURE 11.3 *A skyclad Jain monk and a Jain nun in India, November 2004.*

is allowed only two possessions (the *pichhi,* a peacock-feather whisk-broom) and a *kamandalu* (a wooden water-pot).

In accordance with their practice of nonviolence, all Jain monks and nuns use a broom to clear their path of insects to avoid trampling them. Ascetic practices for Jain monks and nuns include celibacy, limited food intake, fasting, rejecting possessions, and contemplative and meditative practices. In addition to denial of material comforts, Jain ascetics practice non-attachment, learning to let go of relationships such as family. Their practices are aimed at letting go of physical pleasures and negative emotions, as well as their attachment to their body. This includes *santhara* or *sallekhana*—starving unto death when old or terminally ill, whereby they gradually withdraw from all physical needs including food and drink in an effort to minimize the accumulation of karma which would impact their rebirth.

Head shaving is often connected with an ascetic lifestyle. The shaving of hair becomes a symbolic giving up of a previous way of life and a renunciation of worldly desires. For Jain and Buddhist nuns, shaving the

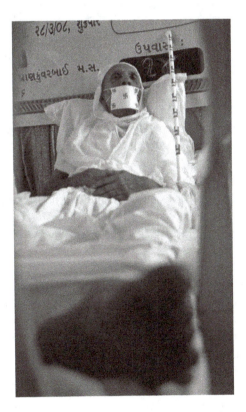

FIGURE 11.4 *A Jain nun practicing* santhara *at an* upashray *(Jain ashram) in Mumbai, on April 6, 2008. Credit: PAL PILLAI / Stringer, via Getty Images.*

FIGURE 11.5 *Yudit Greenberg with Jain nuns in Allahabad, India, on their three-year walk to impart their teachings of nonviolence, February 2015. Courtesy of David Greenberg.*

head signifies rejection of sexual desires, as well as symbolic renunciation of family life, and a dedication to chastity and a single-minded pursuit of spiritual enlightenment.

While both Jain and Buddhist nuns shave their heads, Jains also have the optional practice of hair removal by plucking hairs from the scalp rather than simply cutting or shaving them. Through these rituals, practitioners both outwardly and inwardly display their devotion and religious status to the community by embodying one of their core principles of detachment from desires and the physical form.

Among Jain ascetics, there is a large population of nuns and other women practitioners. Similar to the social structure in Hindu and Buddhist societies, lay people are called "householders," raising families and supporting the material needs of the monastic community. Lay Jains generally adhere to a strict vegetarian diet, and practice their rituals at temples. It is a great honor for them to share their meals with local monks and nuns. They believe that their support of nuns and monks who have taken the sacred vows, helps to mitigate some of their own karmic burden, enabling them to pursue the ascetic path in the next life with the opportunity to achieve spiritual liberation.

Buddhist asceticism

During the time of the Buddha, between the sixth and fifth centuries BCE, there were a variety of ascetic groups who strove to attain liberation employing extreme forms of self-mortification, including rejecting clothes and wandering naked, and eating once a week. Early in his life, it is reported that the Buddha was influenced by such trends, and adopted extreme forms of asceticism in his search for liberation and enlightenment. Later in his life, he came to realize that neither extreme self-mortification nor extreme sensual indulgence is the appropriate means toward spiritual realization. Rather, he taught his disciples that instead of such extremes, which did not lead to his enlightenment, they should cultivate self-discipline and self-control through the "eightfold path:" right views, intention, speech, action, livelihood, effort, mindfulness, and concentration; this is what he termed, "the middle path," a path which lies between the two extremes.

For monks and nuns who are intent on achieving nirvana and are capable of a more intense spiritual regimen, he specified additional techniques as elaborated in Theravada canonical texts and referred to as *dhutanga* (literally, shaking off defilements; renunciation). During Theravada ordination ceremonies, the newly ordained monk or nun is taught the four *nissaya* ("resorts"), practices that originated at the time of the Buddha: begging for alms, wearing recycled robes, dwelling at the foot of a tree, and using fermented cow urine as medicine. *Dhutanga,* consisting of thirteen practices, is considered the foremost ascetic path in Buddhism, setting the boundaries between what is accepted and other more extreme forms of self-mortifications that were practiced in earlier times. While directed toward monks, the rigorous practices of *dhutanga* are additional to the austerities of ordinary monastic life.

Although not compulsory, *dhutanga* serves to define the limits of asceticism, and are intended for adepts who wish to address their deepest attachments, for example food, sleep, or comfort. It includes wearing recycled patchwork robes, possessing only three robes, seeking alms, not excluding any house while begging for alms, eating at one sitting, eating only from the alms-bowl, refusing all further food, living in the forest, living under a tree, living in the open air, living in a cemetery, being satisfied with any humble dwelling, and sleeping in the sitting position (without ever lying down). Adopting these enables the adept to reduce one's physical needs and helps rid oneself of pride, greed, and aversion, which constitute the main poisons on the path to liberation. Furthermore, ascetic practices help in the cultivation of positive feelings such as love, compassion, equanimity, mental purity, and the happiness found in being attentive to and bringing happiness to others. Mahayana Buddhists follow Theravada ascetic practices which are called in their tradition, *dhutaguna*, with minor modification regarding food and wool clothing. Despite the Buddha's teachings of moderation or the middle path, in many Buddhist cultural contexts, it is the most ascetic individual who is the most revered.

The ascetic practices as prescribed in Buddhist teachings do not define the spiritual path, but rather, prepare the seeker to eliminate all forms of attachment. The purpose of cultivating ascetic practices in Buddhism is not to subjugate the body to unnecessary suffering, but to improve one's meditation abilities aimed toward the abolition of *dukkha*, or suffering, as well as attaining nirvana. What enables Buddhist adepts in their pursuit of enlightenment is the structure of the monastic life, which offers them a regulated life of study, meditation, and self-discipline in the company of other monks or nuns, similar to the monastic lifestyle pursued in other religious traditions.

When reviewing the intentions and practices of spiritual adepts across religions and cultures, we find a number of similarities regarding practices such as celibacy, fasting, and poverty. We note from their scriptures, and from hagiographies of their founders, that they adopted or recommended a path of renunciation. While the vows and practices of celibacy, fasting, and poverty are common to renunciants in Christianity, Jainism, and Buddhism, the motives and telos underscoring these radical forms of spirituality are different.

The purpose of ascetic practices in Buddhism and Jainism is to achieve detachment from the physical world so that the adept can be free of distraction that would prevent them from achieving enlightenment. Whereas for Christians, the purpose of ascetic practices is to do penance for one's evil body and emulate Christ's suffering, in order to purify their body and soul for the reward of joining with Christ in the afterlife.

Asceticism in Zoroastrianism, Judaism, and Islam

Asceticism has not been accepted by all traditions as a mark of spiritual excellence. In fact, as a lifestyle of renunciation of the body, it is looked upon with suspicion in religions such as Zoroastrianism, Judaism, and Islam, traditions that affirm the goodness of creation and physical pleasures within their ethical frameworks. While all three religions identify physical pleasure with divine blessings, Zoroastrianism in particular denounces asceticism and opposes ascetic tendencies that inflict pain and suffering upon the body, and practices such as celibacy and fasting.

While these traditions provide strict rules of purity and impurity, these rules are not intended to proscribe physical pleasures; rather, purity laws contribute to social order and cohesion. In Zoroastrianism, eliminating pollution and restoring purity are also seen as part of the cosmic struggle against evil. Yet such rules do not denounce the body, nor advocate for asceticism as a disciplinary action against the body. In comparing Zoroastrian, Jewish, and Muslim attitudes toward asceticism, a common practice for all three religions is their acceptance and even preference for their clergy to be married. They view marriage as an important institution, which in no way interferes with one's spiritual growth, even for their spiritual leaders. Zoroastrian teachings explicitly reject ascetic practices and do not attribute any spiritual benefits to them; quite the contrary, fasting and celibacy are seen as antagonistic to their life-affirming beliefs.

In ancient Judaism, there was an ascetic practice for the Nazirite (one who is "consecrated"). The vow of the Nazirite required abstaining from wine, vinegar, grapes, and raisins, and to refrain from cutting one's hair and/or beard. However, this practice ended after the biblical period. An early Jewish group in ancient Israel—the Essenes, which were later known as the Dead Sea Sect— separated themselves from the rest of the Jews by living in isolation in the desert, embracing celibacy and following a strict regimen of purification rituals and restricted diet.

The Jewish calendar includes six designated fasting days that serve as rites of penance and mourning. These include Yom Kippur, the Day of Atonement, in which Jews observe a twenty-five hour fast as part of the High Holidays rituals, and Tisha B'Av, which commemorates the destruction of the First and Second Temples. Despite rabbinic aversion to extreme forms of self-mortification and self-denial, some medieval pietists and Kabbalists followed rigorous ascetic practices such as fasting. Some Kabbalists believed that ascetic practices could help hasten the messianic era, and therefore they spent the entire week fasting, rendering only the Sabbath a day of comfort and joy. While in certain times and contexts, Jewish thinkers have endorsed ascetic practices, Jewish attitudes and teachings in general accept moderation and balance over acts of renunciation.

The key figures of Islam and Judaism integrated spirituality with family life. Abraham and Moses, the two most significant figures of Judaism, were both husbands and fathers. The central figure of Islam, Muhammad, was also a husband and father. In addition, the early key religious women of Islam were wives and mothers, not virgins or celibate ascetics, which provides highly religious Islamic women a spiritual exemplar on the basis of family life.

Despite its rejection of celibacy, we can identify ascetic practices in Islam. In the Shia Islamic tradition, asceticism is expressed in flagellation performed in parades every year to commemorate the martyrdom of Imam Hussein, the grandson of the prophet Muhammad. While many hit themselves on the chest, in some countries, flagellation is done using chains and knives.

FIGURE 11.6 *Shiite Muslims taking part in a self-flagellation ritual to mark the festival of Ashura in Delhi. Credit: Daniel Berehulak / Staff, via Getty Images.*

The month-long fasting of Ramadan, one of the five pillars of Islam, requires complete abstention from food, drink, sexual intercourse, and smoking from the break of dawn until sunset during the entire month. The Qur'an explains that this "fast is prescribed to you . . . that you many learn piety and righteousness" (2:183). In addition to normative Islamic prayers and Ramadan, the early Sufis also emphasized ascetic practices as part of their path toward union with Allah. The very name of this mystical movement refers to the rough woolen robe worn by them. An ascetic life for the early Sufis included introspection and meditative practices, fasting, the denial of luxury, and for some, withdrawing from the world. By the ninth century, there was a shift away from a life centered around austerities, to the belief that exemplification of divine love is superior to all other practices. This new focus helped popularize Sufism throughout the Muslim world.

Questions for review and discussion:

1 What made a life of suffering so appealing to women in the medieval period?

2   What role did the doctrine of "original sin" play in shaping gender roles in the Church?

3   Does the medieval penchant for embodied suffering have relevance for Christians today?

4   Does the Sacrament of Penance still have relevance in contemporary society?

5   Why is Penance accompanied by bodily punishments?

6   How do the aims of ascetic practices of Jains and Buddhists differ from those of Christians?

7   Is it easier for women to maintain their vows of celibacy? Why or why not?

8   Illustrate how the concept "mind-body dualism" (see Introduction) is represented in religious views and practices of asceticism. Why have women been identified with the body, in contrast with men who have been identified with the mind?

9   Is the Jain vow and practice of *sallekhana* in alignment with their dedication to nonviolence? Why or why not?

10   Should rules developed in ancient times still apply to modern life?

1, 3, 5, 6, 8, 10

Glossary

Anchorites-Christian hermits who withdrew from society. This ascetic practice which entailed living in cells that were attached to churches, became widespread in Europe during the Middle Ages.

Beguines-lay Christian women in the thirteenth century who expressed their religious devotion through ascetic practices such as poverty and caring of the poor and sick.

Celibacy-the state of abstaining from marriage and sex for spiritual reasons; officially taking a vow as part of the requirement for membership in a monastic community.

Digambara-one of two major sects in Jainism whose members are men who shun clothes and are therefore always naked. It is distinguished by its extreme ascetic practices, including shunning all worldly possessions, limited intake of food, and fasting.

Essenes-ascetic Jewish groups in Palestine, also known as the Dead Sea community from the second century BCE to the first century CE. Sharing a belief in the imminent coming of the messiah, its members withdrew from conventional life, many became celibate, and all adhered to a strict regimen of purity practices and fasting.

Nazirite-a person who took a vow of abstinence from alcohol, cutting hair, and touching a corpse to dedicate himself to God. This was practiced in ancient Israel.

The Passion-in Christianity, refers to the sufferings of Christ. Recitations of the Passion narratives from the Gospel of Mark are performed during Holy Week.

Penance-an act of repentance or punishment, either self-imposed or ordered by a Church authority; considered a sacrament by the Roman Catholic, Eastern Orthodox, and Anglican Churches.

*Santhara-*a Jain ascetic practice of gradual withdrawal of food and drink when one is old or terminally ill; considered to be a nonviolent process of dying with the aim of minimizing one's accumulation of karma.

Shvetambara-a major sect in Jainism whose monks and nuns wear white garments. Their ascetic practices include celibacy, fasting, and meditation.

Stigmata-the miraculous appearance of body marks, blood, and sores that correspond to the crucifixion wounds on Christ's body. Were believed to be received by Christian saints and were particularly popular in the medieval period.

Telos-an ultimate object or aim.

Cost of the death through burial falls on the living
↳ economic aspect

Muslims will never cremate →
Body needs to be intact for day of judgement

Cremation
↳ not available for Muslims

Honoring the human body
↳ why

Practices continue to change
↳ cremation
Hinduism (purity and pollution)

Death = polluted nature

Fire → purifyer

Death and the Afterlife

In this chapter, we will reevaluate the link between our physical bodies and our spiritual goals in light of the experience of death and our beliefs in the afterlife. We will clarify religious and ethical world views in our examination of burial and cremation practices. These include the sacredness of the body and the environment, notions of purity, as well as beliefs in physical resurrection (Zoroastrianism and the Abrahamic religions), or the view that human bodies are temporary vessels for souls (Hindu, Jain, and Buddhist religions). We will also address indigenous beliefs in the spiritual power that the deceased exert on their families, and the rituals that express awe and veneration for their ancestors. We then turn to other beliefs in the afterlife, exploring notions of heaven and hell as well as notions of reincarnation and the cessation of physical existence. Finally, we will review contemporary issues related to death, such as the controversy and debate regarding assisted suicide, and the increasing popularity of cremation around the world.

Concern for the body after death is an essential tenet in many religions that can be traced to ancient times. The importance of a proper burial is the central point in the ancient Greek play *Antigone,* written by Sophocles over four centuries before the birth of Jesus. Antigone defies King Creon's order denying her brother proper burial rites after he dies in a battle against the king. Although her defiance will result in her own death sentence, Antigone believes that only through the proper burial rites will her brother be able to enter the underworld. This conflict between Antigone and King Creon over burial rites sets the framework for this tragic play.

In the Abrahamic religious traditions (Judaism, Christianity, and Islam), the customary means of disposal of the human body for thousands of years has been the physical burial of a corpse in the earth. For Hindus and Buddhists, however, cremation is typically preferred. Followers of the Persian religion, Zoroastrianism, on the other hand, reject both burial in the ground and cremation; for them, the only accepted way is "sky burial," exposing the

FIGURE 12.1 *Zoroastrian Tower of Silence, Yazd, Iran, Middle East, Ggia, via Wikimedia.*

corpse for the purposes of excarnation, (or the removal of the flesh by vultures or wild animals) by using the *dakhma* ("tower of silence"). This practice stems from their notions of purity and pollution.

Beliefs about the afterlife of the soul or eschatology vary greatly. In some religions such as Catholicism, doctrines about heaven and hell are required to be accepted by believers (catechisms). In other traditions such as Judaism, textual representations of the afterlife of the soul are not doctrinal or particularly systematic. Beliefs about the afterlife can also be linked to cultural and philosophical notions of cosmic time. Accordingly, in traditions such as Judaism, Christianity, and Islam, cosmic time is conceived of in linear terms; for Eastern traditions such as Hinduism and Buddhism that believe in reincarnation, time is cyclical. The Buddhist and Hindu understanding of rebirth contrasts sharply with Jewish and Christian understanding of resurrection. Whereas in the Abrahamic religions, an individual's resurrection is in the original body, Hinduism and Buddhism believe that rebirth occurs in a new body or form, depending upon one's karma.

Judaism

Burial

In Judaism, respect for the physical body is paramount and this precept extends beyond life. The body of the deceased is traditionally washed before burial. The custom of washing the corpse is based on Mishnah Shabbat 23:5 which specifies what duties to the corpse may be performed on the Sabbath: "one may do all that is necessary to a corpse on the Sabbath (anoint and wash), provided one does not move the limbs." A more elaborate rite of purification is performed by some Jews based on Ecclesiastes 5:15 "as he came so shall he go," with the belief that a person is bathed at birth and should be bathed at death. This purification entails laying the corpse on a flat board while water is poured over it. The body must be buried completely free of any jewelry. The corpse is dressed in linen shrouds that resemble the garments worn by the priests in the ancient Temple (Exod. 28:40-43).

Due to the high level of respect for the physical body in Judaism, autopsies are discouraged, unless they are required by law. This respect for the corpse also requires that the corpse be buried, not cremated, which would be a desecration of the body. Deuteronomy 34:6 is often cited as a precedent for burial: "God buried him [Moses]." Since the body of an important prophet such as Moses was buried, burial has been adopted as the required method. Genesis 3:19 is also cited as an argument for burial: "In the sweat of your face shall you eat bread, till you return unto the ground; for out of it were you taken; for dust you are, and unto dust shall you return."

When it comes to the actual burial, interment generally takes place as soon as possible after death and without embalming. Deuteronomy 21:23-24 is often cited as a source for the tradition of a quick burial, even though this text is specifically about the burial of a criminal who was hung from a tree. The timing for a burial is swift, often the day of death. Corpses are typically buried in plain wooden caskets. Wood decomposes and therefore does not prevent the body itself from returning to the earth. In Israel today, many are buried without a coffin or casket. Outside of Israel, a small packet of earth from Israel is spread inside the coffin.

Cremation is specifically prohibited by Jewish law. In the Hebrew Bible, cremation was designated only for criminals. Leviticus 20:14 speaks of burning the wicked: "and if a man take with his wife also her mother, it is wickedness: they shall be burnt with fire, both he and they; that there be no wickedness among you."

Mourning

The rituals of mourning begin immediately after the burial. The *shivah* (Hebrew: seven) is the seven days of mourning for the immediate family members. The mourners stay at home for the duration of the seven days; traditionally, extended family and community members provide them with meals. Customs include sitting on low chairs or even on the floor and reciting prayers for the dead. It is a great *mitzvah* (good deed) to visit a mourner's home. A traditional way of approaching the mourner during *shivah* is with the saying, "May God console you, together with all mourners of Zion and Jerusalem." The second stage of mourning is called *shloshim* (thirty days) during which time a mourner may not marry; men do not shave or cut their hair during the thirty days. Those mourning a parent also observe a twelve-month period counted from the day of death. During this period, the mourners continue to recite the mourner's kaddish (prayer) as part of the synagogue services. Often Orthodox Jews will refrain from attending festive occasions where music is performed.

The afterlife and resurrection

There is no direct reference in the Torah to the afterlife. This could have been a result of knowing of, and desiring to distinguish themselves from, Egyptians' obsession with the afterlife. The metaphors of bones of the dead in Ezek. 37:1-14 and Isa. 26:19 are often understood symbolically as referring to the restoration of the exiled community. The dead are often described as residing in *sheol* which refers primarily to the grave. In rabbinic literature, the notion of gehenna is introduced, as a temporary place where the wicked are punished. While somewhat rectified in rabbinic Jewish writings, the remarkable silence on this subject contrasts with the New Testament and the Qur'an where there are explicit doctrines of heaven and hell. The period referred to by the phrase *olam ha-ba* (the world-to-come) begins with the resurrection and the beginning of the messianic era. In the Talmud, there is a humorous story about Moses teaching Torah all day; for the righteous people, this is heaven; for the evil ones, it is hell.

Although the Jewish tradition, especially the Bible, generally places more emphasis on life rather than the afterlife, rabbinic Judaism accentuated the belief in resurrection. In the Middle Ages, rabbi and philosopher Moses Maimonides summarized the beliefs of the Torah and the Talmud in his Thirteen Principles of Faith, with his final principle being the belief in the resurrection of the dead which is juxtaposed with the belief in the messiah. Also, the belief in resurrection entails the idea that body and soul are a single entity, both essential to the notion of a human being. A rabbinic parable makes this point quite clear:

Antoninus said to Rabbi, "The body and soul could exonerate themselves from judgment. How is this so? The body says, 'The soul sinned, for from the day that it separated from me, lo, I am like a silent stone in the grave!' And the soul says, 'The body is the sinner, for from the day that I separated from it, lo, I fly in the air like a bird.'" He answered him, "I will tell you a parable. To what is the matter likened? To a king of flesh and blood who had a beautiful orchard and there were in it lovely ripe fruit, and he placed two guardians over it, one a cripple and the other blind. Said the cripple to the blind man, 'I see beautiful ripe fruit in the orchard. Come and carry me and we will bring and eat them.' The cripple rode on the back of the blind man and they brought and ate them. After a while the owner of the orchard came and said to them, 'Where is my lovely fruit?' The cripple answered, 'Do I have legs to go?' Answered the blind man, 'Do I have eyes to see?' What did he do? He placed the cripple on the back of the blind man and judged them as one—so also the Holy Blessed One brings the soul and throws it into the body and judges them as one" (San. 91a–b).

Jewish daily prayer includes the belief in the resurrection of the dead and informs the burial society's scrupulous attention to burying the body intact, in expectation of resurrection in the messianic era.

Christianity

Burial and mourning

The Christian tradition of burial is founded upon the Jewish tradition at the time of Jesus and the evolving belief in resurrection. As Jews of the first century BCE buried their dead, the early Christians continued to follow similar practices. Narratives such as the burial of Moses, the text of Leviticus in which the wicked alone are "burnt with fire," and the reference to returning to dust in Gen. 3:19 provide textual justifications for burial.

Furthermore, Jesus himself was buried in a tomb, solidifying the burial tradition for Christians. In the New Testament, Lk. 23:52-53 states that after Jesus died, "this man went to Pilate and asked for the body of Jesus. Then he took it down and wrapped it in a linen shroud, and laid him in a rock-hewn tomb." The same is reported in Mt. 27:58-60, Mk 15:42-46, and Jn 19:38-42. The gospel of John specifically notes that, "they took the body of Jesus, and bound it in linen clothes with the spices, as the burial custom of the Jews" (Jn 19:40). Each of these gospels sets forth the burial precedent for Christians.

After death, Christians observe a variety of rituals, depending on one's denomination and country. An important ritual practiced by both Catholics and Protestants is the "visitation" (also known as the wake), the custom of viewing the body of the dead which is placed in a casket. The wake is often held at funeral homes a day or two days prior to a funeral. Christians also practice embalming, especially in preparation for the wake. Embalming the body involves removing of bodily fluids and applying formaldehyde-based chemical solutions that will delay the decomposition of the body. The body is then cosmetically prepared for viewing by styling the hair, applying makeup, and setting the facial features. The practice of burial after death for Christians includes prayers at the church and the graveside. The Catholic observances consist of the Funeral Mass led by a priest, who also presents a statement of committal of the body back to the earth, and concludes with a prayer. Protestant Christians do not have a prescribed period of mourning. Generally, the period of time from the death to the burial is considered the time of mourning. For Catholics, the period of mourning is dependent upon one's relationship to the deceased, and is manifested, among other things in the black clothing one wears during the heavy period, which is the first thirty days after death. For all family members, the first thirty days after death are considered the heavy mourning period. After that time, spouses are expected to mourn for additional eleven months; parents or children spend six months and siblings are expected to spend three months in mourning following the initial thirty days. Other family members are expected to spend thirty days in mourning.

FIGURE 12.2 *(a) Day of the Dead, Oaxaca, Mexico, November 2, 2015. Courtesy of Carolina Castaneda (b) Day of the Dead, Oaxaca, Mexico, November 2, 2015. Courtesy of Carolina Castaneda.*

Resurrection

Of utmost importance, however, for the practice of burial is the belief in physical resurrection. Upon Jesus's resurrection, he is manifest in his earthly body. "The Lord has risen in deed, and has appeared to Simon" (Lk. 24:34). The resurrected Jesus is not merely a spirit, but a physical being who walks and eats (Lk. 24:39-43; Jn 20:26-28; Mt. 28:8-10). Had his body been cremated or otherwise destroyed, this physical resurrection would be problematic.

For individual adherents of Christianity, it is not only the resurrection of the body of Jesus that is important, but also the potential for one's own resurrection. In Lk. 7:11-17, a deceased man is miraculously returned to life by Jesus, and he sits up and speaks. In the Gospel of John, Lazarus is resurrected four days after he died (Jn 11:38-44). A young girl is raised from the dead in Mt. 9:18-25. These physical resurrections, like that of Jesus's resurrection, provide a compelling argument for the preservation of the physical body, in as much as possible.

Theological debate continues regarding resurrection in Christianity: Does resurrection occur with a physical human body or as a spirit in heaven? While most believe that Jesus's resurrection was through a physical human body, does this apply to others? The New Testament discusses resurrection as a spiritual process. In 1 Cor. 15:42-44, the resurrected body is a spiritual body: "So also is the resurrection of the dead. It is sown in corruption; it is raised in incorruption: It is sown in dishonor; it is raised in glory: it is sown in weakness; it is raised in power: It is sown a natural body; it is raised a spiritual body. There is a natural body, and there is a spiritual body." In the "Apostle's Creed," a fourth century declaration of Christian beliefs, Christians affirm: "I believe in . . . the resurrection of the body and the life everlasting." Today, most Christians believe that "life everlasting" refers to a life in heaven.

As early Christians embraced the tradition of burial, by the fourth century the practice of cremation generally ceased in the Roman Empire. Its status as a forbidden rite was strengthened in the year 789 when, in an effort to further distinguish Christianity from paganism, Charlemagne made cremation illegal.

In the centuries after Charlemagne, Christian acceptance of cremation came slowly. In the Middle Ages, some Christians argued for cremation, yet its acceptance was negligible. Whether it was for purposes of hygiene, convenience, or land preservation, cremation advocates slowly began to gain influence. With the age of industrialization and the growth of densely populated cities, the scarcity of suitable land for burial made cremation a more practical alternative. By the late 1800s, cremation was considered acceptable for Protestant Christians.

For Roman Catholics, the ban on cremation ended in 1963 under the revised Code of Canon Law. Under this revised law, cremation is permitted so long as it does not occur for reasons contrary to Christian faith. The 1983 Code of Canon Law (Book IV, Part II, Title III, Canon 1176) states: "The Church earnestly recommends that the pious custom of burying the bodies of the deceased be observed; nevertheless, the Church does not forbid cremation unless it has been chosen for reasons contrary to the Christian doctrine." In other words, although burial is still preferred, cremation is not forbidden. Previously, under the 1917 Canon Law, cremation was only permitted in times of plague or natural disaster when rapid disposal of bodies was a necessity.

Christians of the twenty-first century continue to wrestle with the concepts of physical and spiritual resurrection and consequently the debate regarding the appropriateness of burial or cremation persists.

Beliefs in purgatory

The doctrine of purgatory, while not explicit in the Bible, arises from the synthesis of three Catholic beliefs: (1) human beings are sinners, no matter how virtuous one tries to live, and so it can be assumed that most people will die with some unforgiven sins tainting their souls. (2) God is loving and merciful toward souls, and (3) God is just and would therefore make the punishment commensurate with the sin. Juxtaposed with the justification provided by biblical passages, Roman Catholic theologians inferred that there would be a "third place," aside from heaven and hell, in which the typical person, with the not-wholly-wicked-but-not-wholly-good soul, could go to suffer bodily torment until they are purged of the stain of their sins, and thus be purified to enter heaven. It did not seem just that an individual who had indulged in a minor sin, such as petty theft, would burn in hell forever next to a soul that had committed murder.

Among the many charges leveled against Roman Catholics by Protestants is that purgatory is a non-biblical destination for souls after death. Roman Catholics, however, defend the doctrine of purgatory using biblical verses, including verses from the Book of Maccabees. In 15:41-46, soldiers are exhorted to pray for forgiveness for the souls of their fallen comrades, several of whom had hidden idols in their clothes before battle. If there is no chance of changing the condition of the soul after death, why would anyone pray for the souls of the dead? The Book of Maccabees was extricated from the biblical canon for Protestants by Martin Luther, but it is part of the Latin Vulgate Roman Catholic Bible.

Both hell and purgatory use fire in their operations, but the fire in purgatory is meant to purge and cleanse souls of their sins. Souls subjected to the

FIGURE 12.3 *Souls in purgatory. Credit: BSIP / Contributor, via Getty Images.*

torment of purgatorial fire are believed to be grateful for this cleansing, because it is temporary, and a merciful God is cleansing and preparing them for everlasting life. The fires of hell, on the other hand, are only punitive; they will never end and the condition of the soul upon which it is inflicted will never change. There is a period of time in which the soul must burn in purgatory to be cleansed of its sins, depending on the number and severity of its sins. It is believed that prayers for the dead may be able to shorten this time in purgatory, and hasten the soul's entrance into heaven. Thus, it is the obligation of the living to pray for mercy on the souls of the dead, according to Catholic doctrine. The doctrine of purgatory still exists in the Catholic Church, but is currently far less a focus of spiritual practice. Catholics routinely request that prayers and masses be said for the dead, but it is rarely mentioned that the purpose of the prayer is to free a soul from purgatory.

Christian views on heaven

The goal of Christianity is eternity in heaven after death. The most complete description of heaven in the New Testament is found in Chapter 21 of the Book of Revelation, in which even the number of gates and the building materials are specified. Despite this description, there are varying interpretations among Christian denominations of what heaven is like. The single point of agreement between them is that heaven is not like the kitschy dwelling place of harp-wielding, toga-clad postmortem souls floating around on clouds that is so frequently depicted in popular culture.

The Roman Catholic view, as clarified by Pope John Paul II in 1999, is that heaven "is neither an abstraction nor a physical place in the clouds, but a living, personal relationship with the Holy Trinity. It is our meeting with the Father which takes place in the risen Christ through the communion of the Holy Spirit." This blissful union is the "heavenly reward" that the believer may attain after death, but only through the grace of God. Furthermore, the *Catechism of the Catholic Church* teaches that in addition to communion with the Trinity, in heaven the believer will be in the company of the Virgin Mary, the angels, and "all of the blessed." This will occur "when the form of this world has passed away." It emphasizes that heaven is a "state" of the incorporeal soul, not a physical place. It states that few details describing heaven are provided because words and human concepts cannot accurately describe the reality of heaven.

Protestant views of heaven are more varied, but the descriptions provided are short and general, similar to their Catholic counterparts. Some Protestants believe that souls in heaven will have celestial bodies, but others do not. Some Protestants believe that the soul of the dead will arrive in heaven immediately after death, and others believe that the soul will sleep until Judgment Day. The main point of almost all Protestant beliefs about heaven is that it is the place where the "justified" go after death, that they will be in the presence of Jesus Christ, and that there will be no pain or sadness. Protestants believe that there is nothing they can do to ensure their admittance into heaven other than to accept Jesus Christ as their savior.

Islam

Muslim view of treating the corpse with utmost respect is in keeping with the spirit of the Qur'anic verse, "We have honored sons of Adam" (Qur'an 17:70). Islamic practice therefore treats the human body with respect not only when a person is alive, but also when he or she is dead. Following Judaism and Christianity, early Muslims adopted the tradition of burial of corpses. One Hadith affirms the practice of burial: "The Prophet said 'bury them with their blood'." Burning the deceased or discarding bodies to be eaten by wild beasts is considered sacrilege and abhorrent and, therefore, forbidden. Similar to the Jewish tradition, the body is bathed and dressed in shrouds. If possible, burial occurs on the same day as the death. The body does not need to be buried in a coffin.

It is an obligation of the Muslims as a community to ensure that every Muslim who dies is properly washed, dressed in burial shrouds, and buried. Prayer for the deceased is performed after the body is dressed and before it is taken to the grave. The importance of partaking in the funeral is also advised in the following Hadith: "Visit the sick and walk with the Janazah (funeral), it will remind you of the hereafter." After the funeral, most family members observe a three-day mourning period. The widow however, has an extended mourning period of four months and ten days following the death of her husband, and generally stays at home during this period while family and friends take care of her basic needs.

Muslims believe that there will be a day of judgment when all humans will be divided between the eternal destinations of paradise and hell. On the last day, the world will be destroyed and Allah (God) will raise all people from the dead to be judged. Until the day of judgment, deceased souls remain in their graves awaiting the resurrection.

The resurrection that will take place on the last day is physical, as Allah will recreate the decayed body: "Could they not see that God who created the heavens and the earth is able to create the like of them?" (Qur'an 17:100). On the last day, resurrected humans and *jinn* (supernatural creatures) will be judged according to their deeds. One's eternal destination depends on balance of an individual's good to bad deeds. The person is either granted paradise, where they enjoy spiritual and physical pleasures forever, or condemned to hell to suffer spiritual and physical torment.

The Qur'an specifies that those who fight for God are ushered immediately into heaven; those who are enemies of Islam are sentenced immediately upon death to hell (2:159; 3:169). Heaven, or paradise (firdaws), also called "The Garden" (Janna), is a place of physical and spiritual pleasure, with lofty mansions, delicious food and drink, including wine, and virgin companions called *houris*.

Hell, or *Jahannam*, is mentioned frequently in the Qur'an. It has seven doors (39:71; 15:43) leading to a fiery crater of various levels, the lowest of which contains the tree Zaqqum and a cauldron of boiling pitch. The level of hell depends on the degree of offenses. Suffering is both physical and spiritual.

Hinduism

For Hindus, the physical body is dispensable after death and has no significance; therefore, there is no need to preserve it. Hindus generally cremate bodies within a day after death. Death is death of the body only, not of the soul. There are no monuments to the dead; one's ultimate destiny is in the future.

The soul is either reincarnated or merges with the Supreme Soul, thereby achieving *moksha* (liberation). In the Bhagavad Gita, we read about death and reincarnation:

> For one who has taken his birth, death is certain; and for one who is dead, birth is certain. Therefore, in the unavoidable discharge of your duty, you should not lament. This is the cycle of birth and death. . . . As the embodied soul continually passes, in this body, from boyhood to youth to old age, the soul similarly passes into another body at death. The self-realized soul is not bewildered by such a change (Chapter 2).

When death seems imminent, a priest is contacted, mantras are recited, and the body is commonly transferred to a grass mat on the floor. A small amount of water from the holy Ganges River is placed in the dying person's mouth. Traditionally, the body is washed by family members. A lit oil lamp, as well as a picture of the deceased's favorite deity, is kept by the deceased's head. For the *abhisegam* (holy bath), the body is washed in a mixture of milk, yogurt, *ghee* (clarified butter), and honey. The body may also be washed in purified water, and those washing recite mantras. After the washing is complete, the big toes are tied together, the hands are placed palm-to-palm in a position of prayer, and the body is wrapped in a plain white sheet. If the person who died was a married woman who died before her husband, she is dressed in red.

Hindus generally hold a brief wake before cremation. The body is displayed in a simple casket. *Vibuti* (ash) or *chandanam* (sandalwood) is applied to the forehead of a man, and turmeric is applied to the forehead of a woman. A garland of flowers is placed around the neck, and holy basil is placed in the casket. During the wake, family and friends gather around the casket and may recite hymns or mantras. The casket is then removed with the feet-end first and brought to the place of cremation.

The casket is carried on a stretcher and walked to the cremation site or transported in a vehicle. The family builds a pyre, places the body on the pyre, the eldest male relative circles the body three times, and the family stays until the body is entirely burned. The day after the cremation, the male relative returns to the cremation grounds to collect the ashes. The ashes are later scattered in the Ganges River, though other rivers are acceptable as well.

The cremation of the deceased marks the beginning of the mourning period, which lasts for thirteen days. During this time, the family of the deceased stays at home and receives visitors. An image of the deceased with a garland of flowers is displayed. Throughout the mourning period, a ritual called *preta karma* is performed, which prevents the spirit of the deceased from becoming a ghost by assisting it in obtaining a new body for reincarnation. One year after the death, the family will observe a memorial event called *sraddha*, which

FIGURE 12.4 *A cremation ceremony in Bali. Courtesy of Jenny Bisset.*

pays homage to the deceased. The event includes inviting brahmins and close friends to the home and providing them with an elaborate meal.

Buddhism

Buddhists, similarly to Hindus, relate to human bodies in a transitory manner. For Buddhists, individuals are reborn on earth in a recurring cycle of life and death and our current life on earth is just one phase of this cycle. They view the opportunity to be born as a human and live a life with purpose, as life should not be wasted. Yet, after this life is over, the body is of little or no importance; rebirth occurs in a new physical form.

In Tibetan Buddhism, monks and nuns are encouraged to contemplate and meditate on the dead body through their central practice, *Maranasati* (death awareness), in order to decrease attachment to it. Since the body is fragile, easy to injure and damage, and will inevitably grow old, suffer, and die, it is vital for Buddhist monks and nuns to recognize their own attachment to this transitory state. To that end, they often attend to the sick and the dying, both to help the person through the process of dying tranquilly and to contemplate the changes that occur as the corpse starts to putrefy. Additionally, Buddhist monks and nuns practice meditation on their own deaths and the state of their bodies after their soul has vacated.

The goal of contemplating suffering and dead bodies is not to deny the body's, but to realize the body's impermanence and constant change. It is believed that the sense of detachment engendered in such meditations will enable the person to experience the decay of the body with calmness, which is essential for future births. In order to die tranquilly, monks and nuns meditate on the stages of the death process, thereby rehearsing their own death. The *Maranasati* meditation includes chants and visualizations of the body from the top of the head to the skin, bones, and internal organs, through which the adept is able to view the body as a tool which must be given up with serenity at the time of death.

As with other religious traditions, the customs of the early leaders are adopted as part of the religious rites. Whereas Moses, Jesus, and Muhammad were buried, Shakyamuni Buddha (also known as Siddhartha Gautama) was cremated, and cremation remains the preferred method of disposing of the body.

This temporary nature of a human life and this cycle of rebirth render the physical body less important in Buddhist rituals for the dead. Still, rituals regarding the deceased often focus on efforts to ensure the dead person is not reborn into a depraved being such as a demon or ghost. There is no haste in the cremation process, and often cremation does not take place until four days after death, during which waiting period it is customary to read from the Bardo Thodol (Tibetan Book of the Dead).

Shinto views of death, funeral rituals, and ancestor worship

The *kami,* the divine entities worshipped in the Shinto faith, are believed to inhabit everything in the natural world, including human beings. Shinto beliefs hold that the *kami* are offended by death, and so funerals are not held in Shinto shrines. Japanese culture sees no conflict between Shinto beliefs and Buddhism, which arrived in Japan in the sixth century CE, and thus, Shinto funerals frequently include the Buddhist practice of cremation. The Shinto tradition contributes several rituals to ensure the comfort of the spirit of the deceased, such as a ritual to conduct the spirit to a temporary shrine and a ritual to purify the location of the funeral.

Rituals for the dead are repeated at ten-day intervals for the first fifty days after death, and then again one hundred days after death. Shinto practitioners believe that the spirits of the dead continue inhabiting the family home during the year following death. It is essentially a transition period, and at mealtime the spirit is offered food. When the year has passed, the spirit is transferred

FIGURE 12.5 *Glass Buddha altars are lit up in Koukokuji temple on July 7, 2016 in Tokyo, Japan. Credit: NurPhoto / Contributor, via Getty Images.*

to the family shrine and joins the spirits of the ancestors. The spirits of the deceased are invited back to the family home on the Festival of the Ancestors, during which the living entertain the dead.

When the spirits are not visiting the family home, they dwell with the *kami* in one of three "other worlds," which are located underground, beyond the sea, or in the mountains. These other worlds are much like the world that the living inhabit, and so the spirits of the dead can keep watch over their families so long as the living revere them by regularly holding festivals in their honor. The *kami* and the spirits of the ancestors can protect and bestow blessings on the family, provided they are worshipped.

Ancestor reverence in Confucianism

Rituals of ancestor worship are central to Confucianism, including elaborate funerals, preparing home and Temple altars, making offerings in honor of the deceased, partaking in annual rituals at the family cemetery, and the Ghost and Tomb Sweeping Festivals. It is believed that the afterlife is similar to the earthly life and therefore filial piety expressed during the life of one's parents should continue after their death. In fact, the Chinese word for filial piety, *xiao*, is the same as the word for mourning. After the funeral, Chinese families set up a home altar on which there is a portrait of the deceased and where daily offerings of fruits and vegetables are made. After the home altar is taken down, it is believed that the ancestors dwell in commemorative tablets, which are pieces of wood inscribed with the name and dates of the deceased. The daily home ritual consists of lighting incense in front of the tablets, while the Temple ritual also includes food offerings.

[handwritten: meaning and purpose of pain]
[handwritten: → negativity]
[handwritten: The way language changes views]

Contemporary issues and practices

[handwritten: community]
[handwritten: → wrong and sinful]

Assisted suicide

[handwritten: associated with sin]

[handwritten margin: → clear definition for death and 0-0-2 life?]

Life is seen as a gift to be treasured and to be lived meaningfully. A biblical teaching expresses this value of life: "I call heaven and earth to witness against you today, that I have set before you life and death, the blessing and the curse. So choose life in order that you may live, you and your descendants" (Deut. 30:19). This verse has been interpreted not only as choosing life over death but also as a calling to embrace a life of good deeds.

For most religions, suicide of any kind is considered wrong and sinful. In fact in Judaism, one who commits suicide is forbidden to be buried inside a Jewish cemetery. Nonetheless, assisted suicide is of considerable debate cross-culturally. Those in favor of assisted suicide argue that it fulfills religious duties for compassion and alleviates suffering. For those who support the right to choose, "Death with Dignity" or "compassionate choice" are preferred terms. "Death with Dignity" tends to refer to the movement as a whole. In the United States, the states of Oregon, Washington, Vermont, and California have passed "Death with Dignity" legislation. In order to be considered eligible for physician-assisted suicide in these states, one must be terminally ill and not expected to live beyond six months. After two oral and one written requests by the patient, the physician may write a prescription for the end-of-life medication that the patient may fill at the pharmacy after forty-eight hours. The cause of death on the death certificate will be listed as the illness that the individual was suffering from, not suicide, and therefore will not affect insurance benefits. As 2016 was an election year in the United States, nineteen states considered Death with Dignity laws during that election cycle. In Canada, following a 2015 Supreme Court decision that ruled that the right to die is a constitutional right, the Canadian Parliament passed Bill C-14 in June 2016. This bill ensures the right to die to Canadians suffering and approaching a "reasonably foreseeable death." Advocates of compassionate choice in Canada are outraged at the "reasonably foreseeable death" clause because

[handwritten margin: → emphasis of destiny and fate "playing God"]

[handwritten: Tension between human agency and will]

it excludes those suffering from incurable and excruciating illnesses, but who are not necessarily near death.

Christianity

All major Christian denominations, except the Presbyterian Church, reject assisted suicide based on the premise that all life is sacred and that the moment of death can only be determined by God. Bringing on death prematurely is viewed as a rejection of God's gift of life and a usurpation of God's power. To assist another in ending his or her life is considered murder. The Presbyterian Church has not yet issued an official position in regard to assisted suicide. While not permitted to terminate life, Catholics, Mormons, Seventh-day Adventists, Baptists, Episcopalians, and United Methodists do not face a religious obligation to continue medical treatment that only promises to minimally prolong life rather than provide a cure.

Judaism

Assisted suicide of any kind is unequivocally rejected based on the belief that human life belongs to God; it is not up to humans to decide when life ends. Jewish teachings state that even one minute of life is of infinite value, therefore, life should be extended as long as possible. Whether or not to prolong the death of a coma patient or an individual in a persistent vegetative state is a highly contentious issue. Some Orthodox rabbis reject the removal of nutrition and hydration from these patients, but will condone the removal of the respirator, claiming that the mark of life is breath, as God put his breath into Adam; if the patient cannot breathe on his or her own, this patient must be considered to be already dead.

Buddhism

Most Buddhists reject assisted suicide based on the belief that it is wrong to destroy life of any kind. However, Buddhism is a religion highly focused on the individual, so there are some Buddhists who believe that assisted suicide may be the most compassionate option. A Buddhist does have the right to reject end-of-life treatment if said treatment appears to be futile.

Islam

Assisted suicide is not permitted in Islam because of the belief in the sacredness of human life. Like Judaism and Christianity, Islam holds that only God has the right and the power to determine the time of death and the length of one's life. Additionally, Muslims believe that end-of-life suffering may be a way to test one's faith or atone for earlier sins, purifying oneself to meet God after death.

Hinduism

There is no unified teaching on assisted suicide in Hinduism, however Hindus believe in karma, leading many to believe that all suffering in this life is attributed to actions in the previous rebirths. Therefore, if someone prematurely ends life via assisted suicide in order to avoid suffering, they will inevitably have to face this suffering in a later life.

Jainism

Unique to Jainism is the practice of *santhara* or *sallekhana*. *Santhara*, fasting unto death, is a ritual in which an elderly person is allowed to choose the time of his or her own death, through the gradual elimination of food and water. Rather than being a taboo practice, Jains believe that *santhara* requires bravery as well as spiritual and physical will power. As in Hinduism, the belief in karma is one of the most important tenets of the Jain faith. The practice of fasting unto death is seen as a way to cleanse karma before death and positively influence the next rebirth.

Jains firmly assert that *santhara* is not an act of suicide. On August 10, 2015, the Rajasthan High Court in India, where the Jain faith developed and where the majority of its adherents still live, ruled to ban *santhara* on the grounds that it should be considered an act of suicide. Jains in India quickly mobilized and by the end of the month had earned back the right to continue the practice of *santhara*, after the Indian Supreme Court overturned the earlier ruling of the Rajasthan High Court.

Cremation and burial: Pragmatics versus tradition

Religious beliefs and rituals, even those dealing with death, can clash with pragmatic needs. From a biological perspective, the prompt disposal of a corpse may prevent the spread of disease. Decomposing bodies may contaminate water supplies, and corpses infected with communicable diseases such as hepatitis, HIV (the virus that causes AIDS), cholera, and Ebola can pass these diseases to the living. However, the hasty burial of a diseased body can conflict with religious practices. According to the New York Times in a December 2014 article "How Ebola Roared Back," the 2014 Ebola outbreak in Western African nations was made more difficult to contain due to burial practices. For many individuals in the infected regions, the practice of washing the bodies of the deceased is important so that they will have a dignified burial and a contented afterlife. Unfortunately, this practice helped spread the highly contagious Ebola virus. From a public health perspective, those combating disease must address the potential conflicts between religious practices, scientific information, and the need for potentially life-saving action.

The dramatic increase in the practice of cremation represents an important shift in Western views toward burial. While in Eastern religions such as Hinduism, Buddhism, Jainism, and Sikhism, cremation is the preferred method of disposing the body, this practice was rare in the West until recently. Since 1958, approximately 3 percent of Americans were cremated; today, the Cremation Association of North America is estimating that over 50 percent will be cremated by 2018, and projects that 70 percent of Americans will choose cremation by 2030. In other countries, such as the UK and Canada, a large majority already chooses cremation.

Many religions that once prescribed a traditional funeral and burial as part of their religious tenets, now allow, or even encourage, cremation as an alternative to burial. The Catholic Church forbade cremation until 1963, and while still recommending burial, is now permitting cremation. Some churches have even built their own columbariums (storage of cinerary urns) to serve their congregations, which increases the convenience of cremation while providing adherents a place to respectfully store remains. Reform Judaism has little objection to cremation, although it normally favors burial. As discussed earlier in the chapter, for reasons of disrespect for the deceased and the belief in the resurrection of the dead, Orthodox rabbis oppose and frown on cremation. Islam, similarly to Judaism, sees cremation as an act which is disrespectful to the deceased, and considers it *haram*, or an unclean act, and a sin.

Religions such as Confucianism with a strong component of ancestor worship usually prohibit cremation, although under Communism, the Chinese have been forced to practice cremation. Cremation in Japan, which was previously seen as a Buddhist practice, has become a secular, nation-wide tradition for economic and public health reasons, and Japan is recognized today as having the highest rates of cremation in the world.

The substantial increase in popularity of cremation in the West is due to significant changes in religious expectations, beliefs, and family life. The increasing number of people who claim to be agnostic or atheist, and those who are not associated with a formal religion, tend to choose cremation. Other factors such as geography also play an important role in people's choices. A hundred years ago, family plots in cemeteries and family graveyards were common because most extended families lived close together for their entire lives. Now people often move away from their birthplaces, making it difficult

most fears point back to the body

uncontrollable element scary

to visit burial places of deceased family members. People also consider cremation for environmental reasons, including the non-biodegradability of materials used to create caskets, and the environmental consequences of dedicating more and more land to cemeteries. Finally, economic factors are also a consideration for many, as cremation is much less expensive than burial. Given current trends, we should expect that cremation will become the standard way to dispense with human remains.

In reviewing beliefs in the afterlife, we recognize that both our philosophical notions of the body and our spiritual goals have shaped our views of death and our practices of disposing of the body. For Zoroastrianism and Abrahamic religions that espouse the belief in a tangible afterlife, the motive for burial has been respect for the deceased person, and the protection of the integrity of the body in anticipation of the resurrection of the dead. For Eastern religions (Hindu, Jain, Buddhist and Sikh religions), the body is a temporary vessel for the soul, and the reincarnation of the soul will provide it with a new body. Cremating the body has been the preferred method of disposing of the body. The ultimate goal in these religious systems is liberation from rebirth and physical existence. We also addressed how Confucian, Shinto, and indigenous beliefs in the spiritual power of the deceased are represented in rituals that honor and revere ancestors. Beliefs in heaven and hell, as well as the build-up of good or bad karma, reflect a post-death punishment and reward system, intended to influence behavior in this lifetime.

widespread cultural fear of death → especially western sense

Questions for review and discussion

1 Discuss traditional burial of Christian bodies and traditional cremation of Hindu bodies. How does each of these practices reflect core beliefs?

2 How does Buddhist meditation of the dead body help prepare the adept for death?

3 What changes have influenced contemporary Christian acceptance of cremation?

4 How do various burial and cremation practices reflect a religion's reverence for ancestors?

judgement day vs. going right to heaven

5 For which religions is a reward of heaven or paradise important? What is the basis for their beliefs in paradise?

6 Does a rejection of assisted suicide contradict religious teachings of compassion?

comfort

eternal paradise with God → heaven

Hell → fire, physical pain

Temporary resting place

Getting rid of the fear of death is done through disoatachment of the body

christianity and muslim both have heavens

fear, eternal, drastic, emotions

Glossary

Embalming-preserving a corpse from decay, often in preparation for the wake.

Eschatology-the belief in the afterlife and the final destiny of souls.

Gehenna-a place where souls are purified or punished during a period of twelve months after death. Derived from the biblical reference to Gehinnom—the Valley of the Son of Hinnom, located outside the Old City of Jerusalem where some of the kings of Judah sacrificed their children by fire.

Judgment Day-a central belief in Judaism, Christianity, and Islam that human begins will be judged based on their actions.

Maranasati-death awareness; a central meditation in Tibetan Buddhism which uses visualization techniques to contemplate on the nature of death.

Paradise-a place of harmony; the Garden of Eden.

Purgatory-a Roman Catholic doctrine defining an intermediate state after physical death where the souls of sinners expiate their sins before going to heaven.

Santhara-a Jain ritual of making an oath of fasting unto death with the goal of achieving *moksha* or liberation from rebirth.

Shivah-formal mourning period of seven days after a funeral in Judaism.

Sky burial-the Zoroastrian practice of exposing the corpse for the purposes of excarnation, the removal of the flesh by vultures or wild animals by using the dakhma (tower of silence).

Wake-a Christian ritual of viewing the body of the deceased prior to burial.

Fire
↳ purification

meditation → going to a
→ letting go off a   transcended state
"broken tool"

↳ dead body is → Deattachment
not useful in   from the
the cycle   fear of
the unknown
Deattachment from   (being
the body →   death)
importance
of afterlife
↳ awareness that
their "legacy" is not
compassion and death   over

Selected Bibliography and Further Readings

Introduction

Beauregard, Maria. and O'Leary, Denyse. *The Spiritual Brain: A Neuroscientist's Case for the Existence of the Soul*. New York: HarperOne, 2007.

Berger, Peter L. *The Sacred Canopy: Elements of a Sociological Theory of Religion*. Garden City, NY: Anchor Books, 1969.

Bourdieu, Pierre. *Outline of a Theory of Practice*. Cambridge, UK: University of Cambridge Press, 1977.

Brown, Peter. *The Body and Society: Men, Women, and Sexual Renunciation*. New York: Columbia University Press, 1988.

Bynum, Caroline Walker. *Fragmentation and Redemption: Essays on Gender and the Human Body in Medieval Religion*. New York: Zone Books, 1991.

Coakley, Sarah, ed. *Religion and the Body*. Cambridge, UK: Cambridge University Press, 1997.

Cooey, Paula. *Religious Imagination and the Body: A Feminist Analysis*. New York: Oxford University Press, 1994.

Eliade, Mircea. *Yoga, Immortality and Freedom*. Princeton: Princeton University Press, 2009.

Greenberg, Yudit, ed. *Encyclopedia of Love in World Religions*. Santa Barbara: ABC-CLIO, 2008.

Hick, John. *The New Frontier of Religion and Science: Religious Experience, Neuroscience and the Transcendent*. New York: Palgrave Macmillan, 2006.

Hopkins, Michael. *The Soul in the Brain*. Baltimore: Johns Hopkins University Press, 2007.

Law, Jane Marie, ed. *Religious Reflections on the Body*. Bloomington: Indiana University Press, 1995.

LaFleur, William R. "The Body." In *Critical Terms for Religious Studies*, edited by Mark C. Taylor. Chicago: University of Chicago Press, 1998.

Lakoff, George. and Johnson, Mark. *Philosophy in the Flesh: The Embodied Mind and Its Challenge to Western Thought*. New York: Basic Books, 1999.

McGuire, Meredith B. "Religion and the Body: Rematerializing the Human Body in the Social Sciences of Religion." *Journal for the Scientific Study of Religion*, vol. 29, no. 3 (September 1990), pp. 283–96.

Merleau-Ponty, Maurice. *Phenomenology of Perception*, translated by Colin Smith. London: Routledge, 2002.

Newberg, Andrew. *The Principles of Neurotheology.* Farnham, UK: Ashgate, 2010.

Otto, Rudolph. *The Idea of the Holy: An Inquiry into the Non-Rational Factor in the Idea of the Divine and its Relation to the Rational,* 2nd ed., translated by John W. Harvey. New York: Oxford University Press, 1978.

Synnott, Anthony. "Tomb, Temple, Machine and Self: The Social Construction of the Body." *The British Journal of Sociology,* vol. 43, no. 1 (March 1992), pp. 79–110.

Chapter 1 The Body in Creation Myths

Plato. *Symposium.* Translated, with Introduction and Notes by Alexander Nehamas and Paul Woodruff. Indianapolis and Cambridge: Hackett Publishing Company, 1989.

Reeser, Todd W. *Masculinities in Theory: An Introduction.* Chichester, UK: Wiley-Blackwell, 2010.

Rolston, Holmes, III. *Genes, Genesis and God: Values and their Origins in Natural and Human History.* Cambridge, U.K.: Cambridge University Press, 1999.

Schloss, Jeffrey. and Michael, Murray, eds. *Hesiod's Theogony: from Near Eastern Creation Myths to Paradise Lost.* New York: Oxford University Press, 2015.

Scully, Stephen. *Hesiod's Theogony: from Near Eastern Creation Myths to Paradise Lost.* New York: Oxford University Press, 2015.

Stewart, Sarah, Punthakey Mistree, Firoza, and Sims-Williams, Ursula, eds. *The Everlasting Flame: Zoroastrianism in History and Imagination.* New York: I.B. Tauris & Company, 2013.

Sproul, Barbara C. *Primal Myths: Creation Myths Around the World.* San Francisco: HarperCollins, 1991.

Trible, Phyllis. "Depatriarchalizing in Biblical Interpretation." *Journal of the American Academy of Religion,* vol. 41, no. 1 (March 1973), pp. 30–48.

The *Upanishads,* trans. Patrick Olivelle. New York: Oxford University Press, 2008.

The English Bible: King James Version. New York: Norton, 2012.

JPS Hebrew-English Tanakh. New York: Jewish Publication Society, 2003.

Midrash Rabbah, trans. and ed. H. Freedman and Maurice Simon. London, New York: Soncino Press, 1983.

The *Qur'an.* A new translation by A. Haleem. Oxford, New York: Oxford University Press, 2004.

Chapter 2 Representation of the Divine in Art and Text

The *Bhagavad-Gita.* Trans. Laurie L. Patton. New Delhi: Penguin, 2008.

Cattoi, Thomas and McDaniel, June, ed. *Perceiving the Divine Through the Human Body.* New York: Palgrave Macmillan, 2011.

Clooney, Francis X. *Comparative Theology: Deep Learning Across Religious Borders*. Malden, MA: Wiley Blackwell, 2010.

Daly, Mary. *Beyond God the Father: Toward a Philosophy of Women's Liberation*. Boston: Beacon Press, 1973.

Doniger O'Flaherty, Wendy. *Siva the Erotic Ascetic*. Oxford: Oxford University Press, 1973.

Holdrege, Barbara A. "Body Connections: Hindu Discourses of the Body and the Study of Religion." *International Journal of Hindu Studies*, vol. 2, no. 3 (1998): 341–86.

Jantzen, Grace M. *Becoming Divine: Towards a Feminist Philosophy of Religion*. Bloomington: Indiana University Press, 1990.

Lanzetta, Beverly. *Radical Wisdom: A Feminist Mystical Theology*. Minneapolis: Fortress, 2005.

Lerner, Gerda. *The Creation of Patriarchy*. New York, NY: Oxford University Press, 1986.

Lucia, Amanda. *Reflections of Amma: Devotees in a Global Embrace*. Berkeley: University of California Press, 2014.

McFague, Sallie. *Metaphorical Theology: Models of God in Religious Language*. Philadelphia, PA: Fortress, 1982.

McFague, Sallie. *Models of God: Theology for an Ecological Nuclear Age*. Philadelphia, PA: Fortress, 1987.

Miles, Margaret R. *Image as Insight: Visual Understanding in Western Christianity and Secular Culture*. Boston, MA: Beacon Press, 1985.

Miles, Margaret R. "(Re) Imaging the Divine." *Response*, vol. 41–42 (Fall–Winter 1982): 110–19.

Sommer, Benjamin D. *Bodies of God and the World of Ancient Israel*. New York: Cambridge University Press, 2009.

Snell, Daniel C. *Religions of the Ancient Near East*, New York: Cambridge University Press, 2011.

Srinivas, Smriti. *In the Presence of Sai Baba: Body, City, and Memory in a Global Religious Movement*. London: Brill, 2008.

Umansky, Ellen. "Creating a Jewish Feminist Theology: Possibilities and Problems." In *Weaving the Visions: New Patterns in Feminist Spirituality*, edited by Judith Plaskow and Carol P. Christ, 187–98. San Francisco: HarperCollins, 1989.

Valantasis, Richard, ed. *The Subjective Eye: Essays in Culture, Religion, and Gender in Honor of Margaret R. Miles*. Eugene, OR: Pickwick Publications, 2006.

Chapter 3 Erotic Desire and Divine Love

Barks, Coleman. *The Essential Rumi* (New Expanded Edition). New York: HarperOne, 2004.

Bloch, Ariel and Bloch, Chana. *The Song of Songs: A New Translation*. Berkeley and Los Angeles: University of California Press, 1995.

Chittick, William C. *The Sufi Path of Love: The Spiritual Teachings of Rumi*. Albany, NY: SUNY Press, 1983.

Dimock, Edward. *The Place of the Hidden Moon*. Delhi: Motilal Banarsidass Publishers, 1991.

Prince Ghazi bin Muhammad bin Talal, H.R.H. *Love in the Holy Quran*. New York: Kazi Publications, 2011.

Holdrege, Barbara A. *Bhakti and Embodiment: Fashioning Divine Bodies and Devotional Bodies in Krsna Bhakti*. New York: Routledge, 2015.

Idel, Moshe. *Kabbalah and Eros*. New Haven, CT: Yale University Press, 2005.

Katz, Steven T., ed. *Mysticism and Religious Traditions*. Oxford: Oxford University Press, 1983.

Luibheid Colm, trans. *The Divine Names in Pseudo-Dionysius: The Complete Works*. New York: Paulist Press, 1987.

McDaniel, June. *The Madness of the Saints: Ecstatic Religion in Bengal*. Chicago: The University of Chicago Press, 1989.

Mechthild of Magdeburg. *The Flowing Light of the Godhead*. Translated by Frank Tobin. New Jersey: Paulist Press, 1998.

Miller, Barbara Stoler, ed. and trans. *Love Song of the Dark Lord: Jayadeva's Gītagovinda*, 20th anniversary ed. New York: Columbia University Press, 1997.

Pechilis, Karen. *Interpreting Devotion: The Poetry and Legacy of a Female Bhakti Saint of India*. New York: Routledge, 2015.

St. Teresa of Avila. *The Life of St. Teresa by Herself*. Translated by David Lewis. Digitreads.com, 2009.

Schimmel, Annemarie. *Mystical Dimensions of Islam*. Chapel Hill: University of North Carolina Press, 1975.

Schweig, Graham M., trans. *Dance of Divine Love: The Rasa Lila of Krishna from the Bhagavata Purana, India's Classic Sacred Love Story*. Princeton: Princeton University Press, 2005.

Wolfson, Elliot. *Language, Eros, Being: Kabbalistic Hermeneutics and Poetic Imagination*. New York: Fordham University Press, 2005.

Chapter 4 Body in Religious Ritual

Asad, Talal. *Genealogies of Religion*. Baltimore: John Hopkins University Press, 1993.

Bell, Catherine. *Ritual: Perspectives and Dimensions*. New York: Oxford University Press, 1997.

Bernstein, Anya. *Religious Bodies Politic: Rituals of Sovereignty in Buryat Buddhism*. Chicago: University of Chicago Press, 2013.

Geertz, Clifford. *The Interpretation of Cultures*. New York: Basic Books, 1973.

Grimes, Ronald. *Beginnings in Ritual Studies*. Columbia: University of South Carolina Press, 1995.

Grimes, Ronald. *Deeply into the Bone. Reinventing Rites of Passage*. Berkeley: University of California Press, 2000.

Mauss, Marcel. *The Gift: Forms and Functions of Exchange in Archaic Societies*. London: Routledge, 1990.

Noland, Carrie. *Agency and Embodiment: Performing Gestures/Producing Culture*. Cambridge, MA: Harvard University Press, 2009.

Tottoli, Roberto. "Muslim Attitudes towards Prostration (sujud)." *Studia Islamica*, vol. 88 (1998): 5–34.

Turner, Victor. *The Ritual Process: Structure and Anti-Structure*. Harmondsworth, UK: Penguin, 1995.

Promey, Sally M, ed. *Sensational Religion: Sensory Cultures in Material Practice*. New Haven: Yale University Press, 2014.

Rappaport, Roy A. *Ritual and Religion in the Making of Humanity*. Cambridge, UK: Cambridge University Press, 1999.

Steinmetz, Paul. *Pipe, Bible, and Peyote Among the Oglala Lakota: A Study in Religious Identity*, rev. ed., Knoxville: University of Tennessee Press, 1990.

Zuesse, Evan M. "Meditation on Ritual." *Journal of the American Academy of Religion*, vol. 43, no. 3 (1975): 517–30.

Chapter 5 Food: Laws and Practices

Eaton, Heather. *Introducing Ecofeminist Theologies*. London: T&T Clark, 2005.

Falk, Marcia. *The Book of Blessings: New Jewish Prayers for Daily Life, the Sabbath and the New Moon Festival*. San Francisco: HarperCollins, 1996.

Freidenreich, David M. *Foreigners and Their Food: Constructing Otherness in Jewish, Christian, and Islamic Law*. Berkeley: University of California Press, 2011.

Harvey, Graham. *Food, Sex and Strangers: Understanding Religion as Everyday Life*. New York: Routledge, 2014.

Lovelock, James. *Gaia: A New Look at Life on Earth*. Oxford: Oxford University Press, 2000.

McFague, Sallie. *The Body of God: An Ecological Theology*. Minneapolis, MN: Augsburg Fortress, 1993.

Narayanan, Vasudha. "Water, Wood and Wisdom: Ecological Perspectives from the Hindu Traditions." *Daedalus*, vol. 130, no. 4 (Fall 2001): 179–206.

Raman, Varadaraja V. "Food: Its Many Aspects in Science, Religion, and Culture." *Zygon*, vol. 49, no. 4 (2014): 958–76.

Ruether, Rosemary Radford. *Integrating Ecofeminism, Globalization, and World Religions*. Lanham, MD: Rowman & Littlefield, 2005.

Starhawk. *The Spiral Dance: The Rebirth of the Ancient Religion of the Goddess*. New York: Harperone, 1999.

Tucker, Mary Evelyn. *Worldly Wonder: Religions Enter Their Ecological Phase*. Peru, IL: Open Court, 2003.

Vincentt, Giselle. "Goddess Feminist Ritual Practices and Thealogy." *Martifocus: Cross-Quarterly for the Goddess Woman*, vol. 8, no. 2 (Imbloc 2009).

Zeller, Benjamin E., Dallam, Marie W., Neilson, Reid L., and Rubel, Nora, L., eds. *Religion, Food, and Eating in North America* (Arts and Traditions of the Table: Perspectives on Culinary History). New York: Columbia University Press, 2014.

Chapter 6 Breath, Harmony, Health and Healing

Balzer, Mandelstam Marjorie. *Shamans, Spirituality, and Cultural Revitalization: Explorations in Siberia and Beyond.* New York: Palgrave-Macmillan, 2012.

Barnes, Linda and Susan, Sered, eds. *Religion and Healing in America.* New York: Oxford University Press, 2005.

Csordas, Thomas J. *The Sacred Self: A Cultural Phenomenology of Charismatic Healing.* Berkeley: University of California Press, 1994.

——. *Body, Meaning, Healing.* New York: Palgrave Macmillan, 2002.

Desai, Prakah. *Health and Medicine in the Hindu Tradition.* New York: Crossroad, 1989.

Eddy, Mary Baker. *Science and Health with Key to the Scriptures.* Boston, MA: Christian Science Board of Directors, 1994.

Foucault, Michel. *The Birth of the Clinic: An Archaeology of Medical Perception.* New York: Random House, 1973.

Jain, Andrea R. *Selling Yoga: From Counterculture to Pop Culture.* New York: Oxford University Press, 2014.

Kakar, Sudhir. *Shamans, Mystics, and Doctors.* Chicago: University of Chicago Press, 1991.

Lewis, I. M. *Ecstatic Religion: A Study of Shamanism and Spirit Possession.* New York: Routledge, 2003.

Mitchell, Stephen. *Tao Te Ching: A New English Version.* New York: HarperCollins, 1988.

Numbers, Ronald and Darrel, Amundsen, eds. *Caring and Curing: Health and Medicine in the Western Religious Traditions.* New York: Macmillan, 1986.

Prakah Desai. *Health and Medicine in the Hindu Tradition.* New York: Crossroad, 1989.

Rahman, Fazlur. *Health and Medicine in the Islamic Tradition.* Chicago: ABC International Group, 1998.

Schumm, D, and Stoltzfus, M, eds. *Disability and Religious Diversity: Cross-Cultural and Interreligious Perspectives.* New York: Palgrave Macmillan, 2011.

Singleton, Mark, and Goldberg, Ellen, eds. *Gurus of Modern Yoga.* New York: Oxford University Press, 2013.

Urban, Hugh. *Zorba the Buddha: Sex, Spirituality, and Capitalism in the Global Osho Movement.* Berkeley: University of California Press, 2015.

Chapter 7 Purity and Pollution

Bashford Alison. *Purity and Pollution: Gender, Embodiment and Victorian Medicine.* New York: Palgrave Macmillan, 1998.

Broshi, Magen. "Qumran and the Essenes: Purity and Pollution, Six Categories." RevQ 22/3 (2006): 463–74.

Choksy Jamsheed K. *Purity and Pollution in Zoroastrianism: Triumph over Evil.* Austin: University of Texas, 1989.

Douglas Mary. *Purity and Danger: An Analysis of the Concepts of Pollution and Taboo.* London: Routledge, 2003.

Gavin, Flood. *The Ascetic Self: Subjectivity, Memory and Tradition*. Chicago: Cambridge University Press, 2005.

Gross, Rita M. "Menstruation and Childbirth as Ritual and Religious Experience among Native Australians." In *Unspoken Worlds: Women's Religious Lives in Non-Western Cultures*, edited by Nancy Auer Falk and Rita M. Gross. San Francisco: Harper and Row, 1980.

Hanegraaff , W. J., and Kripal, J, eds. *Hidden Intercourse: Eros and Sexuality in the History of Western Esotericism*. Boston: Brill, 2008.

Fonrobert, Charlotte Elisheva. *Menstrual Purity: Rabbinic and Christian Reconstructions of Biblical Gender*. California: Stanford, 2000.

Meyers, Carol. *Households and Holiness: The Religious Culture of Israelite Women*. Minneapolis: Fortress, 2005.

Meyers, Carol. *Rediscovering Eve: Ancient Israelite Women in Context*. New York: Oxford University Press, 2013.

Petrovic, Andre, and Petrovic, Ivana. *Inner Purity and Pollution in Greek Religion: Volume I: Early Greek Religion*. Oxford: Oxford University Press, 2016.

Powers, Marla N. "Menstruation and Reproduction: An Oglala Case." *Signs: Journal of Women in Culture and Society*, vol. 6, no. 1 (autumn 1980): 54–64.

Smyers, S. "Women and Shinto: The Relation Between Purity and Pollution." *Japanese Religions*, vol. 12, no. 4 (1983).

Chapter 8 Gender and Sexuality

Alpert, Rebecca. *Like Bread on the Seder Plate: Jewish Lesbians and the Transformation of Tradition*. New York: Columbia University Press, 1997.

Boyarin, Daniel. *Carnal Israel: Reading Sex in Talmudic Culture*. Berkeley: University of California Press, 1993.

Cabezón, Jose Ignacio, ed. *Buddhism, Sexuality, and Gender*. Ithaca, NY: SUNY, 1992.

Eilberg-Schwartz, Howard and Doniger, Wendy, eds. *Off with Her Head! The Denial of Women's Identity in Myth, Religion, and Culture*. Berkeley: University of California Press, 1995.

Geller, Pamela L. and Stockett, Miranda K, edited. *Feminist Anthropology: Past, Present, and Future*. Philadelphia: University of Pennsylvania Press, 2006.

Kripal, Jeffrey. "Sexuality." In *Encyclopedia of Religion*, vol. 12, edited by Mircea Eliade. New York: Collier Macmillan, 1987.

Mernissi, Fatima. *Women and Islam: An Historical and Theological Enquiry*. Cambridge, MA: Blackwell Publishers, 1991.

Pagels, Elaine. *Adam, Eve and the Serpent*. New York: Vintage Books, 1988.

Parrinder, Geoffrey. *Sexual Morality in the World's Religions*. Oxford: Penguin, 1996.

Plaskow Judith. *Standing Again at Sinai*. San Francisco: Harper and Row, 1990.

Stimpson, Catharine R., and Herdt, Gilbert, eds. *Critical Terms for the Study of Gender*. Chicago: University of Chicago Press, 2014.

Tougher, Shaun. *The Eunuch in Byzantine History and Society*. New York: Routledge, 2008.

Urban, Hugh B. *Tantra: Sex, Secrecy, Politics, and Power in the Study of Religion*. Los Angeles: University of California Press, 2003.

Weiser-Hanks, Merry E. *Christianity and Sexuality in the Early Modern World: Regulating Desire, Reforming Practice.* London: Routledge, 2000.

White, David Gordon. *Kiss of the Yoginī: "Tantric Sex" in its South Asian Contexts.* Chicago: University of Chicago Press, 2003.

Chapter 9 Marriage and Reproduction

Bennett, Linda Rae. *Women, Islam and Modernity: Single Women, Sexuality and Reproductive Health in Contemporary Indonesia.* New York: Routledge, 2005.

Broyde, Michael J., ed. *Marriage, Sex and Family in Judaism.* Lanham, MD: Rowman & Littlefield Publishers, 2005.

Cott, Joan. *Politics of the Veil.* Princeton, NJ: Princeton University Press, 2007.

Dhar, Rajib Lochan. "Intercaste Marriage: A Study from the Indian Context." *Marriage & Family Review*, vol. 49, no. 1 (01 January 2013), pp. 1–25.

Doniger, Wendy. *The Laws of Manu.* Delhi: Penguin India, 2000.

Eilberg-Schwartz, Howard and Doniger, Wendy, eds. *Off with Her Head! The Denial of Women's Identity in Myth, Religion, and Culture.* Berkeley: University of California Press, 1995.

Fournier, Pascale. *Muslim Marriage in Western Courts: Lost in Transplantation.* New York: Routledge, 2016.

Jordan, Mark D. et al., ed. *Canon, Tradition, and Critique in the Blessing of Same-Sex Unions.* Princeton, NJ: Princeton University Press, 2006.

Korteweg, Anna and Selby, Jennifer, eds. *Debating Sharia: Islam, Gender Politics, and Family Law Arbitration.* Toronto: University of Toronto Press, 2012.

McGinity, Keren R. *Marrying Out: Jewish Men, Intermarriage, and Fatherhood* (The Modern Jewish Experience). Bloomington: Indiana University Press, 2014.

Oehlschlaeger, Fritz. *Procreative Ethics: Philosophical and Christian Approaches to Questions at the Beginning of Life.* Eugene, Oregon: Cascade Books, 2010.

Pierceson, Jason. *Same-Sex Marriage in the United States: The Road to the Supreme Court and Beyond.* Lanham: Rowman & Littlefield Publishers, 2014.

Chapter 10 Marking and Modifying the Body

Barilan, Yechiel Michael. *Jewish Bioethics.* New York: Cambridge University Press, 2014.

Cole-Turner, Ronald, ed. *Design and Destiny: Jewish and Christian Perspectives on Human Germline Modification.* MIT Press, 2008.

Cole-Turner, Ronald, ed. "The Singularity and the Rapture: Transhumanist and Popular Christian Views of the Future." *Zygon*, vol. 47 (2012): 777–96.

Eilberg-Schwartz, Howard. *People of the Body: Jews and Judaism from an embodied Perspective.* Albany, New York: SUNY Press, 1992.

Harari, Yuval, Noah. *Homo Deus: A Brief History of Tomorrow.* Harper, 2017.

Hoffman, Lawrence A. *Covenant of Blood: Circumcision and Gender in Rabbinic Judaism.* Chicago: University of Chicago Press, 1996.

Kurzweil, Ray. *The Singularity Is Near: When Humans Transcend Biology*. New York: Penguin, 2005.

Rubin, Lawrence. "Tattoos and Body Piercings: Adolescent Self-Expression or Self-Mutilation?" *Psychology Today*, July 2, 2009.

Bryan, S. *Turner Religion and Modern Society: Citizenship, Secularization and the State*. Cambridge: Cambridge University Press, 2011.

Youssouf, Samia. "Female Genital Mutilations: A Testimony." *The European Journal of Contraception and Reproductive Health Care*, vol. 18, no. 1 (2012): 5–9.

Chapter 11 Asceticism

Brown, Peter. *The Body and Society: Men, Women and Sexual Renunciation in Early Christianity*. New York: Columbia University Press, 1988.

Bynum Caroline Walker,. *Holy Feast and Holy Fast: The Religious Significance of Food to Medieval Women*. Berkeley: University of California Press, 1988.

Clark, Gillian. "Women and Asceticism in Late Antiquity: The Refusal of Status and Gender." In *Asceticism*, edited by Vincent L. Wimbush and Robert Valantasis. Oxford: Oxford University Press, 1998.

Flood, Gavin. *The Ascetic Self: Subjectivity, Memory and Tradition*. Cambridge, UK: Cambridge University Press, 2004.

Glucklich, Ariel. *Sacred Pain: Hurting the Body for the Sake of the Soul*. New York: Oxford University Press, 2001.

Hick, John. *An Interpretation of Religion: Human Responses to the Transcendent*, 2nd ed. New York: Palgrave Macmillan, 2004.

Hollywood, Amy. *Sensible Ecstasy: Mysticism, Sexual Difference, and the Demands of History*. Chicago: University of Chicago Press, 2002.

Jantzen, Grace. *Power, Gender, and Christian Mysticism*. New York: Cambridge University Press, 1995.

Kripal, Jeffrey J. *Authors of the Impossible: The Paranormal and the Sacred*. Chicago: University of Chicago Press, 2010.

Long, Jeffery D. *Jainism: An Introduction*. London: I.B. Taurus, 2009.

Muller, F Max, trans. *Wisdom of the Buddha: The Dhammapada*. Sweden: Wisehouse, 2016.

Roebuck, Valerie J., trans. and ed. *The Upanishads*. Delhi: Penguin, 2004.

Scarry, Elaine. *The Body in Pain: The Making and Unmaking of Worlds*. New York: Oxford University Press, 1985.

Wimbush, Vincent L. and Valantasis, Richard. edited. *Asceticism*. New York: Oxford University Press, 1998.

Chapter 12 Death and the Afterlife

Becker, Carl B. *Breaking the Circle: Death and the Afterlife in Buddhism*. Carbondale: Southern Illinois University Press, 1993.

Bynum, Caroline Walker. *The Resurrection of the Body in Western Christianity, 200-1336*. New York: Columbia University Press, 1995.

Cuevas, Bryan. *Travels in the Netherworld: Buddhist Popular Narratives of Death and the Afterlife in Tibet*. Oxford: Oxford University Press, 2008.

Gordon, Matthew. *Islam: Origins, Practices, Holy Texts, Sacred Persons, Sacred Places*. New York: Oxford University Press, 2002.

Hussain, Amir. *Death, Dying, and the Afterlife: Oxford Bibliographies Online Research Guide*. New York: Oxford University Press, 2011.

Le Goff, Jacques. *The Birth of Purgatory*. Chicago: The University of Chicago Press, 1984.

Marinis, Vasileios. *Death and the Afterlife in Byzantium: The Fate of the Soul in Theology, Liturgy, and Art*. New York: Cambridge University Press, 2017.

Scheffler, Samuel. edited by Niko Kolodny. *Death and the Afterlife*. New York: Oxford University Press, 2013.

Segal, Alan F. and Alles, Gregory D. *Life after Death: A History of the Afterlife in the Religions of the West*. Doubleday, 2004.

Taylor John, H. *Death and the Afterlife in Ancient Egypt*. Chicago: University of Chicago Press, 2001.

Thurman, Robert. *The Tibetan Book of the Dead: Liberation through Understanding in the Between*. New York: Bantam, 1994.

Thanissaro, Bhikkhu. "Contemplation of the Body." *Dhamma Talks and Writings of Thanissaro Bhikkhu*. Dhammhatalks.org, March 1, 2004.

Index